Herald INTERNATIONAL Tribune

Guide to
Business Travel
in ASIA

Herald INTERNATIONAL Tribune
Guide to
Business Travel
in ASIA

Robert K. McCabe

PASSPORT BOOKS

Trade Imprint of National Textbook Company
Lincolnwood, Illinois U.S.A.

Dedication

Sandra Raymond
and
Lester and Marion McCabe

Contributors: Judith Bonavia, Beijing and Shanghai; Allen Dawson, Bangkok; Robert King, Taipei; Dinah Lee, Canton; Lin Neumann, Manila; Terry Trucco, Tokyo and Osaka; and Paul Zach, Singapore and Jakarta.

Many good friends along the way helped immeasurably to smooth my path. In Hong Kong: Dr T.M. Moles, Harvey Leve, Burt and Lily Levin, Steve Hutton, John Tkacik, Dinah Lee and Patrick Smith. In Seoul: Paul Ensor, Dr and Mrs Horace G. Underwood, and Shin Jae Hun. In Manila: F. Sionil Jose and Max Soliven. In Kuala Lumpur: James Clad. In Rangoon: U Myo Swe. In Canton: Joachim Burger. In the United States: Peter Bird Martin.

My deep thanks go as well to those at home base in Hong Kong, particularly to Dawn Low, Suzanne Lee and Lucilla Kao, as well as to other Hong Kong friends: Derek Davies, Dirk Brink and James Smith. In Macau: Henri Vong and Kip de Shazo. In Singapore: Anthony and Josephine Kan. In Brunei: Mary Ambrose and John Hoover. In Bangkok: James Willwerth and Nay Htun and especially Mrs Ankana Gilwee. In Manila: Cindy Lilles, Steve Lohr, Bill Chapman, Graham Lovell and Sandra Burton. In Jakarta: John and Martha Holdridge, Daisy Hadmoko, Richard Pascoe, Peter Millership and Michael Schuetzendorf. In Denver: Dr Kenneth N. Bredesen. In Washington: Walter C. McCabe. In Paris: Thomas A. McIvor and Jean Pasqualini.

Foreword

This book has been created for the specific purpose of helping business people to travel with maximum ease in the capitals of Asia. Equipped with this guide, even the first-time business visitor will discover that the East is an area he or she can visit with confidence. Those more familiar with the region will also discover that this collection of useful information contains much that is new.

This is not simply a book the *International Herald Tribune* recommends or endorses. It is also a guide which one of our most experienced journalists, Bob McCabe, has worked on from first page to last, using material from a broad selection of Trib readers who frequently do business in Asian cities. With the help of other journalists, he has checked and cross-checked their suggestions and comments. He has studied the ways they side-step annoyances or time-wasting hurdles. And he has delved into their secret discoveries and tested preferences. The resulting book is one which should provide a unique service to all who use it.

This book has been published in the year of the *International Herald Tribune's* Centennial celebrations. When publication of this daily newspaper began in Paris one hundred years ago, Europe was said to be 'where the action was'. Today, as we move into our second century, we are participating increasingly in the rapidly evolving life of a new and dynamic Asia. The IHT has been printed in Asia daily by satellite transmission since 1980 and, as this is written, the IHT is selling over 30,000 copies each day throughout the region. This may not yet make us an old Asia hand, but it has given us a chance to make many friends in the region, to grow ever more convinced of its endless fascination and exciting potential, and, we trust, to put us in a position where we can usefully share some of our observations about travelling in Asia with friends and readers the world over.

Lee W. Huebner
Publisher
International Herald Tribune

HOW THE CITIES RATE

	Communications	Congestion	Efficiency	Hotels	Economy	Food	Nightlife	Culture	Weekends	Totals
Hong Kong	10	7	10	9	7	8	10	7	8	76
Tokyo	10	5	10	10	1	8	10	10	8	72
Seoul	10	7	8	8	7	6	8	8	6	68
Taipei	7	6	7	7	8	10	8	7	7	67
Singapore	10	7	10	10	2	7	5	4	7	62
Osaka	10	5	9	7	2	6	8	4	8	59
Manila	7	5	5	7	8	8	8	5	6	59
Bangkok	5	3	4	8	7	8	8	6	6	55
Jakarta	6	4	4	8	8	6	6	5	6	55
Beijing	3	5	6	6	6	5	3	10	8	53
Canton	6	5	6	8	7	6	3	3	5	49
Kuala Lumpur	7	5	5	8	3	6	3	5	4	46
Brunei	8	8	4	8	3	6	1	4	4	46
Shanghai	2	3	4	1	9	2	3	6	2	32

The author, in a clearly doomed attempt to spotlight the best Asian cities from the business traveller's point of view, offers the above, for the sake of argument only. Ratings are on the usual 1-10 scale. (Bali and Macao, among other locations mentioned in the guide, are not included here because they are not primary areas for doing business.)

Contents

Bangkok	1
Beijing	15
Brunei	31
Canton	38
Shenzhen	49
Hong Kong	53
Macau	69
Jakarta	75
Bali	86
Kuala Lumpur	89
Manila	99
Osaka	112
Seoul	123
Shanghai	134
Singapore	146
Taipei	160
Tokyo	169

Introduction

Writing an introduction to a book on East Asian travel is much less fun than actually introducing someone to the region. And from the moment Sandra and I stepped off our Air France 747 in Bangkok (she for the first time) to the time we returned home to Paris a year later, our Oriental travels were 99% pure joy.

Not 100%; no journey ever goes that well. So I will admit that although we ourselves disembarked at Bangkok that October day, our luggage went on to Tokyo. But it was delivered to our hotel the next day, none the worse for its journey to Narita, and that was the last time in more than a year that our suitcases went astray.

For Sandra, East Asia was new. For me, coming back after nearly 20 years away was both exhilarating and unsettling: the former because the region is in the midst of enormous and generally positive change, the latter because so much of my well-loved Old Asia had vanished. Change is all-pervasive out here, and it's mostly positive. Most residents believe quite coolly that theirs is the land of the future, and more and more Westerners are beginning to agree.

It is the cities of Asia, not the countrysides, that have altered most dramatically. And it was in Hong Kong, where I'd lived for half the Sixties, that I was comprehensively struck by this phenomenon. 'This is my turf,' I announced to Sandra as we stepped off the Star Ferry onto Hong Kong Island. 'You'll love it.'

I was lost in less than two minutes.

In my defense, I should explain that no single urban area in Asia has changed its look more thoroughly and more astonishingly than Hong Kong's Central District. Unless it is Tokyo's Shinjuku, or Singapore's Orchard Road, or Jakarta's Jalan Thamrin. And the list need not stop there.

Economically and sociologically, the changes are just as far-reaching. Consider the surprisingly widespread participation by Malays in Malaysia's economic growth today. Two decades ago, that sphere was wholly dominated by local Chinese. Or wonder at the economic revolution in China itself, where once-poverty-stricken peasants no longer lust after mere wristwatches and bicycles but instead work to earn VCRs and in some cases private autos.

Or weigh the casual statement by a Brunei tribal chieftain, as we talked in his longhouse deep in the Brunei jungle, that his son had just finished his university education in England.

An American ambassador in the area sums it up this way: Asia is dynamic, Europe is static. A Malaysian diplomat says quite matter-of-factly that Asia is where the future is. Despite the slowdown of the mid-Eighties, over the long run I think they'll be proven right. Increasingly, the world is buying Asia's products. The American trade imbalance with Japan alone is $50 billion. US-Asia trade totals surpassed US-Europe totals in 1980 and now are a third greater. Japan's automobiles are running rival Europe's products right off the road. Hong Kong is the world's third most important financial center, after New York and London.

Behind all this dynamism is the sheer size of Asia—something difficult to comprehend not only for the average Liechtensteinian, say, but for Britons or Frenchmen or even—dare one say it—for many Americans.

Consider population, for example: there are more than 1.5 billion people in Asia (citing only those nations whose capitals are represented in this book), compared to 331 million in the European Economic Community (EEC) and 235 million in the United States. Asia's land area is 3.6 billion square kilometers, compared to the 2,254,215 square kilometers of the EEC nations and the 9,372,614 square kilometers of the United States. Per-capita GNP averages $4756.36 in Asia (including China's $290 and Brunei's $21,140, both shocking figures in different ways), compared to the EEC's $7,977 and the United States's $14,090. Six of every ten persons in the world are Asian.

Just as daunting is Asia's diversity; linguistically, ethnically and socially. So are the ways of life, the degrees of affluence and, indeed, of education. Perhaps the greatest single uniting factor is the English language, spoken with varying degrees of fluency by leading politicians, civil servants, businessmen and journalists in every city cited in this volume.

All those people, all that diversity, all that rising productivity— all those fresh new appetites. The revolution of rising expectations is being replaced by one of rising hedonism: the appetite for BMWs in Hong Kong, say, must be seen to be believed. There's lots of business to be done in Asia.

For the visiting executive, the increasing emphasis on *haut posh* may come as something of a welcome surprise. Yes, prices are high for hotels and food; but no, not wildly out of line with prices in Europe. And Asia's new hotels are the world's fanciest. Many of the finest occupy their own private parks. In Jakarta, Bangkok and Manila there are hotels that amount to mini-cities, with a broad selection of restaurants, gymnasiums, tennis and squash courts, mini-golf, jogging paths neatly laid out through park greenery, luxurious pools and good shopping arcades.

For some travelers, there's a drawback: one is sheltered in these enclaves from the depressing urban realities outside the gates. But not necessarily from the local folks: for the successful Indonesians and Thais of Jakarta or Bangkok, the mini-city is a highly desirable place to see and be seen.

So are the other hotels, from the giants like Singapore's new Westin-Raffles City complex, or Tokyo's New Otani, to the smaller gems like Bangkok's Oriental, Hong Kong's Mandarin, Macau's Oriental or Tokyo's Okura. There are personal favorites like Singapore's Goodwood Park, or Bali's Tanjung Sari, Canton's China Hotel or Asia's grande dame, the Manila Hotel. And city for city, dollar for dollar, one cannot go wrong with the superb hotels run by Hilton's Asia-Pacific group. They're everywhere and they're very good.

That said, remember that room prices in Asia tend to be very flexible indeed. Not during high season. This varies from city to city, and when the rush is on, one pays top dollar. (Examples: Hong Kong and Canton, during the spring and autumn trade fairs). More often, prices can be bargained down dramatically, by sometimes more than 50% in cities like Bangkok and Singapore in summer and early fall. A business friend advises: 'Walk up to the reception desk, place your card in front of the clerk and ask for 40% off. You'll be surprised at how often they'll grant it.'

And when checking out, go over bills carefully. Not only to make sure the promised discount was actually granted, but to be sure one is not being charged for someone else's splurge in the Grill. Computerization makes hotel bills appear accurate, but mistakes still occur. Examine all receipts. Count shirts when they come back from the laundry. And keep a very sharp eye on minibar charges: there's lots of sloppiness here. (To avoid this problem, some travelers simply ask that their minibar stock be removed on arrival).

As one might expect in a distinctly male-oriented part of the world, few Asian hotels have caught on to the idea that it's good business to cater to the increasing number of European and American women traveling on business. Questioned on this point, most hotel spokesmen (and spokeswomen) quickly denied that they discriminated against women, thus neatly missing the point. But some hotels, including the Ritz and Lai Lai Sheraton in Taipei and the new Tokyo Hilton, have already taken positive action.

These hotels, for example, make a point of screening incoming phone calls for their women guests. They seat lone women diners discreetly and brush off pests. All offer special gift toiletries to female guests and make a point of ensuring a good supply of clothes hangers designed to accommodate women's clothing.

Most of the hotels listed in this book have good business centers, with equipment that ranges from telex and cable machines to facsimile machines and computers. All will find temporary secretarial and translator assistance. The newer hotels, unsurprisingly, are generally much better equipped for business travelers than the older ones.

And the newer ones are also much more apt to offer fairly lavish sports facilities, from gyms (kitted out with all the latest muscle-building equipment) to large swimming pools, saunas and steam baths. Many have squash and tennis courts; some even have bowling alleys. But for golf and sailing, introductions to the local clubs are needed. Sometimes the hotel can help, sometimes not—and the traveler thus may be forced to accept the hospitality of business contacts.

Business acquaintances can also help out if one falls ill. A personal recommendation to a doctor is to be preferred to that of one's hotel, though in a couple of cases during our year of travel in Asia the hotel doctor turned up trumps. Note: hotel doctors tend to be expensive.

If one is very lucky, one may escape Asia's foods unscathed. In international-standard hotels, the food-preparers are closely supervised and the chances of catching the runs accordingly less. But most travelers can expect to be grounded by stomach trouble for a day or two along the way. To play safe, have a shot of gamma globulin before departure: it's less expensive than a bout of infectious hepatitis. Other shots usually aren't necessary. Exception: For trips to remoter parts of Indonesia or the Philippines, doctors may advise taking anti-malaria tablets.

Water: Hotels supply boiled drinking water as a matter of course. Though tap water is perfectly drinkable in some cities, one may not want to risk a stomach upset. One very viable alternative is local beer, or hot tea.

Food and drink: Most Asian food, to this traveler at least, is extremely palatable. By now most Westerners, in restaurants in their home cities back in Europe and North America, have been exposed to Cantonese and Sichuanese cuisine, to at least a few Japanese and Thai dishes, and perhaps even to some of the delights of Malaysia and Indonesia. Things taste even better in their homelands, and most leading hotels offer fine local dishes. Don't feel confined to hotel menus, however. In this book, we have tried to point you toward good local restaurants in each city. Give them a try.

With Asian meals, locally produced beer, or tea, goes well. In Hong Kong and Singapore, Chinese hosts will offer you brandy right through the meal. (Be cautious.) Asian beer is generally excellent: Kloster in Thailand, Angker in Indonesia, San Miguel in Manila and Hong Kong, Sapporo in Japan and Tianjin in China are all highly recommended.

Western (or 'continental') food in Asia isn't top-notch, despite noble efforts by all varieties of imported chefs. Neither is it inedible. But it's vastly overpriced. One feels one is paying for the decor, which can be awfully twee. Asian food is often a better choice.

For wine-lovers, there are problems. Many European wines simply do not travel well. Nor do they survive sometimes erratic Asian storing and handling. And prices are exorbitant: count on paying twice as much—for mediocre European wines—in Asia. California wines are cheaper.

If wine is essential, try China's Dynasty and Great Wall brands, produced in China by Sino-French combines. The whites are fairly dry, and quite palatable, the reds scrappy. The Chinese also produce fortified rice wines that are somewhat heavy, with some resemblance to sherry. These are served warm. Japan's *sake* is a bit lighter and preferred by many Westerners. South Korea produces quite good whites and so-so reds under the Majuwang label. Remember, by the way, that Asia-produced wines are about as expensive as their heavily taxed Western equivalents.

The usual European tipples—scotch and bourbon, sherry and port, gin, vodka and rum—can be found just about everywhere. Prices generally are just short of being outrageous (particularly in hotel minibars) as the direct result of the near-confiscatory duties, imposed by greedy governments on imported booze in most parts of Asia. Cognacs are both expensive and in lavish supply, a direct consequence of the Chinese community's fascination with the stuff.

Most Asian spirits such as arrack and Thai whisky should be avoided, though a taste will satisfy curiosity and probably won't cause brain damage. Most Japanese whisky, on the other hand, is not all bad, and the best of it is fairly palatable.

The single most daunting Asian spirit is China's *mao-tai* (or *gao-liang*, in Taiwan), made from millet and an assortment of other grains. Its taste of gasoline and burned rubber (with, one is forced to believe, hemlock) emphatically does not deter Chinese hosts from offering it in huge quantities at official banquets.

Foreigners who face long bargaining sessions the next day should be particularly wary of the stuff, for it causes dragon-sized hangovers. Though Chinese hosts will rarely admit it, their aim often is to get guests potted while escaping unscathed themselves and thus earning a decided advantage for the next morning's negotiations.

Thus: sip, don't gulp. Resist all challenges to drain the glass. When the host lifts his glass and says 'gan-bei' (bottoms up), smile, lift a glass in turn and reply 'sui-byan' (do as you please), and drink sparingly. Remember that in Asia, duplicity is depthless: that clear liquid in your host's glass may be only water, not *mao-tai*. Reverse trickery is perfectly okay under Asian rules: spill a drink onto the table, the floor or the host; pour it into flowerpots, teapots or the ubiquitous orange softdrink glasses.

But never be rude. Politeness is one of Asia's eternal verities. Compliments and gracious gestures will carry the foreign visitor a long way toward his goals; a loss of temper is very bad news indeed.

Good manners, in fact, are one of Asia's few unchanging standards, from top hotels to tribal long-houses. In just about everything else, change is the supreme fact, and the pace of change, accelerated by the area's thirst for high technology, is discouragingly rapid. Much of the information in this book, gathered in the mid-Eighties, may be dated soon. But be sure that a new edition will appear with all deliberate speed, to keep up with the area's changing realities.

This book was written after visits by the author to all cities covered, aided by a corps of correspondents who know their individual cities well and who in almost every case have lived many years in those cities. All are Western journalists: their nationalities range from American to British to Australian. All speak the language of their city of residence. Their reports bring to this book an enormous amount of knowledge, professional competence—and *joie de vivre* as well.

That said, the author alone is to be blamed for errors of omission and commission alike. In succeeding issues of this book, we hope to broaden our coverage both geographically and intellectually. Suggestions from readers, along these or other helpful lines, will be welcomed.

Bangkok

Angels and Others

In the Asia love-hate league, Bangkok is tops. One of the continent's most permissive cities, it's also one of the most frustrating. Here's a city where everything goes—except for traffic and telephones. Where every couple of years the streets vanish under water for weeks at a time. Where the smog is so thick it's nearly edible. And where the people are so downright charming that one forgives them all, every time, for the periodic impossibilities of their city.

But don't let that charm fool you. The Thais are capable of smiling through the most horrid of adversities, but they are also capable of switching to violence at the snap of a finger. Foreigners (*farangs* in Thai) have not yet figured out why the dreadful traffic (always just inches from gridlock during the day) does not cause bloodshed at every intersection. One *farang*, running an hour late on a key day of appointments, tried three times to alert his contacts by calling from public phones along the streets he was traversing at a meter per hour. The phones, naturally, did not work, nor did the phones of shopkeepers who offered to help. At last, he ran into a bank and sent a telex. The answer—'Let's have supper instead'—came back in three minutes. The dreadful traffic has one great utility, however: it's the perfect excuse for absolutely anything except perhaps bad breath.

Bangkok can't blame its traffic jams on urban tangles left over from ancient times. The city is only 200 years old, younger in fact than many cities in Europe and the Americas. The city's official name is not Bangkok, but Krung Thep (City of Angels). How many residents? The capital officially has a population of about 5 million, but there are perhaps 3 million unregistered jobseekers who have flooded in from the countryside.

Thai written history goes back about 1500 years. Some believe that the Thais were forced south from China by the Han Chinese. Most Thais are Buddhist (90%), and King Bhumibol Adulyadej himself is protector of the faith—and of the seven other state religions as well. Thais are intensely nationalistic, and at least part of this pride is traceable to the fact that the country was never colonized, as were all of its neighbors. The pride very definitely extends to the King and the Royal Family. Derogatory remarks about them are punished—and heavily—by law. But questions about the royals are welcome. Simply let the Thais express any opinions.

Most tourist publications tell readers not to touch anyone on the head; not to cross legs so that the sole of the foot points to anyone; to speak softly and avoid any

1

BANGKOK

display of temper; and to beckon people with the fingers held down, not up. The tourist books are right, but Thais give foreigners a lot of leeway in such matters. Perhaps the best advice is the golden rule: the Thais are very good at it.

Spotlight

There's nothing quite like heavy, Asian yellow gold to spice up a spouse. And Bangkok is a fine place to find it. But don't buy at a jewelry shop. Instead, take a drive down to Vaowaraj, which means Chinatown and is the name of the quarter's main street.

Here's where the capital's legal gold shops are most plentiful. They seem to be everywhere: open to the street, no frills, unemotional Chinese clerks handling thousands of dollars worth of the precious stuff. Prices are posted. There's no haggling on the basic cost. But the street price is tied to world gold prices, so quotations change often.

Because exporting gold in ingot form is difficult, most gold is sold in the form of bangles which can be taken anywhere. So look over the designs. There are bracelets and brooches, rings and necklaces—and statues in gold as well. Something tasteful in a Chinese god, say, will set you back a lot. Prices vary according to workmanship. The average cost runs from about US$10 to a maximum of $20 an ounce over the price of the gold itself.

Who buys the gold? Not many farangs. Instead, the customer next to you is likely to be a housewife, salting away a bit more security in the form of a new bracelet. Or a businessman buying a bracelet's worth of affection from his latest mistress. Or a smart dowager who knows that gold is always in good taste.

Warning: As noted, avoid buying gold at jewellery shops—unless you must purchase a setting for a ring. In this case, remember that Thais have their own system of counting carats, and it is two or more points below what they call the 'International standard'. Thus Thai 24 carat gold is 20 carats by usual standards. Always ask.

● Arriving

Bangkok's Don Muang Airport is not the most maddening in Asia—there are several competitors, including Taipei and Hong Kong. But waiting times at both immigration and customs can be absurdly long. Thailand advertises itself as 'the land of smiles' but there are very few at Don Muang. A new international terminal, due for completion in the near future, may speed processing a bit.

Most visitors routinely receive permission to stay for 14 days. Extensions are extremely time consuming. If more time is needed, it's easier on the nerves to fly to Penang, for example, and pick up another 14-day permit. An alternative is to pick up a 2-month tourist visa, available for $15 at all Thai embassies.

Do *not* obtain a non-immigrant visa. Holders of such visas cannot leave Thailand without a tax clearance, obtainable only after incredibly complicated red tapery at the Finance Ministry.

Don Muang Airport folks usually are very good at recovering lost luggage. Your airline representative will help get the search started and almost all misplaced items will reach your hotel in 24 hours.

Transportation into town is best arranged via the limousine service run by Thai Airways International. Cost: about $18. Contact the desk just past Customs. Ignore the clamoring touts: they'll have you on your way to a fifth-class hotel almost instantly.

Brace yourself for a long ride into central Bangkok. Traffic is usually brutal. At the best of times the ride will take an hour, and the scenery is depressing.

● Transportation

Bangkok traffic is fierce. Only optimists will schedule two appointments in the morning—unless they're in the same building. Thus an airconditioned hotel sedan is recommended, if only because it makes the smoggy, slothlike traffic a bit more bearable. Prices vary for these cars, but count on at least $10 an hour. Slightly cheaper are the private drivers who wait outside many major hotels. Most are relatively honest and haggling is painless.

Street cabbies are a reckless and often dishonest lot and should be avoided if at all possible. In any case, haggle fiercely before starting a journey. This will fend off ugly scenes at the end of a trip. Meters do not exist. Tips are built into fares: don't tip unless the service has been exceptional.

Avoid the motorized three-wheelers called tuktuks. Buses are downright risky. And most strolling is unrewarding. Thai blocks tend to be about a kilometer long, and Bangkok's high temperatures and high humidity will turn one's legs (and everything else) to water almost immediately.

● Money

The Thai currency unit is the *baht*, broken down into 25 and 50 *satang* coins. There are one and 5 *baht* coins as well, and bills come in the following denominations: 10, 20, 100 and 500. The best place to change money is with a licensed money changer. Banks will give a slightly lower rate. Hotel money changers give much lower rates.

● Tipping

The 10% rule applies generally—if a service charge has not been added to your check. For extra services, 20 *baht* is adequate. Instant fame comes to the tourist unwary enough to offer a 100 *baht* tip. Don't tip cabbies unless service has been extraordinary.

● Communications

Bangkok really isn't out of touch with the world, but there are times that it seems that way. Domestic phone service is about the worst in Asia. Many hotels still require that their operators handle all calls. And if direct city dialing has been installed, one waits—and waits—for a line. International calls go through with less than a hour's delay, and quality is usually good. Public phones are all but useless. Telex cummunication, on the other hand, works pretty well.

● What to wear

Bangkok is *hot*. Wear cottons. For evenings in better restaurants, men wear jackets or the relatively new and practical formal men's shirt that resembles the Filipino *barong tagalog*. Women dress a bit more formally in the evenings as well—and should beware of icy air-conditioning. Bangkok's tailors are good, and often less expensive than in Hong Kong, should extra shirts or frocks be needed.

Chiang Mai, in the northern hills, can be cool in the evenings. Bring a sweater.

● Languages

Thai is the national language, and it is not particularly easy to pick up. English works in most of Bangkok's restaurants, shops and hotels, but is barely useful upcountry. Shouting is not advised. Sign language sometimes works. Several Chinese dialects (Mandarin, Cantonese and Chuichow) are spoken in the larger cities.

● Doing business

*Business hours: Government and private offices generally are open between 08:30 and 16:30, with an hour off for lunch at noon. Banks close at 15:30.

*Business counsel: Aside from the many chambers of commerce in Bangkok, the government's Board of Investment (BOI) offers generally excellent service to potential investors. Its 'one-stop center' for investors isn't quite as efficient as BOI would like it to be, but it offers sound advice and is empowered to give major investment breaks to foreign business people. The BOI is located on Larn Luang Road, tel. 222–8161.

*Another asset for inquiring investors is the Board of Trade, which shares an address and phone number with the Thai Chamber of Commerce: 150 Rajabophit Road, tel. 221–3351.

● Other government offices:

Ministry of Commerce, Sanamchai Road el. 221–0835; Ministry of Industry, Rama VI Road, tel. 281–1067; Export Service Center, 22–77 Rachadapisek Road, Bng Khen, tel. 511–5066.

Useful phone numbers

● Embassies:

Nearly all diplomatic missions in Bangkok are equipped to give commercial advice. The US Embassy, for example, maintains a large commercial section in the Kian Gwan Building, 140 Wireless Road, tel. 252–5040, across the road from the main embassy ofices. Its library keeps normal business hours and is open to all nationalities.

● Embassy telephone numbers:

Argentina, 234–6911.
Australia, 286–0411.
Austria, 286–3011.
Bangladesh, 391–8069.
Belgium, 233–0840.
Bolivia, 392–4870.
Brazil, 251–2989.
Bulgaria, 390–2326.
Burma, 233–2237.
Canada, 234–1561.
Chile, 391–8443.
China, 279–7075.
Czechoslovakia, 234–1922.
Denmark, 286–3932.
Dominican Republic, 521–0737.
Egypt, 252–6139.
Finland, 252–3636.
France, 234–0950.
Germany (West), 286–4223.
Greece, 314–7333.
India, 392–4161.
Indonesia, 252–3135.
Iran, 251–4925.
Iraq, 278–5335.
Israel, 252–3131.
Italy, 234–9718.
Japan, 252–6151.
South Korea, 234–0723.
Laos, 286–0010.
Malaysia, 286–1390.
Nepal, 391–7240.
Netherlands, 252–6103.
New Zealand, 251–8165.
Norway, 392–1104.
Pakistan, 252–7036.
Peru, 233–5910.
Philippines, 391–0008.
Poland, 391–0668.
Portugal, 234–0372.
Romania, 252–8515.
Saudi Arabia, 233–7941.
Singapore, 286–211.
Spain, 252–6112.
Sri Lanka, 251–2789.
Sweden, 234–3891.
Switzerland, 252–8992.
Turkey, 251–2987.
United Kingdom, 252–7161.
USA, 252–5040.

USSR, 234–9824.
Vatican, 233–9109.
Vietnam, 251–7102.
Yugoslavia, 391–9090.

● **Chambers of commerce:**

These organizations offer general business advice, oriented toward citizens of the countries they represent.
American Chamber of Commerce, 140 Wireless Road, 251–9266.
British Chamber of Commerce, 302 Silom Road, 234–1140.
Chinese Chamber of Commerce, Sathorn Road North, 211–2369.
Franco-Thai Chamber of Commerce, 140 Wireless Road, 251–9386.
German-Thai Chamber of Commerce, 699 Silom Road, 233–9113.
Italian-Thai Chamber of Commerce, 2013 New Petchburi Road, 314–6101.
Japanese Chamber of Commerce, Ploenchit Road, 252–0178.

● **International airlines:**

Aeroflot, 233–6965.
Air France, 233–7100.
Air India, 233–8950.

Alia, 235–4800.
Alitalia, 233–4000.
British Airways, 252–9871.
Burma Airways, 234–9692.
Cathay Pacific, 235–6022.
China Airlines, 251–9656.
Egyptair, 235–8964.
Garuda, 233–0981.
Gulf Air, 235–0416.
Iraqi Airways, 233–3271.
Japan Air Lines, 234–9105.
KLM, 235–5150.
Korean Air Lines, 234–0283.
Kuwait Airways, 251–5855.
Lao Aviation, 233–7950.
Lufthansa, 234–1350.
Malaysian Airlines, 234–9795.
Pakistan International, 234–2961.
Philippine Airlines, 233–2350.
Polish Airlines, 235–2223.
Qantas, 234–4951.
Royal Brunei, 234–3110.
Royal Nepal, 233–3921.
SAS, 252–4181.
Sabena, 235–5940.
Saudi Arabian Airlines, 233–7630.
Singapore Airlines, 235–1570.
Swissair, 233–2930.
Thai Airways, 282–7640.

Shopping

The rule is simple: Buy Thai. The range of local textiles and handicrafts is mouthwatering and the prices are decent once you've haggled a bit. Avoid, however, Thai products made for export (Levis, Arrow shirts, Cannon towels): you'll save no money at all on these.

Perhaps the best value is that old perennial, Thai silk. It comes in a rainbow of colors, patterns and weights, and is altogether delightful for clothing, table cloths, upholstery, wall coverings and just about anything else.

Still the best place to buy silk, as it has been for decades, is the Thai Silk Co. Ltd. Founded by Jim Thompson, an OSS agent in Thailand during World War II, this firm offers the most expensive silk in town. It's also of the best quality. Thompson vanished in the Cameron highlands of Malaysia in 1967, and the mystery of his disappearance has never been solved. But his shop at 9 Suriwong Road remains a delight to the eye and a memorial to the man.

There are two other topnotch Thai silk shops: Design Thai (304 Silom Road) offers fine Thai cottons; and Star of Siam (2194 Charoenkrung Road, Yanawa). Beware of the smaller shops. Some of their offerings are not pure silk and will not stand up well.

Gems and precious stones abound in Bangkok shops and should be regarded with a jaundiced eye—and loupe! Some of these stones are Thai, others are smuggled over the border from Burma, which is a source for some of the world's best gems. But *caveat emptor* remains the rule.

One may, for example, be shown a selection of flawless rubies or sapphires. If they are indeed flawless, they are fakes; made by salvaging the 'dust' left when gems are cut, then compressing it into molds. On the world market, these fakes are worth $5 per carat.

Gem dealers are expert at the hard sell. In general, the harder the sell the more dubious the merchandise. If you must buy, be guided by local friends. And haggle mercilessly.

Tailors abound in Bangkok, and most are reasonably reliable. But they are copiers, not designers: you must show them precisely what you want or risk looking ever so slightly clownish. Shop around and do not accept the first price quoted. Prices in arcades of top hotels (such as the Oriental) are flatly outrageous. Prowl the shops, and take your time. It should be noted that Bangkok tailoring, aside from the banditti, is considerably cheaper than in Hong Kong. Its quality, however, may not be as high.

Antiques are tricky. Thai firms manufacture some of the world's most convincing fakes. Even experts have been fooled. The prudent course, if one decides one cannot live without that lifesize teak horse, is to pay handicraft prices for it. If the seller claims it's really antique and charges accordingly, walk away. (*Exception:* Peng Chen, on Suriwong Road, which has superb antiques and will help obtain the necessary export permits. Expensive, of course.) In general, Thai wood carvings make appealing gifts.

Bronzeware seems to be another perennial purchase in Bangkok, but it can produce much disappointment. Again, be guided by your Bangkok friends: quality varies enormously. Thai pewter is more expensive, and not as good, as Malaysia's Selangor products.

▶ Hotels

The Great Room Glut began here in 1982 and hasn't yet ended. For the wise business traveler, this offers a splendid opportunity for price negotiations. There are moments during the year in which your favorite hotel may be full—but these moments will pass rapidly. A 25% room price reduction is normal—try for 50%. Or 75%. You may get it, depending on the degree of desperation of the moment.

Once installed in one's room—or suite—travelers will be stunned by the high quality of service. Bringing a guest in for the night, however, will cause difficulties in first-class hotels, although after a bit of eyebrow-raising most will simply ask your newfound friend to register.

Hotels listed here accept major credit cards and offer the usual top-class amenities: swimming pool, executive business centers and shopping.

The Oriental, Oriental Avenue, tel. 236–0400, telex TH ORIENTL 82997. This quite simply may be the best hotel in the world, as far as several respected polls are concerned. The experience of 100 years shows throughout the old and new wings, service is excellent and facilities superb. Room prices are high, but reductions (particularly in summertime) are possible. Its superb riverside location can seem a bit far from business areas, particularly given Bangkok's frustrating traffic. Two pools, business center, sports center.

Ambassador, 8 Sukhumvit Road, Soi 11, tel. 251–0404, telex TH 82910. The largest (1,000 rooms) in town, it's favored by Japanese executives because of its straight-ahead, no-nonsense service and its huge selection of restaurants featuring most major cuisines of the world.

Regent, 155 Rajdamri Road, tel. 251–6127 telex TH 20004. Opened in 1982 (as the Peninsula) and billed as the most luxurious hotel in town, the Regent has worked hard ever since to catch up with the Oriental. It is one of the world's most beautiful hotels. Its superscale Rajdamri Suite (priced at $2250 per day) features among other things an 18-person dining room, six bedrooms and a living room almost big enough for tennis. Health center, outdoor pool; its faintly out-of-way location offers calm after the city's pandemonium.

Dusit Thani, corner of Rama IV Road and Silom Road, tel. 233–1130, telex TH 81170. When the hotel room glut began, this lofty (26 floors) hotel went through a renovation that combined every two rooms into one, making its rooms the city's largest. Nicely located, it has Lumpini Park just across the road for joggers and strollers, and a block the other way is Patpong, Bangkok's unrestrained adult play area. Business travelers have a wing reserved for them, free of children and tourists.

Erawan, 494 Rajdamri Road, tel. 252–9100, telex TH 82189 ERWAN. Run by the national government, the Erawan remains the address for official guests (who enjoy a sumptuous seven-room teak suite). But the hotel in general has slipped significantly in recent years and may be renovated soon.

Montien, 54 Surawong Road, tel. 233–7060, telex TH 81038. One of the older (1960s) luxury hotels, the Montien is well located in a major business area and fronts on nightlifey Patpong.

Hilton, Nai-Lert Park, 2 Wireless Road, tel. 251–0123, telex 72206 HILBKK. Opened in 1983, it occupies its own lovely flowered park, offers several good restaurants and is one of the more spectacular Hilton Asia stars. Direct-dial phone system. The grill, and the Ma Maison French restaurant, are recommended.

Tawana Sheraton, 80 Surawong Road, tel. 233–5160, telex TH 81167. Located in the Patpong area, it welcomes nightlifers who frequent the lively disco. Indoor pool.

Hyatt Central Plaza, 1695 Phaholyothin Road, tel. 541–1234, telex 20173 HYATTBK. Big and new, it's the closest first-class hotel to the airport, but a bit far from business areas. Hugo's grillroom is recommended. Regency Club, health center with tennis and jogging.

Shangri-La, 89 Soi Wat Suan Plu, New Road, Bangrak, tel. 236–0280, telex 84593 SHANGLA TH. Eight bars and restaurants, health club with pool, tennis and squash, business center.

Siam Intercontinental, Rama I Road, tel. 252–9040, telex TH 81155 SIAMINT. Another hotel with its own park and thus a favorite of joggers. Rooms tend to be spare and functional. Pool.

Royal Orchid Sheraton, Captain Bush Lane, off New Road, tel. 234–5599, telex 84491. Sheraton took over management of this well-located riverside hotel in early 1985. Four restaurants, business center. Located beside River City, a large new shopping center.

Restaurants

● Thai

D'Jit Pochana, Three locations: Oriental Hotel annex, tel. 234–8620; 20 Sukhumvit, tel. 391–3586; and 1802 Phaholyothin Road, tel. 279–5000. The best Thai food in town, many claim. Large menus featuring most classic Thai dishes; fast service. Dining under the stars on the riverside opposite the Oriental (free ferry) is particularly recommended. Try the spicy shrimp soup called Tom Yum Gung, and warn the waiter if you have not yet adjusted to truly fiery food. Also recommended, though not on the menu, is the incredible volcano chicken. When it arrives at the table, move your chair back about a meter and stay alert.

Bussaracum, 35 Soi Pipat 2, tel. 235–8915. Perhaps a step up in terms of elegance from D'Jit Pochana, it offers fine curries (try the Penang version) and 'dancing shrimps'—dancing because they're hot off the griddle. First-class service by some of Bangkok's best waitresses and Thai classical music—on tape and barely audible.

Thon Thub Rub, Sukhumvit Soi 8, tel. 252–5145. As pleasant as Bussaracum, save that the music is live. Just across the street from the Ambassador Hotel.

Tap Kaew, Asoke-Din Daeng Road, tel. 245–2075. Outdoor dining in a huge garden, good food, and lively Thai company. Bring a Thai-speaker along—not much English spoken, although the menu is in English and Chinese as well as Thai.

● Western

Nick's Number One, 1 Sathorn Road, corner of Wireless Road, tel. 286–2258. A Bangkok landmark since the early Fifties, located in an old mansion, Nick's is the oldest European restaurant in town. Nick Jero died in 1984 but his Thai widow rules with an iron hand and quality is still tops. Great atmosphere, fine steaks.

Neil's Tavern, Soi Ruamrudee, tel. 251–5644. Opened by the former chief chef of Nick's Number One, offers good steaks and seafood and ranks with Nick's as a favorite of the foreign community. The restaurant opened on July 20, 1969. And who was Neil? The place is named for Neil Armstrong, first man on the moon.

Charly's, 66 Sathorn Road, tel. 234–9035. Swiss continental, expensive and just passable. Good cheeses, though.

Le Metropolitan, 135–6 Soi Gaysorn, near President hotel, tel. 252–8364. French in cuisine, French in decor, owned by Corsican Pierre Mengi, who has many tales of Indochina to tell. *Bouillabaisse* and *lapin à la moutarde* are favorites. Popular with Bangkok's French colony.

La Normandie, Oriental Tower Hotel, penthouse, tel. 234–8620. Generally first-rate French cooking, fair (but terribly expensive) wines and *un peu* snob—tie required in the evening. Fine pastry. Splendid river view.

The Two Vikings, Soi 35, 2 Sukhumvit, tel. 391–1970. Gone are the superb smörgasbords of yesteryear, but the herring is still terrific. The basic continental menu is always good. Fine service, elegant decor, very expensive. Closed on Sunday.

● Chinese

Hoi Tien Lau, 308 Suapa Road, tel. 221–1685. Good Cantonese food, bright and noisy, spotty service. Tasty *dim sum* snacks at lunchtime, served by a seemingly endless parade of pretty Bangkok girls.

Shangrila, 154 Silom Road, tel. 234–2045. Cantonese and Chiuchow cooking, noisy, bright. Good Beijing duck, beggar's chicken. Private rooms upstairs.

Rose La Moon, Soi Asoke, 165–5 Sukhumvit, tel. 391–7351. No frills but great food. Try the squab roasted in coffee grounds, the dish that 'made' this restaurant; also the imported bamboo fish served steamed and whole, or the fried (yes) iceberg lettuce. Not many foreigners and lots of locals, so reserve.

Tien Tien, Patpong Road, tel. 234–8717. Very good Cantonese food, set off by perhaps the sulkiest, most chaotic service in Bangkok. Packed nontheless, mostly by local Chinese who will put up with a lot for a good meal. Try the barbecued duck, any of the seafood dishes or the noodles.

Scala, Siam Square, opposite Scala cinema, tel. 250–1633. Western decor but good Cantonese food, and the best Beijing duck in town. Why? Because it's real duck—most restaurants use goose. And it is beautifully cooked.

● Japanese

Daikoku, 960 Rama IV Road, opposite Lumpini Park, tel. 233–1495. One of the best in Bangkok, Japanese-run right down to the waitresses, and expensive ($75 per person is not unusual), Daikoku offers the usual Japanese menu (*tempura*, *sushi*, *sashimi* and *sukiyaki*) and prepares it very well indeed.

● Korean

Arirang, 106–8 Silom Road, favored by local Koreans.

Koreana, 488–50 Siam Square, tel. 252–9308. Best *kimchi* (spicy cabbage) in town.

New Korea, Sukhumvit Soi 15. Best *bulgogi* (barbecued beef) in town.

● Indian

Himali Cha-Cha, 1229/11 New Road, tel. 245–1561. Tandoori Moslem food, kebabs.

Cafe India, 460/8 Surawong Road, tel. 284–1384. Moslem food, good curries.

■▶ After hours

There are a million stories about Bangkok's nightlife, and perhaps 1% are false. The variety, color and liveliness are pretty much as advertised, and while serious trouble can be found by the earnest seeker, the usual damages are only hangovers and flat wallets.

Where's the action? Patpong is the place to start—and often to finish as well. Located in mid-city near several top-rated hotels, the Patpong area now consists of three narrow streets called, for convenience, if not topographical accuracy, Patpongs One, Two and Three. Patpong One has been a favorite hangout since before the boom days of the Vietnam War. The other two are newer but no less lively. Patpong Three has several gay spots.

Ripoffs? There are indeed places that will take advantage of drunks, and some of the girls have been known to be less than straight with late-hour customers. Visitors are advised to exercise reasonable caution. (And a Bangkok resident advises visitors to avoid picking up 'friends' on the streets: those delicious Thai girls strolling about are usually boys.)

Prices are high in most places, but there are ways to keep the bills low. Try Thai whiskey, for example: it is called Mekhong, has a low alcohol content (30%) and is inexpensive. Local beer is good. Kloster, a full-bodied lager, is a favorite. Another is Singha, a heavier beer that has something of a reputation for hitting hard. A third local beer, Amarit, resembles ale.

Evenings out usually involve more than one stop. A formal business circuit may involve an hour or so at the nightclubs of the larger hotels—the Ambassador, for example, or the clubs at the Dusit Thani, Royal Orchid or Bangkok Palace. The Cafe de Paris (Surawong Road) is a popular nightclub stop. It's expensive ($5 to $7 a drink) but the show's not bad.

From here on into the night, it's useful if not essential to have a Bangkok friend as guide, drinking buddy or master of the revels. One unusual local amusement is the so-called 'no-hands' restaurant. You must ask a Thai friend to arrange this diversion, which involves having a succession of pretty young Thai women come to your private room to stuff goodies into your mouth, while you think deeply about what to do with your hands. Cost: $60 apiece or so.

Appetites partly appeased, many will head for Patpong. Recommendations are difficult, because many bars change hands rapidly. But some, such as the Grand Prix GoGo Bar, the Mississippi Queen Rock'n'Roll Bar and the Super Star GoGo Bar and (yes!) Coffee Shop have lasted under the same owners since the late Sixties. These spots aren't cheap; nor are the hostesses, but the right combination of smooth charm and coarse bills can do wonders for one's social life.

Another method of easing tension involves a call on one of Bangkok's legendary massage parlors. Here, a Thai friend or at least a tip from a fellow *farang* (foreigner) will be most helpful in pointing you in the best direction. Pay in advance for your bath and massage. Extras can be discussed later, depending on the degree of stress.

And then there are the discos, as popular here as they are elsewhere in Asia. It's best to bring a partner; Bangkok discos are not much use for meeting people, if only because they may be the loudest in the world. Try the Bubbles, in the Dusit Thani hotel, or Diana's at the Oriental, or the discos at the Ambassador or Manhattan hotels.

For old-fashioned quiet drinks and conversation, count on the Oriental's Bamboo Bar, the lobby bar at the Hilton, or Patpong's Executive Lounge, Lucy's Tiger Den or Cloud Nine. The Stoned Crow on Soi Cowboy is another possibility.

There are several after-hours spots, and only a Bangkok chum can guide you properly here. But one late-night spectacle is, as it has been for years, the coffee shop at the Grace, where many ladies of the evening gather to greet the morning. It's a sight to stir the blood, if you can still keep your eyes open.

Sights and sounds

Royal Palace and Emerald Buddha: The palace complex is open from 09:30 to 12:00 and 14:00 to 16:00 daily. Guides show visitors the Chakri Palace, built in 1782 in an oddly pleasing combination of Thai and Victorian styles, now used only for formal receptions. *Warning:* For men, jackets and ties are required; for women, slacks and shorts are prohibited. The Wat Phra Keo houses the Emerald (really jasper) Buddha, probably the most important Buddha image in Thailand.

Wat Po (Temple of the Reclining Buddha): This huge Buddha image, with its feet beautifully inlaid with mother-of-pearl, is in a temple just south of the Royal

Palace.

Floating market and **Temple of Dawn**: A boat tour takes visitors through the *klongs* (canals) of Thonburi, across the river from the central city, where canalside life is vivid. The Temple of the Dawn (Wat Arun) which offers a pleasant view of the river, is usually included on these tours. Best to start by 07:00, before the thermometer soars.

National Museum: One of the largest—and best—in Southeast Asia, this museum offers a fine overview of Thai history down through the centuries, as well as many superb Buddha images. Huge, and not air-conditioned; near the Royal Palace.

Jim Thompson's House: The home of the famed silk merchant and ex-OSS agent who vanished in 1967, the building was assembled from parts of six traditional-style Thai houses. Much of Thompson's superb Thai art collection is displayed. Open Monday through Friday, 09:30 to 15:30. Near the National Stadium.

Snake Farm and **Pasteur Institute**, corner of Rama IV and Henri Dunant Roads: Venom from poisonous snakes is extracted here and made into serum. 'Milking' at about 11:00 daily. Fangs for the memories...

Crocodile Farm: Located about an hour's drive from central Bangkok, this offers more crocodiles (perhaps 1,000) than anyone really needs to see. Croc wrestling several times a day—the crocodiles always lose. Small zoo, refreshments, kitsch. Open daily.

Rose Garden, Suan Sam Phran, about 90 kilometers from the city: Instant Thailand: daily demonstrations of Thai dancing, sword fighting, cockfighting and handicraft-making. There's also an 18-hole golf course, several restaurants and a hotel.

Ayutthaya, 80 kilometers from the city: This former Thai capital (1350–1767), is about two hours by bus from the capital and can also be reached by train and, most pleasantly, by water. Boat trips offer a fair meal and good views of the countryside en route. Though restoration continues, many beautiful temples and palaces can now be visited.

Weekends

Chiang Mai: It's called the Rose of the North for several reasons, not least because its young women are reputedly the comeliest in Thailand. Reachable by air (US$50, one hour) and by train (US$45, overnight from Bangkok), Chiang Mai is a cool and pleasant weekend retreat. The better hotels (Hyatt Orchid, Rincome and Chiang Inn) have pools, and golf and tennis are easily arranged. Visit hill tribe villages, the pleasant royal palace at Phuping and plod the 300 steps up Doi (Hill) Suthep to Wat Prayong. (For particularly good luck, buy a cage of sparrows (*Baht* 40 for 9) at the foot of the steps and release them at the top. Much Buddhistic merit will accrue to you). Fair selection of handicrafts (umbrellas, textiles, carvings and pottery) at nearby villages. Haggle.

Golden Triangle: Worth seeing if only for the area's newsworthiness, the area can be reached by air from Bangkok in two hours. Stay at the Wiang Inn (Chiang

Rai) and hire a guide/chauffeur to drive up to Mae Sai, on the Burmese border, and then over bad roads to the Golden Triangle itself—the point at which Burma, Thailand and Laos meet on the banks of the Mekong. Colorful opium caravans are hard to find, but then the heavily armed smugglers are known to be touchy about observers. At Mae Sai, smuggled gems (rubies and sapphires) from Burma can be bought. *Caveat emptor*.

Phimai: Built by Khmer Kings in the 8th Century, this smaller version of Angkor Wat has been rebuilt recently by UNESCO. Until the current Cambodia government once again opens war-battered Angkor to Western visitors, Phimai will be the best alternative. Suggestion: rent a bungalow in nearby Khao Yai National Park through the Tourism Authority of Thailand (tel. 281–0372) and enjoy the park's plentiful wildlife. Phimai can be reached by auto in seven hours from Bangkok. Alternatively, fly to Korat, and rent a car for the remaining 30 miles.

The Bridge on the River Kwai: Seventy miles from Bangkok, this is best reached by tour bus, which can be arranged through your hotel. Impressive Allied Cemetery, marking graves of the Allied war prisoners who died building the bridge and railway for the Japanese military. Japanese visitors seem strangely fond of 'Bridge' t-shirts.

Pattaya: Once Thailand's best beach resort, Pattaya has been overbuilt and its age is showing. And the beach is polluted occasionally by a nearby oil-unloading platform. Among the best hotels is the Royal Cliff, which has a private beach and a good pool. Pattaya is a two-hour drive from Bangkok: hotel limos charge US$100 one way, but your hotel can arrange a bus trip (air-conditioned) for about US$15 round-trip. A good restaurant is Dolf Riks, which offers a fine *rijstafel*. Watch out for ripoffs among renters of water scooters, who often falsely accuse renters of damaging equipment. Para-sailing can be fun, but check rigging carefully: maintenance is spotty.

Hua Hin and **Cha Am:** Just across the Gulf of Siam from Pattaya, and two hours south of Bangkok, these towns are altogether more pleasant than their noisier cousin but are almost completely lacking in nightlife. At Hua Hin, the Royal Garden Hotel is new and pleasant. Cha Am, just a bit north of Hua Hin, has a similarly relaxed atmosphere: try the Regent Cha Am Hotel. Beaches in both towns are excellent.

Phuket: Thailand's handsomest beach resort, almost two hours south by air from the capital. Beautiful white sand beaches, quiet coves and just enough night life. Rent a boat and visit the fantastic limestone islands, many with explorable caves. Particularly worthwhile are the islands of Ko Peepee Lek and Ko Peepee Yai, which have a great selection of tiny hideaway beaches. Good hotels include the Phuket Island Resort and the Pearl, both with reservation offices in Bangkok.

Sports

The Thais tolerate some sports imported from the West: tennis, golf, even bowling and basketball. But the sports they love best are their own—and these are violent.

Most spectacular is Thai boxing (*muay Thai*), which has heavy overtones of the martial arts. Everything goes: not only fists are weapons. So are elbows, knees and feet. Any part of the body can be hit. The amount of action packed into the usual five-round brawl is spectacular. There are fights almost every day and admission is inexpensive. Betting is permitted at both major stadiums: Lumpini (on Rama IV Road) and Rajdamnoern, on Rajdamnoern Road.

But Thai boxing is only part of the fight scene in Bangkok. Sports fans here can watch fellow human beings clash with swords, for example, which is another stylized branch of the martial arts.

Or with kites. From February to April, kite flyers engage in aerial combat at Pramane Park, near Wat Phra Keo. So-called 'female' kites (small and agile) clash with huge 'male' kites: the strings are coated with glass shards and the trick is to saw through your opponent's string before he cuts yours.

Fighting fish: Bouts may be found at the Weekend Market, where owners match their multicolored male Siamese Fighting Fish in fights, to the death, amid much illegal betting. One fan says that when bowls containing fighting fish are placed side by side, the fish will batter themselves to death against the glass unless a screen is placed between the bowls.

Fighting cocks: Again, the Weekend Market may produce a bout. But because the betting—an integral part of cockfighting—is illegal, a certain amount of discreet questioning may be necessary. There are more opportunities to see good fights outside Bangkok.

Fighting beetles: Take one large horned male beetle, several inches long. Introduce him to another male, while a female of the species is nearby. Result: a long (sometimes more than an hour) battle, with much betting, that ends when one tips the other on his back.

Fighting crickets: Mostly for the kids, this involves male crickets and is particularly popular at the start of the rainy season, in July, when insects abound.

One popular Thai sport that does not involve combat is *Takraw*, which consists of kicking a ball made of tightly woven rattan among a group of players. The idea is to keep the ball in the air: any part of the body can be used except the hands. Immensely graceful.

On the import side of the sporting ledger, there are the following:

Horse racing: Through most of the year, there is high-quality racing on the weekends at the very posh Royal Bangkok Sports Club, on Saturdays, and at the equally fancy Royal Turf Club, on Sundays. Racing enclosures are open to the public, but entry to private club precincts must be arranged by a Bangkok friend (very strict).

Golf: There are a dozen courses of varying quality within the Bangkok area. Business associates, or the hotel concierge, will make the necessary introduction.

Tennis: Several of the better hotels have their own courts, and there are many private tennis clubs as well. Ask the hotel manager, or a business contact, for an introduction.

Beijing

Skyscrapers and Hutungs

Just off a modern Beijing expressway, a group of men—some poor, some not—gathers almost every day. With them, in cages, or flying free but tethered to wrists by a bit of string, are their fat, sassy and rather lovely birds. And as the surf of shiny Japanese sedans and smoking diesel trucks thunders past, the talk here is of birds and their manifold virtues, as it has been for centuries when Beijing birdlovers flock together.

In the same way, Beijing endures the assaults of modernity, stubbornly preserving its centuries-old beauty. The camel caravans that crowded its rubbled streets a century ago are now long gone. So are its wonderful walls, with their watchtowers and splendid ornamented gates. And so are palanquins and pigtails. (There still are queues in contemporary Beijing, but they're the waiting kind.) Traffic jams are now routine. So are high-rise buildings—this is the city where buildings higher than two stories were once forbidden by imperial edict.

But Beijing still remains essentially a city of the narrow, secretive hutungs, alleys lined with high walls whose occasional doorways permit fleeting glimpses of the crowded and cluttered lifestyle of Beijing's people.

In courtyards and lanes and public parks, young and old still practice 'taijiquan' exercises at dawn. Others sing favorite Chinese opera arias, or fish (with a permit of course) or play another in a long series of games of Chinese chess.

Private enterprise, a feature of Beijing life until it was ruled out of order by the communist government, is once again very much the order of the day. Party newspapers applaud entrepreneurs. Peasants pour into the city's free markets every morning, laden with grains and fresh produce and anything else—such as freshwater crabs or horse-hoof shavings for fertilizer—that will produce a bit of profit.

And the city's beauty, ignored for decades, is beginning to reappear. Leafy trees line many streets and flowering shrubs blossom along the edges. Huge sums are being spent on restoration of historically important buildings, temples, churches and mosques.

One of the most compelling reminders of old Beijing's beauty, in fact, is the newly restored Liulichang, a narrow little street southwest of the center, long famous for its antiques, books and paintings. Today the street stands as one of

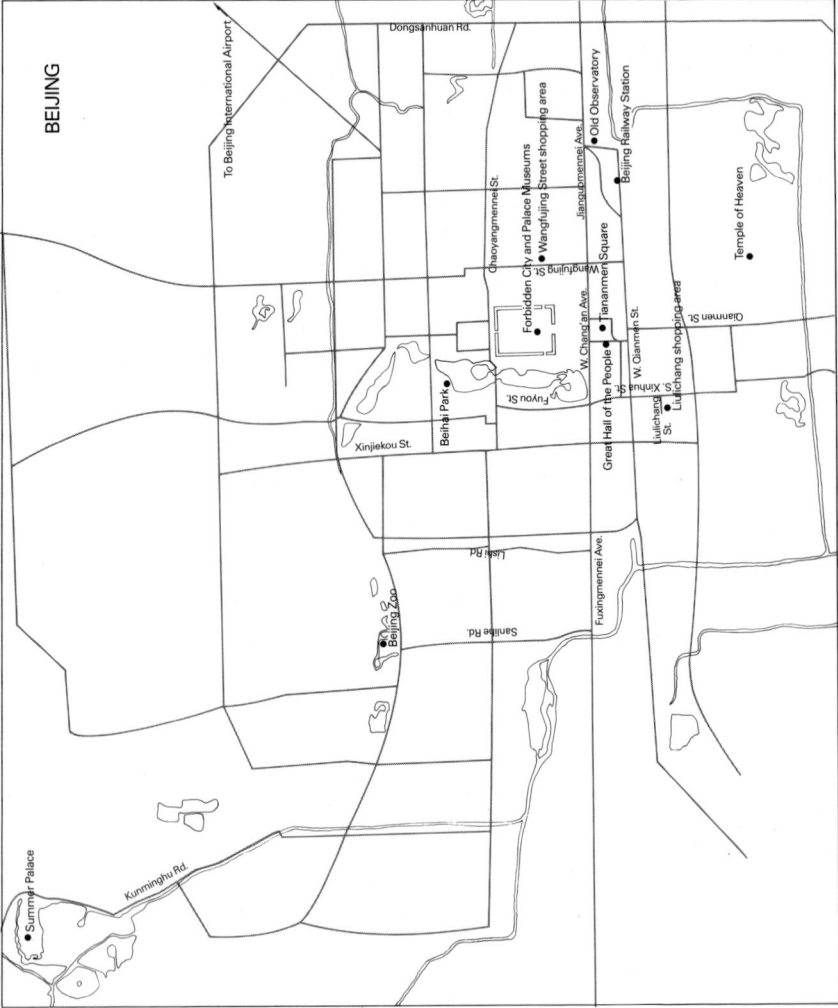

BEIJING

Dongsanhuan Rd.

To Beijing International Airport

Chaoyangmennei St.

Forbidden City and Palace Museums

Wangfujing Street shopping area

Jianguomennei Ave.

Old Observatory

Beijing Railway Station

Wangfujing St.

Temple of Heaven

W. Chang'an Ave.

Tiananmen Square

Great Hall of the People

W. Qianmen St.

S. Xinhua St.

Qianmen St.

Liulichang shopping area

Xiulichang St.

Beihai Park

Fuyou St.

Xinjiekou St.

Lishi Rd.

Fuxingmennei Ave.

Sanlihe Rd.

Beijing Zoo

Kunminghu Rd.

Summer Palace

the few reminders of what the city, once so beloved by residents and foreigners alike, must have looked like a century ago.

Proud of its past though it may be, Beijing keeps an eye firmly fixed on the modern world. In spite of low monthly wages (which average about 70 yuan), most people still seem to have enough money to buy the 'four precious things'—color television sets, video recorders, refrigerators and washing machines—and to throw expensive wedding banquets for their sons and their daughters.

And the young are beginning to embrace modern lifestyles with winning abandon. Surreptitious, private disco parties are a current fad: the kids dance to tapes smuggled in from Hong Kong and Taiwan. Japanese 'punk' clothing is something to kill (almost) for. So are jeans, trench coats, sunglasses and snapbrim hats. The total effect is noisy, sassy and very colorful indeed...more than slightly reminiscent, in fact, of those cheerful birdlovers that form so firm a link to the harmonies of ancient Beijing.

Spotlight

The dazzling architecture and symmetrical beauties of the Forbidden City might plausibly argue corresponding harmonies in the lives of the rulers. Not so. Most of the several sons of heaven (16 Ming emperors, 13 Qing) who lived within the walls saw considerably more tragedy than happiness during their reigns—though a few managed to enjoy themselves thoroughly.

Consider, for example, the Ming emperor Jia Jiang (1522–66), who converted the Qianqing Palace into a giant bedroom, installing 27 beds. In one year alone he had more that a thousand maidens between the ages of 8 and 14 brought into that palace. For amusement, he shuttled about the grounds in a goatcart. Another vigorous emperor was the Manchu emperor Kang Xi (1662–1722), who had 35 sons and 20 daughters, was an accomplished scholar and administrator and set rigorous standards of education for his progeny. Hong Xi, a Ming emperor who ruled only briefly, was sharply rebuked for spending his time with his concubines instead of mourning his late father.

Considerably less pranksome was Ming emperor Xuan De (1426–35), who stuttered so miserably that he was ashamed to appear at court, or even converse with officials. Ming emperor Wan Li (1573–1620) was grossly obese (due perhaps to a glandular disorder), was thought to be an opium addict and was so disagreeable that he once frightened a Grand Secretary into first wetting himself, then falling into a fainting fit which lasted for several days.

And then there was Qing emperor Xian Feng (1851–61), who was struck by lightning, and his successor Tong Zhi (1862–74), who was so unhappy that he sought out the company of prostitutes and died of syphillis (or, as officially recorded, smallpox).

Perhaps the saddest end was that of the reform-minded Qing emperor Guang Xu (1875–1908), who was locked up by his malevolent aunt, the Dowager Empress Ci Xi, and died either of tuberculosis contracted in his cell or from poison administered by the empress herself.

● Arriving

Until the late 1950s, approaching Beijing overland was a stunning experience: its forty-foot-high deep-red crenellated walls rose out of the plain like angry dragons as travelers neared the gates. But in 1958, over-zealous city planners razed those walls, saddening the world's romantics and destroying much of the city's ancient beauty.

In perfect accord with this aseptic attitude is Beijing's colorless new airport, built more than 20 kilometers northeast of the capital and opened in 1979. The airport handles both international and domestic flights. Though crowded at times, it is reasonably efficient.

Most business travelers will be met at the arrival area by representatives of their sponsoring organizations. If not, money can be changed at the Bank of China counter inside the customs area. Taxis are at the exit doors. The usual fare into town is between Yuan 25 and 30: bargain a bit but don't expect much yielding. Shuttle bus service to town varies between poor to nonexistent. Usual time of journey is just under one hour.

Train arrivals should simply follow the crowd toward the main exit. Allow the ticket puncher a jab at the ticket as you leave, then join the queue at the taxi kiosk just outside. There's usually a good supply of cabs.

● Orientation

Beijing ('northern capital' and previously spelled Peking), the capital of the People's Republic of China, has a population of about 8 million and an area of about 16,000 square kilometers. Through its 3,000 years of recorded history, the city's orientation was primarily political, but since the communist government came to power in 1949 the economic sector has expanded. Visitors find, however, that the city's most memorable single quality is the extraordinary richness and beauty of its historical artifacts: palaces, temples and museums.

● Transportation

Save for the truly sporting, visitors find that taxis are the best way to get around Beijing. Public transport is slow and often overcrowded, bus and subway stops are dauntingly spread out. Beijing hotels and offices are not centrally located, for the most part, and distances are long. (For the extremely adventurous, bicycles can be hired at a shop opposite the Friendship Department Store, tel. 592391.)

Though Beijing taxis do not cruise the streets hunting passengers, they are usually plentiful at all major hotels, the railway station, the Friendship Department Store and the International Club. Still, it's a good idea to simply hire a cab for the day: this practice is called 'bao che' and rates vary according to time and distance. For example, the driver of a small French taxi settled for six hours at Yuan 80.

At least two firms offer telephone taxi service, but plan on 15-to-30-minute delays. The largest fleet is directed by Capital Taxi Co., tel. 557461 (their dispatchers speak English). The Peking Car Co. will also send taxis to you (tel. 557661). Both companies will also rent chauffeur-driven cars.

Rental cars are also available from the US-based National Car Rental Co. (tel. 556-531, telex 22337) as well as China International Travel Service (CITS), tel. 554192. Self-drive cars are sometimes available but not recommended for the inexperienced.

● Money

Credit cards now are accepted in several top-rank Beijing hotels, but make a point of confirming this when registering. Many of larger Beijing shops accept credit cards.

For the most part, however, business visitors will use the Foreign Exchange Certificates (FECs), issued by the Bank of

China's many offices in exchange for travelers' checks or foreign currency. FECs are denominated in notes of 100, 50, 10, 5 and 1 *yuan*, and 5 and 1 *jiao*. These certificates may soon be phased out, officials say.

FECs are welcomed by local residents, who use these notes to purchase imported goods at the government's foreign-currency stores. This in part explains the presence of touts outside many major hotels, offering high premiums for FECs in exchange for the national currency. Remember that such transactions are illegal, and that national currency (*renminbi*, or people's money) is not accepted from foreigners in payment for, say, hotel bills, or for air and rail tickets. Some large hotels simply double their rates for *renminbi* payments.

Renminbi, however, can be used by foreigners for purchases in some shops and restaurants. Its basic unit is the *yuan*, which breaks down into 10 *jiao* (also called *mao*). There are 10 *fen* to each *jiao* or *mao*. Bills: 10, 5, 2 and 1 *yuan*; coins, 5, 2 and 1 *fen*.

● Tipping

Tipping is outlawed in China. Service charges are added to bills in the larger hotels. A very few cabbies can now bring themselves to accept tips, but hotel workers usually refuse. Try a smile and a word of thanks, instead.

● Communications

Telephone service (international and domestic) is improving in Beijing, but patience and supple dialling fingers are still required. It's rare, for instance, that you'll reach your contact on the first attempt. Phones in newer hotels are dial-equipped, but international direct-dial service is not yet available. Important: To reach numbers abroad, it's much quicker to place the call yourself rather than await incoming calls. Ask your hotel operator to handle this task. (If a hotel operator is not available, call the international operator yourself, at 337431; calls for the provinces can be booked at 334320).

> Note: Public phone booths have begun to appear on Beijing's streets.

A very few hotels in Beijing offer telex facilities, notably the Great Wall, Jianguo, Lido and Beijing. Others plan to add this service soon. Business centers such as those at major Asian hotels outside China are rare.

For help with photocopying and the like, ask your bank's Beijing branch, or your embassy, for advice.

Postal branch offices exist in nearly all major hotels. Postal service is generally reliable, though a bit slow.

● What to wear

Beijing has four distinct seasons—two pleasant and two difficult. Clothes for the lovely spring (late March to May) and fall (September to early November) are those you'd wear informally in Paris or New York. Winters can be bitter, and while central heating in new buildings is adequate, sweaters and even long underwear can be useful at times. Good heavy coats, down-filled vests and jackets, and splendid fur hats can be purchased in Beijing, and large sizes are more readily available here than in Shanghai or Guangzhou. Winters are also very dry and one's skin tends to parch: cold cream is useful.

Summers are hot and humid: cottons are recommended.

As in other parts of China, styles are informal. Some of Beijing's fast-track executives, however, are adopting the western jacket-and-tie uniform for business meetings.

> Note: Beijing's dreaded dust storms have abated somewhat, thanks to large-scale tree-planting outside the city, but in March and April they still occur.

● Languages

Mandarin (*putonghua*, or common speech) is Beijing's basic dialect, and in fact the standard language for all China. (The Beijing-born, however, can be picked out by their distinctive, almost snarled 'r' sounds). English is not yet widely spoken outside the major hotels and restaurants, although the study of foreign languages—and especially of English—is more and more popular. Shop signs in central Beijing are often in English as well Chinese.

● Doing business

*Working hours: Mondays through Fridays, 08:00 to 12:00, 14:00 to 18:00. Saturdays, 08:00 to 12:00, and sometimes an afternoon stint as well.

*Businesswomen will not be annoyed by the Chinese. Other foreigners are the only persons who might make nuisances of themselves.

*A most useful guide to business practices is *China*, by Robert Delfs, Thomas D. Gorman and Owen D. Nee Jr., US$60.00, published by the Far Eastern Economic Review, Hong Kong.

*Temporary office facilities are still at a premium. Visiting businessmen—and many resident foreigners as well—make their hotel rooms double as offices.

*Secretarial and typing services are offered by Dietz Business Services, Ltd., International Club, Guoji Julebu, tel. 522566.

*Business cards should have Chinese translations on the reverse side. Use the simplified characters, not the traditional style used in Taiwan. Cards can be printed at the Foreign Languages Printing House, Erligou, Xiqiao, tel. 893218.

*Drink only boiled water (*kaishui*). Hotels provide carafes of water safe to drink.

*Electrical current in China is 220 volts, 50 cycles.

*Beware of taking the Chinese toast 'Gan Bei' (Bottoms Up) too literally.

Simply reply 'Sui Bian' (roughly, 'Drink as you please, but I am trying to stay sober'). Chinese hosts occasionally consider it their duty to drink their guests under the table—and mao-tai hangovers are dreadful.

*There are no golf courses yet in Beijing, but plenty of tennis is available. And lots of ice skating in the winter.

*Jogging is highly popular, all year around.

*The narrow, ancient hutungs that run between Beijing's wide main thoroughfares derive their name from an old Mongolian word meaning 'the passageway between yurts'.

*Booking onward travel in Beijing is time-consuming and temper-trying. It's best left to your hotel, or to your sponsoring business agency. China International Travel Service (CITS), 2 Qianmen East Road, tel. 554192, will handle international and domestic bookings but tend to be very slow. Air tickets can be purchased at CAAC (China's national airline), 117 Dongsi West Road, tel. 553245 (domestic) and 557319 (international). Telephone communication with CAAC is often unproductive.

*Remember that flights to Hong Kong are always heavily booked. It may be worthwhile going to the airport and hoping for a last-minute vacancy. An alternative is flying to Canton, then going on to Hong Kong by plane (30 minutes) or train (three hours).

*Train tickets should be purchased at Beijing Railway Station. There's a special booking office for foreigners inside the main hall, left of the entrance.

*If you plan to throw a feast for Beijing friends, reserve two or three days in advance, and stipulate the amount per head you wish to pay. This is called the 'biao jun' and can be very high indeed should you wish to offer shark's fin soup, fresh abalone or bear's paw—all great delicacies.

Useful phone numbers

● Trade offices:

American Chamber of Commerce, c/o General Electric Co., 522491.

Canada-China Trade Council, 507766, ext. 1109.

Italian Institute for Foreign Trade, 595261, ext. 146.

Japan-China Association for Economy and Trade, 521605.

Japan-China Economic Relations and Trade Center, 507766, ext. 3008.

National Council for US-China Industrial Exchange Inc., 890721, ext. 835.

● Foreign trade corporations:

Arts and Crafts, 552187.

Cereals, Oils and Foodstuffs, tel. 558831.

Chemicals, 891289.

Foreign Trade Transportation Corp., 893566.

Light Industrial Products, 556749.

Machinery and Equipment, 556749.

Medicines and Health products, 503344.

Metallurgical Equipment, 550197.

Native Produce and Animal Byproducts, 554124.

Silk, 558831.

Textiles, 553793.

● Churches:

A non-denominational Christian service in English is held every Sunday (except for the first Sunday of the month) at 10:00 in the US Embassy's Bruce Building. Enquiries: tel. 522033.

● Catholic services:

St. Joseph's Church, Wangfujing Street, service for foreigners at 08:00 Sundays, tel. 556287.

Beijing Cathedral, 141 Qianmen Street, foreigner's mass at 09:30, tel. 336470.

● Protestant services:

Church at 21 Dongdan North Street, service at 09:00 every Sunday, in Chinese, tel. 555086.

Church at 57 Xidan Street, services at 09:00 every Sunday, in Chinese, tel. 664027.

● Emergencies:

Capital Hospital, tel. 553731, ext. 217 (Foreigner's Section, ext. 274, or 251). There is also a clinic for foreigners Monday through Saturday. Call ext. 565 or 568.

Ambulance service, tel. 555678. Police Emergency, 110.

● Airlines:

Aeroflot, 523581.

Air France, 523894.

British Airways, 523768.

CAAC, 558861, ext. 2521 (reservations: domestic, 553245; international, 557319).

CAADPRK (North Korea), 523981.

Ethiopian Airlines, 523285.

Iran Air, 523285.

Japan Air Lines, 523457.

JAT (Yugoslav), 523486.

Lufthansa, 522626.

Pakistan International, 523274.

Pan Am, 595261, ext. 135.

Philippine Airlines, 523992.

Swissair, 523284.

Tarom (Romanian), 523552.

Thai, 523174.

Beijing Airport, switchboard for foreigners' enquiries, 522931.

● Embassies:

Afghanistan, 521582.

Albania, 511120.

Algeria, 521231.

Argentina, 522090.

Australia, 522331.

Austria, 522061.

Bangladesh, 522521.

Belgium, 521736.

Benin, 522741.

Brazil, 522740.
Bulgaria, 522232.
Burkina Faso (Upper Volta), 522550.
Burma, 521302.
Burundi, 522328.
Cameroon, 521828.
Canada, 521475.
Central Africa, 521789.
Chad, 521296.
Chile, 521522.
Colombia, 523377.
Congo, 521644.
Czechoslovakia, 521530.
Denmark, 522431.
Ecuador, 523158.
Egypt, 521825.
Equatorial Guinea, 523679.
Ethiopia, 521782.
Finland, 521753.
France, 521331.
Gabon, 522810.
Germany (East), 521631.
Germany (West), 522161.
Ghana, 521319.
Greece, 521277.
Guinea, 523649.
Guyana, 521337.
Hungary, 521431.
India, 521908.
Iran, 522040.
Iraq, 523385.
Ireland, 522691.
Italy, 522131.
Japan, 522361.
Jordan, 556531, ext. 1215.
Kampuchea, 521889.
Kenya, 552231, ext. 1636.
Korea (North), 521186.
Kuwait, 522182.
Laos, 521224.
Lebanon, 522197.
Liberia, 523549.
Libya, 523278.
Luxembourg, 556175.
Madagascar, 521353.
Malaysia, 522531.

Mali, 521704.
Malta, 523114.
Mauritania, 521396.
Mexico, 522574.
Mongolia, 521203.
Morocco, 521796.
Nepal, 521795.
Netherlands, 521731.
New Zealand, 522731.
Niger, 522261.
Norway, 522261.
Pakistan, 522504.
Peru, 522178.
Philippines, 522794.
Poland, 521325.
Portugal, 552497.
Romania, 523315.
Rwanda, 522193.
Senegal, 522545.
Sierra Leone, 521446.
Somalia, 522312.
Spain, 521967.
Sri Lanka, 521861.
Sudan, 523715.
Sweden, 521770.
Switzerland, 522381.
Syria, 521372.
Tanzania, 521491.
Thailand, 521903.
Togo, 522202.
Tunisia, 522435.
Turkey, 522650.
Uganda, 521708.
United Kingdom, 523731.
USA, 522033.
USSR, 522151.
Venezuela, 521259.
Vietnam, 521131.
Yemen (Arab Republic), 521362.
Yemen (Peoples Democratic Republic), 521558.
Yugoslavia, 521562.
Zaire, 521360.
Zambia, 521554.
Zimbabwe, 523795.

Shopping

During Beijing's long centuries as an imperial capital, treasures accumulated and craftsmen arrived from all over the Orient to produce new delights for the rulers. Somehow, the treasures never ran out: as one declining family slowly disposed of its valuables, another on the rise bought its jades, bronzes, ceramics and silks.

Even today, a few prizes still exist. Beijing's antique stores are always worth a close look. Though goods dated before 1795 usually cannot be exported, there are some lovely though newer items that can be taken along. Authenticity is guaranteed by the government's wax seal; prices are firm.

Handicraft items are still a good buy in Beijing, though craftsmanship today is not as high as in the days of dynasty. Silks, antiques, carpets and furs are good buys. There are several important shopping areas, and all are worth a browse. But for short-time visitors, the big Friendship Store on Jianguomen Street, near Jianguo Hotel, is recommended. The variety is enormous—rivalled only in Hong Kong—and there's a packing and shipping service as well.

The Friendship Store is open seven days a week, as are most other large stores in Beijing and elsewhere in China.

For the energetic, the long Wangfujing Street shopping area can be good fun. This is Beijing's most popular shopping street. Stores usually are crowded, though the goods on sale don't differ much from those in Qianmen Dajie and Xidan, the other important shopping places. Center of attraction is the big department store called Baihuo Dalou, which stocks a wide range of consumer goods.

Just across the street is the Dongfeng Market, a warren of small shops since Qing Dynasty days, where buyers can find paintings, carpets, porcelain, old furniture and handicrafts.

Nearby is the Beijing Arts and Crafts Store, at 200 Wangfujing, which has Beijing's largest selection of traditional handicrafts: puppets, kites, toys, paper cutouts, lacquerware, cloisonné and bamboo wares. The best-quality goods are on the top two floors. There's also a good selection of carpets here.

Chinese carpets are in fact a good buy, but remember that Beijing products, though handsomer than those of Tianjin, may not wear quite as well. It's also possible that prices may be lower in Hong Kong. Two other Beijing shops specializing in carpets are the Marco Polo Shop and the small Friendship Shop at the Temple of Heaven. Both outlets also stock old carpets from time to time.

Not far from the Temple of Heaven area is the Beijing Arts and Crafts Trust Co., at 12 Chongwenmennei Avenue, which offers a dazzling assortment of European, Chinese and Japanese kitsch, including carpets, theater robes, furniture and old fur coats.

For antiques of all sorts, spend some time prowling the many small shops along Liulichang Street. Beautifully renovated recently, in traditional Qing Dynasty style, its shops sell antiques, porcelains, paintings, bronzes, carvings, seals and books. Prices are high, but authenticity is guaranteed by the governmental wax seal. The single most famous shop in this area is the Rongbaoshai, founded in the 17th Century, which sells fine paintings, notepaper and woodcuts.

More antiques—at higher prices—can be found at the Yueyatang shops in the Beijing Hotel. If you buy an antique without a seal and wish to export it, take it to the Customs Service Office at the Friendship Store. On Monday and Friday afternoons, Customs will inspect and affix seals to purchases...if in fact the items are legally exportable.

Looking for furs? Try the Friendship Store, or the Jianhua Fur and Leather Store at 192 Wangfujing Street. The latter will make garments to order, but allow plenty of time. The furs (fox, ermine, mink, rabbit and astrakhan) are usually bred commercially.

A complete Chinese or Western dinner service can be bought for about Yuan 300 at Hunan Pottery Products Store, or the Jingdezhen Porcelain Shop in Qianmen Street.

Hotels

Despite optimistic predictions over the past few years, hotel rooms in Beijing remain desperately hard to find. New hotels continue to open: about fifty more were in various stages of construction as of 1986. But the shortages continue as more and more tourists, on more and more guided tours, continue to pack all available space. Individual travelers such as businesspersons must take what's left over. Sponsoring organizations can often find rooms for individuals: be sure these reservations are confirmed before boarding your jet in Tokyo or Hong Kong or Paris.

Three hotels—the Sheraton Great Wall, the Lido and the Peninsula Group's Jianguo—are equipped to handle advance reservations made from outside China.

The capital's newer hotels are up to standards maintained outside China, save that service and general efficiency can be eccentric on occasion. And several do not accept credit cards. Enquire.

● A selection:

Beijing Hotel (Beijing Fandian), Changan East Avenue, tel. 500-7766. For years the capital's leading hotel, the Beijing has been eclipsed by some of the newcomers, but remains a most desirable address. The fact that it's available only to those with good connections makes it most desirable to some. Located just around the corner from Wangfujing Street, the city's best shopping area, and a 15-minute walk from Tiananmen and the Forbidden City, the Beijing has a good selection of restaurants (Chinese, European and Japanese), several banqueting halls, bars and coffee shops, souvenir and antique stores. Rooms are large, whether they are located in the old, mausoleum-like West wing or the modern (1974) East wing, and reasonably comfortable. (The East wing has been under more or less steady reconstruction ever since it opened its doors). Telex service for guests only, postoffice, foreign exchange bank.

Beijing-Toronto Hotel (Jinglun Fandian), Jianguomenwai Street, tel. 500-2266. New and well-managed (by Japan Air Lines), this hotel is nicely located near the Friendship Store and the plusher Jianguo Hotel, has more than 600 rooms, a pool and sauna, a good Cantonese restaurant among its several eating places, and is airconditioned. Its odd name is explained by its joint Chinese and Canadian financing.

Diaoyutai State Guest House (Diaoyutai Guo Binguan), Sanlihe Lu, tel. 866152. Built as a state guest house, this hotel opened to foreigners (only to very wealthy foreigners) in the late 1970s. It consists of several elegant guest houses in a lovely garden in western Beijing, about 15 minutes by sleek limousine from Tiananmen. For reasons that await explanation, Diaoyutai means Angler's Rest.

Great Wall Sheraton Hotel (Changcheng Fandian), Donghuan North Road, tel. 5005566, telex 20045 GWHBJ CN. This beautiful new hotel is coming into its own after getting off to a shaky independent start when it opened in December 1983. Now under Sheraton management, staff and service are improving; so is its food. The mass-tour traffic that has jammed its rooms is being cut back, with the aim of making more rooms available to business travelers. The staff is being retrained, with promising results. Restaurant quality is fair. Its superb lobby bar is one of the city's favorite meeting places. So is the new Cosmos night club, with a resident Filipino band. Other features: a pool (with good Sunday brunches), tennis courts, cinema, garage and 24-hour room service. Business services are available.

Jianguo Hotel (Jianguo Fandian), Jianguomenwai Street, tel. 500-2233, telex 22439 JGHBJ CN. A favorite of many business travelers, the Jianguo is liked just as much by Beijing's foreign residents. Its California-style architecture, indoor pool, good restaurants (Justine's) and bars (Charley's) and efficient management (Hong Kong's Peninsula Group) all combine to make it an ongoing hit. Comfortable rooms. Bank and telex services.

Lido Holiday Inn, Jichang Road and Jiang Tai Road, tel. 500-6688, telex 22618 LIDOH CN. Just off Capital Airport Road and only 15 minutes from the airport, the Lido is somewhat distant from central Beijing (about 30 minutes by cab from Tiananmen) but offers plenty of rewards once one arrives. Notable are its big pool and health club, bowling alleys, good dining rooms (fine buffets at Marco's) and secretarial services. The new Juliana's disco is popular. Bank and telex.

Minzu Hotel (Minzu Fandian), 51 Fuxingmennei Street, tel. 668541. An old favorite, now totally renovated and modernized in the mid-Eighties. Fine Chinese and Western food, excellent staff.

Shangri-La Hotel, 29 Zizhuyuan Road, tel. 802-1122, telex 222231 SHABJ CN. FAX 802-1471. This new member of the Shangri-La group opened in 1986 in its 24-story building. All the usual luxuries are on offer, including a pool and health club, several restaurants and bars, and 40 suites. Some rooms and suites are available with offices attached.

Xiangshan Hotel (Xiangshan Fandian), Xiangshan Park (20 kilometers northwest of the city), tel. 285491. When this beautifully designed (by I.M. Pei) hotel opened in 1983, it was hailed by travel professionals and the press alike. Six months later, it was labelled a failure; weak management, its remote location and all-but-untrained staff combined to darken its reputation. Now, the Xiangshan may be on the way back, largely by concentrating its efforts on training and retraining its staff—and for firing (unheard of in China) rule violators. Rooms are big and comfortable, and rates have been cut. Restaurants offer Chinese and Western food, and there's a coffee shop, outdoor pool and health club. Its park setting is lovely.

Xiyuan Hotel (Xiyuan Fandian), Erligou, Xijiao, tel. 890721. The new Eastern wing, opened in 1984, is housed in a 35-story tower topped by a revolving restaurant and bar. There are 700 rooms in the tower, all equipped with television and airconditioning. The old Western wing consists mostly of suites and is housed in low, old-style buildings. Usefully located near the Industrial Exhibition Hall and the Erligou Trade Center.

Zhaolong Hotel, 2 Worker's Stadium, North Road, tel. 502299, telex 210219 ZLHCN. This is one of the first of the city's new wave of hotels, designed to ease the mid-Eighties crunch. Built with funds from Hong Kong shipping millionaire Sir Y.K. Pao and named for his father Pao Zhao-long, the hotel has 270 guest rooms, including several luxurious suites, and nine restaurants, offering Sichuan, Cantonese and Western food. Located near the Sanlitun foreign embassy area.

> Note: In Tianjin, just 90 minutes by train from Beijing, the Hyatt Tianjin: Jie Fang Road North, telephone 31-8888, telex 23270 HYTJN CN.

Restaurants

Beijing duck is not to be missed, but there are those who've come to believe it's now too often either over-rated or poorly prepared. So many of the city's duck restaurants have given themselves over so completely to mass-production that the taste of the bird, if not forgotten, has been ignored in the rush to get the next plateful on its way to the hungry travelers (see below).

Don't be surprised, in other words, if your duck isn't the marvel you've been promised by food writers. Ask resident friends for advice on which duck restaurants are currently taking their duties seriously. A bad duck is considerably worse than no duck at all, and there are more and more bad ducks in Beijing these days. The quacks, one might say, are beginning to show.

Beijing cuisine, in any case, is not all duck and pancakes. Try the delicious Mongolian hotpot (thinly sliced mutton or beef, cooked by dipping it briefly into a savoury soup aboil on your table, then mixed with a do-it-yourself sauce composed of chili and sesame oil, onions and chives, soy sauce, and a dozen other ingredients, then popped into your mouth). The shashlik is superb; so are the deep fried dumplings (*quotie*). Try snacks like *aiwowo* (love nests), made of sticky rice and nuts, or *ludagun* (rolling donkeys) made of rice and red beans in deepfried soybean flour.

Beijing food specifically, and northern food in general, is not so oily and sweet as that of Shanghai, not as light and multi-flavored as Cantonese, and not quite as fiery as Sichuan. Instead, you'll find more grilled and roasted meats, fewer vegetables (if only because these grow more plentifully down south) and wheat noodles instead of rice.

Finally, remember that most of the major hotels offer good food at fair prices—both Western and most Chinese styles. And while you should taste Peking-style food while you're in town, other regional cuisines are well prepared here in the capital. (Dining hours: 10:30 to 13:00; 16:30 to 22:30).

● Beijing Duck

Listed here are several duck restaurants, without comment on the quality. Some are better than others: ask Beijing friends for advice.

Beijing Kaoya Dian ('Big Duck'), 32 Chianmen, upstairs. Tel. 751379.

Beijing Kaoya Dian ('Duck Factory'), Xuanwimen, south of Qianmen Gate, tel. 334422.

Beijing Kaoya Dian ('Sick Duck'— because the restaurant is located near Capital hospital), 13 Shuifuyuan off Wangfujing Street, tel. 554669.

Chongwenmen Kaoya Dian ('Small Duck'), 2 Chongwenmen Street, tel. 750505.

Syin Beijing Kaoya Dian ('Wall Street Duck'), Xinhua South Road, tel. 334422.

Good luck and don't forget to pack lots of Alka-Seltzer.

● Recommended restaurants

Donglaishun Fanzhuang, 16 Donghuamen at north entry to Dongfeng Market, off Wangfujing, tel. 550069. One of the capital's oldest and best restaurants, serving superb hotpot, shashlik and Beijing duck. It's a Moslem restaurant: *don't ask for pork*. Its name means 'Luck From the East' and it has been lucky for gourmets for years. Reserve well in advance.

Fanshan Fandian, Hortensia Island, Beihai Park, tel. 442573. Beautifully situated in an old imperial park, this restaurant specializes in the rare and costly dishes once served to emperors and their empresses. Reserve in advance.

Hongbinlou Fanzhuang, 82 West Changan Street, tel. 656404. Excellent Moslem food, including mutton hotpot, shashlik and—yes—Beijing duck. Delicious fried dumplings. Nice service.

Jinyang Fanzhuang, 241 Zhushikou West Street, tel. 331669. Shaanxi cuisine, inlcuding crispy duck, onion bread and steamed dumplings. A small courtyard built in the traditional style adds to the pleasant atmosphere.

Maxim's de Paris, 2 Qianmen East Street, tel. 754003. A distinct change of pace from noodles and hotpot, but certain high-ranking officials are known to enjoy the nouvelle cuisine and delicate Bordeaux and Burgundies, to say nothing of the chocolate desserts. *Very expensive.* Reserve well in advance.

Sichuan Fandian, 51 Rongxian Hutong, tel. 656348. Once the residence of military dictator Yuan Shih-kai, this is one of the handsomer restaurants in town and its fiery Sichuan food is truly splendid. Expensive.

> Note: For a fast and tasty Western-style light meal, try Minim's, next door to Maxim's (see above) and a favorite haunt of Beijing's fashion models. Another inexpensive spot for Western food is the BACL Catering Center Restaurant, just behind the International club on Jianguomenwai.

▶ After hours

There is nightlife in Beijing, but there's not much of it and it tends to end early. The city has never been called 'the Paris of the East' and seems proud of it. Old Beijing hands, however, remember the dreary years of the Sixties and Seventies and rejoice at all the current action—another illustration of the truth lent by perspective.

Perhaps the most varied evening scene is at the Beijing Hotel, where the lobby bar/coffee shop and the rooftop cafe attract visitors and locals. Charlie's bar at the

Jianguo is another favorite, with a higher proportion of short-time visitors. There are discos at the Jianguo, Great Wall and Huaqiao hotels, but at times local Chinese find admission difficult, especially since a government ban on social dancing was reapplied in 1982. The International Club disco parties are easier to enter.

The embassy circuit offers the usual round of cocktail and dinner parties—fun for the visitor but often boring for the regular participants.

▶ Sights and sounds

Forbidden City (Zijin Cheng) and **Palace Museums** (Gugong), entrance at Tiananmen, tel. 555301: one of the world's great architectural monumemts, the palace was built in substantially its present form during the Ming Dynasty between 1406 and 1420, seriously damaged by Manchu warriors when the Ming Dynasty was overthrown in 1644, then rebuilt in its old splendor 300 years later, during the succeeding Qing Dynasty. The area totals about 250 acres: there are six main palaces, stunning ceremonial halls and countless statues. The effect is unforgett-able. Take at least a half day for your visit, then return. Closed to the public during imperial days, the palace complex was opened to all after the revolution of 1911. The museums display paintings and artifacts from the Imperial collection, as well as recent archaeological finds. These include the Historical Art Museum of the Yuan, Ming and Qing Dynasties, the Hall of Paintings, the Hall of Clocks and Watches and the Museum of Imperial Treasures. Though the exhibits are usually only captioned in Chinese, they are a feast for the eye. Open between 08:30 and 16:50. The ticket office of the Imperial Treasures exhibition closes at 15:15 and the exhibition closes at 16:15.

Tiananmen (Gate of Heavenly Peace), the heart of modern Peking, covering 98 acres: This vast square accommodates the Monument to the People's Heroes and Chairman Mao's Memorial Hall. On the west side is the monumental Great Hall of the People, housing offices of the highest officials of the nation, ceremonial banqueting rooms and a 10,000-seat auditorium.

Museum of the Chinese Revolution and the **Museum of Chinese History**, Tiananmen Square, tel. 558321: The left wing houses photographs and exhibits which illustrate the history of the Chinese Communist Party. The right wing houses a permanent exhibition of China's culture, history and scientific development. The displays are badly lit and captioned in Chinese only, but very extensive. Closed Mondays.

Military Museum of the Chinese People's Revolution, 9 Fuxing Street, tel. 863580: Displays of memorabilia and weaponry covering the history of China's revolutionary army between 1921 and 1949. Closed Mondays. Bring along your passport for inspection at entrance.

Temple of Heaven (Tiantan), Tiantan Road: One of the architectural splendors of the capital. Here emperors prostrated themselves upon its marble terraces in annual prayers to Heaven. Elaborate ceremonials, blessings of rich harvests and dynastic mandate were beseeched at its altars. The blue triple-roofed Ming Dynasty Hall of Prayer for Good Harvests is magnificent.

The centers listed below change their exhibits frequently. Check the newspaper China Daily for details:

Museum of Fine Arts, corner of Wangfujing and Chaoyangmennei, tel. 443720.
Nationalities Cultural Palace, Fuxingmennei Street, tel. 653231.

● **Temples**

(Peking's temples function as religious centers and/or museums).

Confucius Temple (Capital Museum) Guozijian Street, (near Yonghe Gong): In the old Confucius Temple, to which the emperors came annually, are stone tablets with names of successful candidates in state examinations. The halls now house archaeological finds from the Peking area. Closed Mondays.

Lama Temple (Yonghe Gong), Yonghegong Street, tel. 447569: This magnificent architectural complex, once an imperial residence, became the centre of Tibetan Lamaism in Peking in the 18th Century. Today the monks guard a treasure of Tibetan art. Closed Tuesdays and Thursdays.

Source of Law Temple (Fayuansi), Fayuansi Qian Street, tel. 333966: One of Peking's oldest temples, it now houses the Chinese Buddhist Theoretical Institute, a school for novice monks. See the Buddhist statuary, engravings and manuscripts. Closed Wednesdays.

White Cloud Temple (Baiyunguan), Baiyun Road, tel. 367179: An ancient and famous Taoist temple, full of fine relics and architecture. Open Fridays.

Big Bell Temple (Dazhongsi), Beihuan Xi Road, tel. 283543: A small museum temple housing a display of magnificent bronze bells including a giant from the Ming Dynasty (46 tons) which is a national treasure.

Temple of the White Dagoba (Baitasi), near Fuchengmennei Street: The Dagoba dominated the skyline of Kublai Khan's Peking but became a factory during the Cultural Revolution. Precious Buddhist relics, paintings and scriptures are now displayed in its ancient tree lined courtyards.

● **Sites**

The Old Observatory (Guanxiangtai), Jianguomenwai: In the 17th Century, Kublai Khan's observatory was run by Jesuits. They designed its handsome scientific instruments, which are now on display on top of one of the few remaining sections of Peking's old city wall.

Beihai Park: The gardens, pavillions and lake of this beautiful park, once an integral part of Forbidden City life, draw thousands of Chinese daily—iceskating in winter and boating in summer. The summer lotus blossoms are breathtaking.

The Drum and Bell Towers (Gulou and Zhonglou), Dianmenwai Street: The drum and bell boomed the watch hours across many old Chinese cities and these two—the Drum Tower (1420) and the Bell Tower (18th Century)—are fine examples.

Summer Palace (Yiheyuan), 11 kms northwest of the city: Built for the ferocious Empress Dowager, Cixi, in the late 19th Century, as a summer retreat from the Forbidden City, it is a delightful complex of palace architecture and traditional landscaping. Not far distant are remains of the old Summer Palace, the Yuanmingyuan, sacked by French and British conquerors in 1860.

Fragrant Hills (Xiangshan Gongyuan), about 40 kms west of the city: The Manchu (Qing) Emperors loved hunting and this was one of their deer-stocked reserves. It is now a favorite recreation park, especially in autumn when the leaves turn. In the vicinity is the Temple of Azure Clouds (Biyunsi) with its hall of 500 arhats and the Temple of Sleeping Buddha (Wofosi) with its laquered bronze reclining Buddha and ancient cypress trees.

▶ Weekends

Great Wall and **Ming Tombs** (Changcheng and Ming Shisanling): The section of the Great Wall most visited from Peking is Badaling and can be reached in two and a half hours by car. Start early in the morning, before the hordes of tourists (Chinese and foreign) crowd the site. Afterwards, backtrack to visit the thirteen tombs of the Ming Emperors. Take a picnic lunch and eat it at one of the unrestored tombs, and enjoy the peace and beauty of the valley. Restaurant facilities (poor) are available at both sites.

> Note: For those truly in a hurry, China Travel Service operates a helicopter tour of the Great Wall and the Ming Tombs. The starting point is the Lido Hotel, at 07:30, and guests are assured they'll be back in time for lunch. Price: Yuan 150. Tel. 506688, ext. 3388.

The Temple of the Pool and Wild Mulberry and the **Ordination Terrace Temple** (Tanzhesi and Jietaisi): These two ancient temples are situated 45 and 35 kms west of Peking, respectively. The road winds up through the Western Hills, offering spectacular views. The Tanzhesi has a history of over 1,600 years and many stone stupas—the burial site of its revered monks—below the Buddhist temple confirm this.

Peking Man Site (Zhoukoudian), 48 kms southwest of Peking: Those interested in paleontology, and the mystery of the disappearance during the World War II of the Peking Man relics, will enjoy this cave site and museum devoted to its hominoid culture dated 500,000 BC.

Eastern Qing Tombs (Dongling), 121 kms east of Peking: A long day's excursion to one of the sites chosen to bury the Qing imperial family. The Empress Dowager Cixi's tomb is here, along with emperors Shunzhi, Kangxi, Qianlong, Xianfeng and Tongzhi. Take a picnic lunch.

Chengde, 345 kms northeast of Peking: A 6-hour train journey brings you to the imperial hunting grounds of the Manchu emperors, beyond the Great Wall. This was their summer retreat; from here one can sniff the cool air of Manchuria. In a huge wooded hunting park stands the elegant wooden palace of Emperor Kangxi. Beyond, at the base of the surrounding hills, are eight magnificent temples, one being a copy of the Potala at Lhasa. There are several adequate hotels at Chengde.

Qufu (Confucius birthplace): Qufu, in Shandong province, is a small town of great charm, famed for its illustrious son, Confucius, who was born here in 551 BC. His descendants, the Kong family, are still residents. The walled Temple of Confucius (Kongmiao) can be visited. Nearby is the Residence of the Descendants of Confucius and the tombs of the sage and his successive generations. Reaching Qufu involves an overnight train journey to Yanzhou, with a change at Jinan. From Yanzhou, take a bus or car to Qufu, 16 kilometers distant.

Brunei

Brunei is improbable. It is one of the smallest countries of the world (200,000 inhabitants), but its formal name is one of the longest (Negara Brunei Darussalam) and it enjoys one of the world's highest per capita incomes (more than $21,000 at last count) and nearly everyone seems to have a shiny new car. Its capital, Bandar Seri Begawan (once plain old Brunei Town) is a mixture of handsome new air-conditioned buildings and humdrum old-Asia concrete block spacefillers. This may be the age of mass tourism, but Brunei wants no part of it. Explains a diplomat: 'The last thing they want here is half-naked Swedish secretaries romping on the beaches.'

Brunei is reclusive nowadays, but it was not always so. In the late 15th Century, for example, Brunei's seamen ruled all of Borneo and the Sulu archipalego to the north, and once even captured proud Manila. Its great hero of those searoving days, Sultan Bolkiah, is still fondly remembered as the *Nakhoda Ragam* or Singing Captain. But a century later, Brunei was well into its decline, pushed out of maritime trade by the fleets of Holland, Spain and Portugal. Brunei turned to piracy, and drew the consequent punishments. By the late 19th Century, it had been shorn of much of its land and power.

Then, in 1929, British geologists struck oil. After a slow start, the oil began to flow in quantity, and the oil shock of 1973 confirmed Brunei's status. But the effect has not been cheering. Austerity rules. The country's only disco ('and it wasn't much,' recalls an old-timer) withered under a cloud of disapproval and switched off several years ago. Why? Perhaps it's the awesome responsibility of life afloat on a sea of oil. Perhaps it's the consequence of Brunei's conservative brand of Islam. Whatever the reason, Brunei today is not exactly a gusher of laughs.

Except on the water. In the capital's Kampong Ayer (water village), which lies along the riverfront, life is considerably cheerier. Walk down to the river in the late afternoon, after the day's heat has eased. A wooden pier leads out into the bay, now lit by another in the never-ending series of spectacular tropical sunsets. The residents of those houses built on stilts over the water are all here, joking and gossiping, making last-minute purchases of fish or vegetables from stallkeepers. Below, boatmen nudge their slender, astoundingly fast outboard-powered skiffs alongside the pier, calling to prospective customers. The Malay banter is lively, almost raucous. Old men, housewives and children step nimbly down flimsy ladders and leap into the boats. A roar from the motor and the boat's away, white

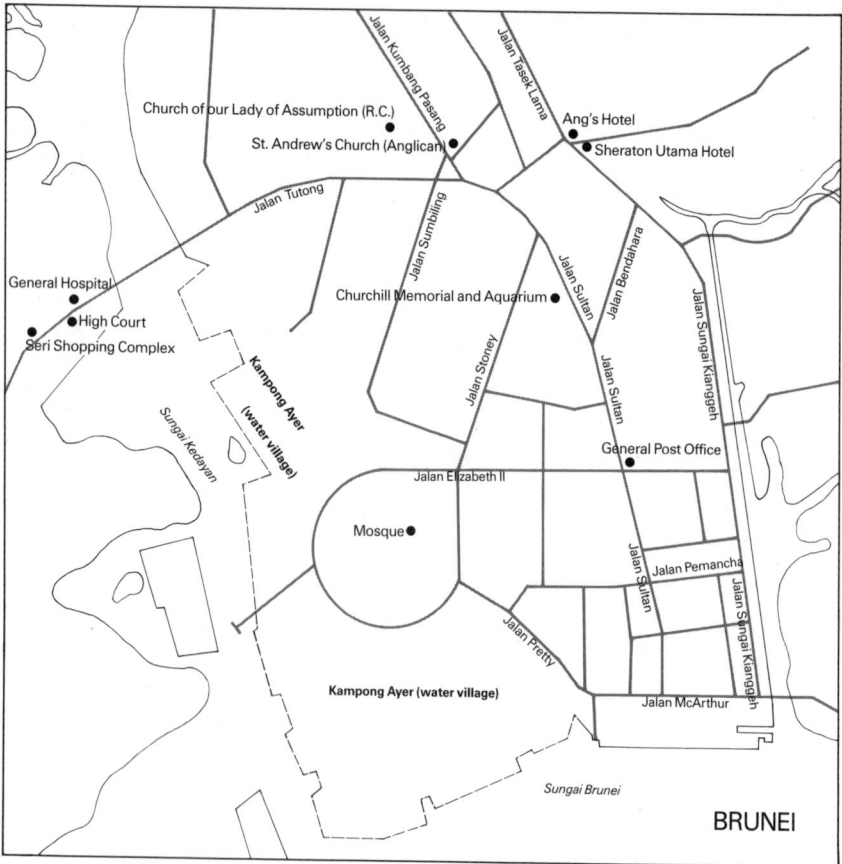

Map of Brunei showing: Church of Our Lady of Assumption (R.C.), St. Andrew's Church (Anglican), Ang's Hotel, Sheraton Utama Hotel, Jalan Kumbang Pasang, Jalan Tasek Lama, Jalan Tutong, Jalan Sumbiling, Jalan Sultan, Jalan Bendahara, Jalan Sungai Kianggeh, General Hospital, High Court, Seri Shopping Complex, Churchill Memorial and Aquarium, Jalan Stoney, Kampong Ayer (water village), Sungai Kedayan, General Post Office, Jalan Elizabeth II, Mosque, Jalan Pemancha, Jalan Sultan, Jalan Pretty, Kampong Ayer (water village), Jalan McArthur, Sungai Brunei, BRUNEI

wake foaming high as it heads toward the shadows of the stilted houses. Almost instantly, another skiff pulls in and loads in its turn. Here is the happy sea-going heart of Brunei.

Back on dry land, in the huge riverfront parking lot where each water dweller keeps his new Toymazsun, there's a conference in progress. Three serious young men are examining a long scratch on a shiny fender. Is it worth repairing? There's no truth, one is assured, in the canard the Bruneians automatically junk their cars after their first scratch. Or even the second. But a *third*....

▬▬▶ Spotlight

Despite the GDP running at just under $4 billion a year in the mid-Eighties and one of the world's highest per capita incomes, Brunei is definitely not another Mideast bonanza scramble. Growth is in the air here, but at an extremely orderly rate. 'No adhockery here,' warns a Western diplomat.

Why? In part, because Brunei became fully independent only in 1984, and its long-range planning has not yet been completed. And its leaders, shaped as they were by conservative British advisers, are committed to step-by-step development. That conservative element in turn makes it difficult to do business in Brunei. For the immediate future, major decisions will be made by the sultan himself, with the aid of only a few advisers. 'Remember that this country is awfully young,' counsels another Westerner. 'They haven't yet developed a corps of really top-notch government officials. The palace is where things get decided.'

For the moment, the Ministry of Development's Economic Development Board is the first stop for many foreign businessmen (S.U.K. Building, Bandar Seri Begawan, tel. 20243). Rather sooner than later, the businessman will probably find he must deal with the officials at the permanent secretary level. That is where most major decisions are made. The Brunei State Chamber of Commerce (tel. 22361) can be helpful.

Because Brunei is small and conservative, the market for huge opportunities is limited. That said, however, Brunei officials are interested in improving the quality of life for their citizens, and construction projects are thus areas of opportunity. So are the so-called 'big ticket' items: a new computer system, for example, or a fleet of police cars or fire engines. Agricultural products may find a market here. And, of course, so will oil industry suppliers.

● Arriving

Brunei, slightly off Asia's main lines of communication, is adequately if not lavishly served by major airlines, including home-based Royal Brunei. The nation's sole international airport, completed in 1973, went through renovation 12 years later. While arriving passengers face something of a hike to the exits, it is otherwise well organized. Visa requirements can be idiosyncratic. In 1985, for example, a visa fee of B$15 (about $US 7.50) for most non-ASEAN travelers was announced only 24 hours before it went into effect. Check the nearest Brunei or British embassy for the latest regulations.

● Transportation

Starting at the airport exit, travelers will find public transport lackadaisical at best. The best advice is to telex ahead, asking your hotel to lay on airport transport. Taxis are often simply not available at the airport, and buses are rare.

If taxis appear, they will not be metered. Arrange fares before starting off. (Airport to central hotel: about B$15.) Because most Bruneians have cars, there's little need for buses around town, though there is the occasional bus transport from the capital down to the oil cities of Seria and Kuala Belait 70-odd miles away.

Traffic jams are few, and most offices are within walking distance of hotels. A word of caution: avoid strolling outside during the heat of the day. Brunei is *hot*.

● Money

The basic unit is the Brunei dollar (B$) which is at par with the Singapore dollar and divided into 100 cents. Bills: B$1, B$5, B$10, B$50, B$100, B$500 and B$1000. Coins: 5,10, 20 and 50 cents.

Brunei and Singapore currencies circulate in the state: Malaysian *ringgits* are accepted only at a discount.

● Tipping

A 10% service charge is built into most hotel and restaurant bills. Another 5% to 10%, depending on merit, is always welcomed.

● What to wear

As in other nations of Southeast Asia, cotton suits and dresses are practical. Brunei is hot and humid year around: temperatures average 28°C and humidity 82%. Casual dress is the rule, save for very formal evening occasions. Safari suits are regularly worn. A note of caution for women: Brunei is a conservative Moslem nation and skimpy clothing is definitely not okay.

● Languages

English is widely spoken in the cities, but Malay is the national language. Several Chinese dialects and native languages (mostly Iban) are also spoken.

● Doing business

The working day starts early, as is usual in the hotter Asian countries: offices open at 07:30 or 07:45 and close at 16:30 or 17:00. Lunchtime occurs between 12:00 and 14:00. Banks: 09:00–12:00 and 14:00–15:00; Saturdays 09:00–11:00. All government offices close on Friday for religious services—and some private offices close then too.

Office facilities: the Sheraton has a small business center and will help find secretaries and translators as needed. Communications: International and domestic phone and telex links work well. The mails are reliable.

■▶ Useful phone numbers

● Airlines:

British Airways, 26860.
Royal Brunei Airlines, 26931.
Malaysian Airlines System, 24141.
Philippine Airlines, 26931.
Singapore Airlines, 24901.

● Embassies:

Australian High Commission, 29435.
British High Commission, 26001.
Indonesia, 21852.
Japan, 29265.
South Korea, 30383.
Malaysian High Commission, 28410.
Philippines, 28241.
Singapore High Commission, 27584.
Thailand, 29653.
USA, 29670.

■▶ Shopping

Limited. Some handsome textiles, and silver and bronze work, can be purchased at the Handicraft Center. Curios, of no particular interest, turn up occasionally at shops in central Bandar Seri Begawan. A better selection of Bornean artifacts is available in either Sarawak's Kuching or in Sabah's Kota Kinabalu, should you be going on to other Bornean cities.

Hotels

● Bandar Seri Begawan

Sheraton Utama, Jalan Bendahara, tel. 44272, telex BU 2306. This is the country's sole top-class hotel: 170 rooms (including suites) at top-line prices; two good restaurants, bar and swimming pool. Opened August 1981.

Ang's, Jalan Bendahara, tel. 23553, telex 2280 BU. Recently renovated. Two restaurants, bar, pool.

Brunei Hotel, Jalan Chevalier, tel. 22373, telex 2287 BU. Sixty rooms, centrally located.

National Inn, Seri Complex, Mile One, Jalan Tutong, tel. 21128, telex 2345 BU. Located in new shopping center. Bar and restaurant. Service flats.

● Kuala Belait

Seaview, Jalan Seria, tel. 32651, telex 3301 BU.

Sentosa, 92–93 Jalan McKerron, tel. 34341. Recently renovated.

Restaurants

● Western

Heritage Restaurant, Sheraton, Jalan Bendahara, tel. 27272. Elegant room, top hotel-standard continental food.

The Grill Room, 22/23 Jalan Sultan, tel. 24908. Perhaps the capital's best: good steaks, fair (but vastly expensive) wines, old English decor, icy air-conditioning, good service.

Maximilian's Restaurant, Ang's Hotel, Jalan Bendahara, tel. 23553. Pleasant surroundings, fair food.

● Chinese

Phong Mun, Teck Guan Plaza. Opened in 1983, good Cantonese cooking. Central location.

● Indian

Regent's Rang Mahel, Mas Pancha Warna Complex, Mile One, Jalan Tutong, tel. 28489. North Indian Moslem.

● Thai

Chao Phaya, Abdul Razak Building, Mile One, Jalan Tutong, tel. 21981. Seafood specialists, Moslem.

● Indonesian

Keri, Seri Complex, Jalan Tutong, tel. 24899. Wide range of Indonesian specialties, Moslem.

After hours

Aside from the pleasant bars at Ang's and the Sheraton, the nearest evening entertainment—as one might expect in this conservative Moslem state—is in Manila.

Sights and sounds

Churchill Memorial: Improbably located far from the scene of Sir Winston's greatest triumphs, this biographical museum illustrates the great statesman's career and offers tape excerpts from his best-known speeches. It also offers, incomprehensibly, recordings of Hitlerian rantings—which fascinate Brunei youngsters.

Hassanal Bolkiah Aquarium: A limited but nicely done collection of tropical marine life as well as fresh-water fish. Particularly appealing giant turtles.

Sultan Omar Ali Saifuddin Mosque: Built in 1958 by the present sultan's father, this is the centerpiece for the state religion. Large (225 feet long and 86 feet wide), it is topped by a golden dome covered with 3.3 million pieces of Venetian mosaic glass. Open to visitors every day but Thursday from 08:00–12:00, 13:00–15:30 and 16:30–17:30, save on Fridays when it can be visited only from 16:30 to 17:30. No shoes.

Brunei Museum: One of the best collections of Chinese porcelain and ceramics in Southeast Asia, housed in a handsome air-conditioned building located in a small park about four miles outside Bandar Seri Begawan. Exhibits of Bornean ethnography, architecture, fishing and hunting. Excellent petroleum exhibit. Well worth an hour or three.

Arts and Handicrafts Center: Supported by the government, this center produces high-quality examples of traditional silver and bronze work as well as silver-threaded and gold-thread weaving. Retail shop. Near city's center.

Kampong Ayer: The 'water village' which lies along the Brunei River at Bandar Seri Begawan is a survival from Brunei's past, when everyone, including the reigning sultan, lived in houses built on stilts over the water. Now, more than 30,000 Bruneians still live (and go to school) in these houses, and have snubbed government efforts to shift them onto dry land. Hire a water taxi (B$5 to B$10 should do it) at twilight to explore the area. Or simply stroll into those parts of the village linked to land by wooden bridges.

The Sultan's Palace (Istana Nurul Iman): Closed to the public save for once-a-year visits just after Ramadan, the palace is reputedly the world's biggest (more rooms than the Vatican, one is told). It was completed only recently, as Brunei moved towards independence from Britain, at a cost estimated well into the millions of dollars. Computer-controlled.

Weekends

There's nothing spectacular available, but travelers with a more than casual interest in their surroundings will be interested in the tribal peoples of Brunei. Several trips to Iban longhouses can be arranged. One useful agency is Travel Centre (Borneo) Ltd, Teck Guan Plaza, Bandar Seri Begawan, tel. 29601.

Kuala Balai: From the oil town of Kuala Balait, a two-hour drive from Bandar Seri Begawan, hire a motorboat from the pier near the central market. The trip to Kuala Balai and its Iban longhouses can be done in less than an hour and leads through deep jungle and swamps. In a clearing near the village, some human skulls are reportedly on display—victims of headhunters. They may still be there.

Labi: Reachable by road are two Iban longhouses, one small and rather new, one older and considerably more interesting. The chief, whose son was educated in London, is a friendly man who will show you through his dwelling. Bring candy for the multitude of kids.

Temburong: This Brunei district is cut off from the rest of the state by a sliver of Sarawak, and is reachable by motorboat from Bandar Seri Begawan to the main town of Bandar. Unspoiled jungle scenery and wildlife is on view here, with more Iban longhouses.

▶ Sports

There's plenty of golf, tennis and sailing available—if you're a member of one of the clubs. Ask your business associates to arrange guest privileges.

The Royal Brunei Yacht Club is headquarters for sailing enthusiasts. New tennis courts are scheduled to be built at several locations, but Brunei's Shell courts at its splendid Panaga Club—at the other end of the state—are currently tops. There's also a good golf course at the Panaga Club. Closer to town, there's the Jerudong Club course. Again, introductions are necessary.

Beyond the hotel pools, there's a good public pool in Bandar Seri Bagawan. More attractive still are Brunei's lovely beaches—scattered along the state's 100 miles of coastline on the South China Sea. Among the more popular beaches are Searsa (windsurfing too), Muara, Jerudong and Seri Kenangan. No introductions are necessary here: simply rent a car and go. Joggers will find the Hash House Harriers well represented. Check the weekly Borneo Bulletin (published in Brunei) for details. Warning: don't jog after early morning hours. Brunei sunlight is fierce.

Canton (Guangzhou)

For centuries Canton has been the West's gateway to China and, with inexorable logic, it has been China's opening on the West as well. (The very name 'Canton' is a Western compression of the Chinese word now romanized as Guangzhou). From the 7th Century onward, the port has been a base for foreign traders, partly because of its superb harbor, partly because emperors in far-off Beijing decreed that the foreign barbarians be limited to Canton and Canton alone.

There are many signs still that the Cantonese prefer being left to themselves in dealing with the foreigners. They have a proverb that neatly defines the city's character: 'The mountains are high and the emperor's throne far away.' That old truth holds today. The mercantile Cantonese can be far more flexible than northerners in dealing with visiting foreign devils, sometimes to the extent of ignoring the letter of the law from Beijing.

The city's famed Trade Fair, held every spring and fall beginning in 1957, helped hone present-day Cantonese canniness. The twice-a-year influx of first hundreds, then thousands of outlanders anxious to pry open China's huge potential market taught the Cantonese much about the vulnerability (and greed) of the outsiders. Though the fair's importance now has slipped a bit as other cities join in the game, Canton's trading finesse is still very much on show.

Beijing's leadership is not unaware of these southern talents. Chinese leader Deng Xiaoping, in 1979, selected Canton's Guangdong Province as the laboratory for his far-reaching economic reforms. Now the province is home to three of the four major Special Economic Zones designated for foreign investment, and for the past several years has been given an unusual degree of autonomy in economic decision-making.

In past centuries, that sort of independence was often grabbed by the Cantonese themselves. The city has long been a port of entry for foreign ideas (democracy and communism among them), and the province has produced its own homegrown rebels as well. Among these notables was Hong Xiuquan, a peasant who transformed his delusion that he was the Risen Christ into the vast and bloody Taiping Rebellion of the 1850s.

Another more recent revolutionary was Dr. Sun Yat-sen, founder of China's Kuomintang Party (which ruled the nation until 1949), equally respected by the Communist Party for his leadership in overthrowing the last dynasty of the long centuries of imperial rule.

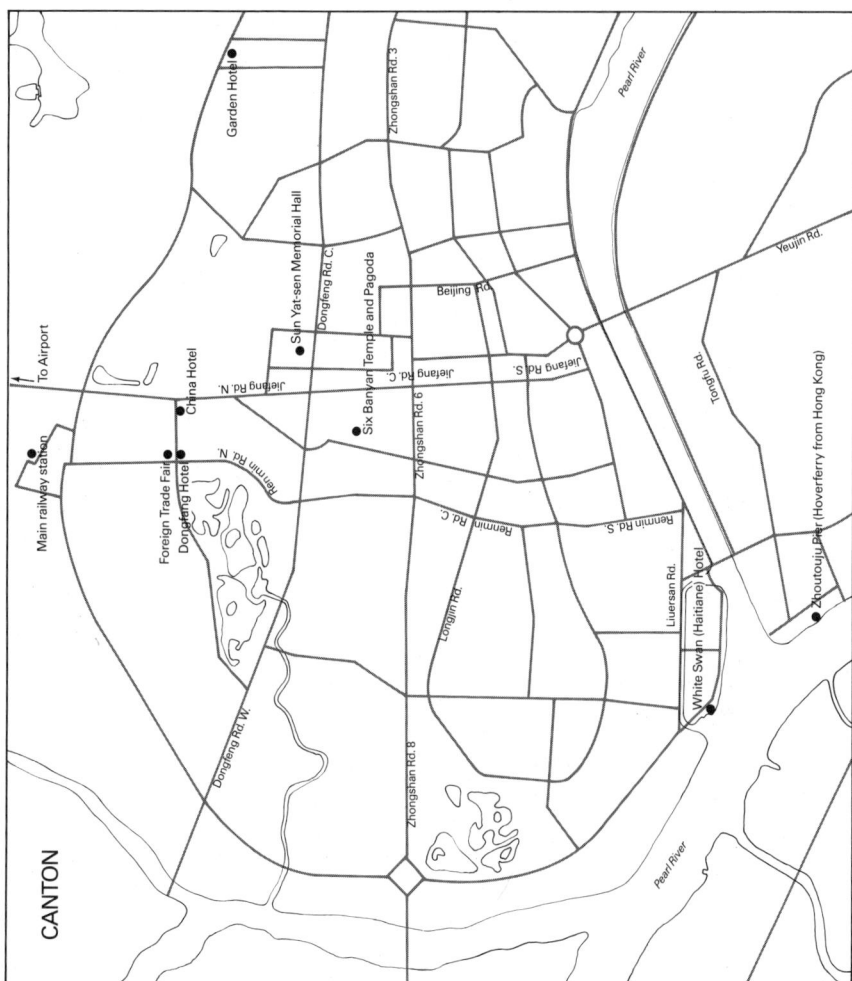

The city itself, verdant, crowded and dilapidated, is China's saltiest. Cantonese take little nonsense from foreigners: their lack of deference is startling to foreigners accustomed to the silken manners of the north. In many ways, Canton today resembles prewar Hong Kong; its low buildings, jampacked alleys, tiny shops, tidal waves of pedestrians and vivid street life all combine to mark it as the archtypical South China port.

That look of long ago, however, is scheduled to disappear. The city now boasts three huge international-class hotels as well as a scattering of new office buildings and apartment blocks (mostly built for foreign businessmen). Discos, of very uneven quality, are springing up. On the planning boards are many more new buildings for offices and factories. Canton, in fact, is now on the cutting edge of change in China. Today's revolution is economic, not political, and all the more far-reaching because of it. 'China will never go through a change like this again,' a resident Westerner said, 'and Canton is the precise center of it all.'

▶ Spotlight

Only a decade ago Canton began to emerge from the deadening years of the Great Proletarian Cultural Revolution (1966–76), an ideological convulsion that did enormous political, economic and spiritual damage to the Chinese revolution. In the 10 years since the GPCR was crushed, Canton has made significant progress: the dark years seem part of a distant past.

For the few foreigners allowed to visit Canton before 1976, however, memories of the city during those difficult years remain strong. Outsiders were rare: a stroll outside the two main hotels (the Love the Masses and the East Is Red) meant braving a rifle range of stares. Guides followed the 'foreign friends' everywhere, partly as insurance against any unseemly 'barbarian' behavior, partly to fend off the staring multitudes.

Nights were dark and quiet, but at dawn hundreds of loudspeakers blaring 'Chairman Mao teaches us not to fear sacrifice' served as alarm clocks. Hotels lacked air-conditioning, television, or private fridges. A call to room service might produce the ubiquitous orange soda or the eternal hot tea, but nothing more.

Nor was there much to see. Sights consisted of politically significant monuments and buildings, and the stilted (and usually inaccurate) recitations by official guides were soporific at best. Museums and churches, more usual tourist fare, were closed by the GPCR.

Very occasionally, there were lighter moments. Some of the younger cadres learned to toss a frisbee with their guests, or taught them how to play *xiaqi*, China's version of chess. There were occasional swimming sessions in old, abandoned diplomatic facilities. One interpreter, who'd had little practice speaking English with foreigners, began every sentence with an emphatic 'So!'. Another would agree to recite Chinese opera segments in exchange for lessons in the lyrics of Bob Dylan and Woody Guthrie.

Those quiet days are long gone now. Foreign t-shirts and pop music are growing common, youngsters march up to practice their English on foreign devils, and Western products are advertised on billboards and shopfronts everywhere. It's reasonable to assume the Western imprint will last. But that of course is what many thought in 1949, just before Canton was sealed off for thirty years.

● Arriving

Canton (Guangzhou in Chinese) has three major arrival points: the airport, the railway station and the ferry pier. Leading hotels, given advance notice, will send a car for arriving guests. Improvident arrivals will find taxis readily available, metered and inexpensive.

Train passengers (express fare one-way from Hong Kong US$26 for a three-hour trip) will go through immigration and customs at the station. Once past that, look for hotel reception desks at the exit. They will arrange transport.

Air passengers (one-way CAAC fare is

US$38 for a 35-minute flight from Hong Kong), may find a hotel vehicle at the exit—or else can take a taxi. Note: Advance flight booking is highly recommended, particularly during the Canton Trade Fair months in autumn and spring.

Coming in by boat (one-way hoverferry fare is US$20 for the three-hour trip from Hong Kong) you will land at a pier just across the Pearl river from the White Swan Hotel.

● Orientation

Canton, for all practical purposes, is the capital of South China. Since the Chinese Communist government came to power in 1949, Canton has been the principal center for foreign trade. Only 182 kilometers (113 miles) northwest of Hong Kong, it is 2300 kilometers south of Beijing and 1800 kilometers south of Shanghai. The population is just under 6 million. It is linked by air and rail to most other major Chinese cities, and to Bangkok and Manila by once-a-week direct flights.

● Transportation

No other Chinese city has a fleet of taxis that can be hailed on the street as well as found at hotels, but cabs can be scarce at rush hours or in the rain. Few drivers speak even rudimentary English, and wise visitors ask their hotel staff to write out destinations in Chinese. Cab fares aren't high, but some taxis (Citroens and Nissans, for instance) charge more than smaller autos.

Traffic is heavy during the day, and you may wish to rent a car and driver if you have several destinations. Your hotel staff can help with this chore.

Avoid public buses and three-wheeled minicabs.

● Money

Chinese currency offers more than a few problems for the first-timer. Relax:

all will become clear in the fullness of time. The currency is called *renminbi* (peoples' money) and its basic unit is the *yuan* (usually called *kuai*). Each *yuan* consist of 10 *jiao* (called *mao*), and each *jiao* consists of 10 *fen* (mercifully called *fen*). Bills: 10, 5, 2 and 1 *yuan*; 5, 2 and 1 *jiao*. Coins: 5, 2 and 1 *fen*.

Banks and exchange offices (all run by the Bank of China) give visitors Foreign Exchange Certificates (FECs) for their travelers checks or foreign currency. (This system will be replaced soon, officials say.) For now, travelers are expected to pay bills in FECs, which were instituted in 1980 in a not-yet-successful attempt to buffer the domestic economy from foreign exchange transactions. FECs, which are denominated as 50, 10, 5 and 1 *yuan*, and 5 and 1 *jiao*, are prized by local residents because imported goods can be purchased only with this special currency.

Warning: Outside all major hotels are touts who will offer you *renminbi* for your FECs (or hard currency) at rates double those offered by the Bank of China outlets. Remember that these transactions are illegal. Nor are they much use to non-Chinese travelers, who find it difficult to legally spend *renminbi*. In major hotels, for instance, rates for *renminbi* payment have been doubled.

● Tipping

Tipping is outlawed in China. Service charges are added to hotel bills. A few cab drivers and hotel workers can now force themselves to accept tips, but most refuse.

● Communications

The leading hotels have reasonably efficient business centers, with the usual telex communications. Telephoning is difficult, however, during working hours. A recent visitor explains that the telephone is still a novelty for most residents of Canton—and novelties are fun only when in constant use. Recommendation: Leave the endless dialling to an assistant and take a cab to see a contact. Or send a telex.

> Note: International Direct Dialling does not yet exist, save for Hong Kong, reachable by dialling '8' before the number.
>
> Note: Canton's breakneck telephone network expansion led to a change in all phone numbers as of July 1, 1985. Now, for all five-digit numbers, dial the first digit twice. Example: CAAC's ticket office, once 34079, is now 334079.

● What to wear

Canton is semi-tropical, and Cantonese tend toward informality. Jackets and ties are discarded after the first formal business meeting during the hot season (April to October). For women, cottons are recommended, and, perhaps because the women of South China traditionally wear trousers, businesslike slacks are perfectly acceptable.

During fall and winter (November to March) heavier clothes such as woolens are useful, as are sweaters in December and January.

Umbrellas are chic during the long summer rainy season.

● Languages

Officially, Cantonese speak the national language (Mandarin to Westerners, *Putunghua* to Chinese); unofficially, but realistically, Cantonese speak Cantonese. This dialect is regularly spoken through most of South China, and in Hong Kong and Macau as well. (Among other differences, its nine tones, compared to Mandarin's four, make it difficult for foreigners to learn).

English is spoken by many trade and tourism officials, with wide variations in

proficiency. There are also amusing variations in accents: some trade officials who specialize in textile dealings have acquired a distinct New York Seventh Avenue accent, while officials who deal with the foreign oilmen working along the coast often pick up a Texan drawl or a Scots burr.

English proficiency declines rapidly once out of the major hotels, and it is wise to ask hotel staffers to write out addresses in Chinese for you. Even the Mandarin spoken in South China has some peculiarities: some foreigners call it Cantorin and classify it as yet another of the thousands of Chinese dialects.

● Doing business

*A so-called 'Foreign Economic Street' opened in 1985 on the ground floor of the Dong Fang (East Is Red) Hotel, just across the street from the Trade Fair grounds. The center groups offices useful to foreign businessmen. Among them:

Bank of China, Zhujiang Trust & Consultancy Co., tel. 669900, ext.1161. Absorbs funds from abroad, invests in projects, provides letters of guarantee.

China State Construction Engineering Co., Guangzhou branch, tel. 669900, ext. 1124. Contracts construction projects in China and abroad, supplies labor to foreign countries.

External Economic Information Consultancy & Service Co., tel. 669900, ext. 1112. Provides external economic consulting service, introduces projects to foreign investors.

Guangzhou Administrative Bureau for Industry and Commerce, division for registration and supervision of foreign enterprises, tel. 669900, ext. 1112. Issues business licenses in the city, advises licensed companies.

Guangzhou Economic and Technical Development, district liaison office, tel. 669900, ext. 1123. Imports and exports products.

Guangzhou Foreign Economic Law Offices, tel. 669900, ext. 1119. Provides legal services for domestic and foreign companies.

Guangzhou Foreign Trade Corp., tel. 669900, ext. 1123. Exports local products, encourages joint ventures.

Guangzhou Friendship Labor Service Corp., tel. 669900, ext. 1118. Provides workers for foreign firms, including interpreters, nurses and clerks.

Guangzhou International Trust and Investment Corp., tel. 669900, ext. 1114. Absorbs funds from abroad, including Hong Kong and Macau, introduces advanced technology and equipment.

Guangzhou Municipal Taxation Bureau, taxation consulting division, tel. 669900, ext. 1115. Interprets tax regulations to foreign and domestic firms.

Peoples Insurance Co., foreign business department, Guangzhou branch, tel. 669900, ext. 1116. Provides many kinds of insurance for domestic and foreign companies.

Yangcheng Certified Public Accountants, tel. 669900, ext. 1117. Provides annual accounting reports for joint-venture and cooperative production companies, provides capital verifications and liquidation reports for these firms.

*Canton Trade Fairs, usually scheduled in March–April and October–November, put enormous pressure on hotel space. Before arriving, confirm travel and hotel reservations not just once but two or even three times. Be prepared, once in Canton, to be shuffled about, particularly if you arrived without a reservation.

*In addition, trade fair weeks produce crowded restaurants and bars and occasional shortages of transportation. Hotel business centers will be jammed.

*Canton's traditional three-hour midday siesta was abolished in 1984; the one-hour lunch is now the standard.

*If you are entertaining Chinese guests at supper, start the affair at 18:00. Do not impose late Western dinnertimes on contacts in Canton.

◗ Useful phone numbers

● Foreign Trade Center switchboard 330–849. Extensions:

Banking and Insurance, 765.
Bookshop, 764.
Customs, 769.
Information, 745.
Photocopy Service, 211.
Post Office, 766, 767.
Restaurant, 760.
Retail Shop, 770.
Telegrams and long-distance calls, 763.

● National import and export corporations:

Animal Byproducts, 887–869.
Arts and Crafts, 334–208 (Export Department, 330–849).
Cereals and Oils, 335–840.
Chemicals, 885–531.
Foodstuffs, 888–220.
Light Industrial Products, 882–101.
Machinery, 331–387.
Metal and Minerals, 885–647.
Native Produce, 884457.
Textiles, 331–750.

● Transport services (freight):

China National Foreign Trade Transportation Corp., 889–625.
China National Chartering Corp., 779–851.
China Ocean Shipping Corp., 551–310.

● Foreign Consulates:

Japanese Consulate-General, 661–195.
US Consulate-General, 669–900.

● Emergencies:

First Municipal Hospital, N. Renmin Road, 333–090.
Public Security Bureau (Foreign Affairs Section), 331–060.

● **Communications:**

Information (local), 04.
Information (international), 06.
Long-distance (domestic), 03.
Long-distance (international), 330-000.
Cables, 334–205. Post Office, 886–615.

● **Travel (air):**

CAAC, tickets, 334–079.
CAAC, domestic reservations, 331–271.
CAAC, international reservations, 333–684.

● **Travel (rail):**

Information desk, 333–333.
East Station, 888–551.
North Station, 777–112.

● **Travel (hoverferry):**

Zhoutouju Pier, 550–314.

● **Taxis Central Office:**

661–251.

● **Travel agents:**

China International Travel service, 333–454.
Dongfang Hotel branch, 669–900, ext. 366.

> Note: Phone numbers from 'The China Guidebook,' by Fredric Kaplan, Julian Sobin and Arne de Keijzer, Eurasia Press, New York.

Shopping

For centuries, Canton's antique and curio shops offered treasures to foreign visitors. But no more. You may run across an interesting buy, or two, but prices are generally lower in Hong Kong and Taipei.

Pleasant gifts for the folks at home can be found at the **Friendship** (foreign currency) **Stores**: one next to the China Hotel, another at the White Cloud (Baiyun) Hotel. There are also interesting shops in the lobby of the White Swan Hotel. Among goods on sale are jade carvings, silk, jewellery, porcelain and ceramics. Men's and women's cashmere sweaters are good value, as is some children's clothing.

Other shops:

Guangzhou Antique Shop, 146 Wendebei Lu, just off Zhongshan Lu. An assortment of old-and-new antiques. Export and prices strictly controlled by the government.

Xinhua Bookshop, 376 Beijing Lu. Canton's largest bookshop offers a good selection of books on art, history and literature, as well as propaganda posters and maps.

Changjiang Musical Instrument Shop, 6–8 Zhongshan Wu Lu. Traditional Chinese instruments are sold here, as well as Chinese opera costumes and some amusing stage props.

Sporting Goods Store, 335 North Beijing Road. A selection of domestically made sports equipment, including badminton and pingpong gear, and jogging suits.

Hotels

There are just three topnotch hotels in Canton; the China, Garden and White Swan. A fourth, the old Dongfang, which housed a generation of hopeful China traders, has now slipped quite a lot.

The China Hotel, Liu Hua Road, tel. 666–888, telex 44888 CHLGZ CN. (Reservations in Hong Kong via New World Hotel, tel. 3--694111). Houses China's first office tower for foreign businesspeople and eight floors of residential apartments, as well as 1017 guest rooms. Close to the Trade Fair. Eighteen food and beverage outlets, including **The Roof** (Western food, tasty, expensive), three Chinese restaurants and a hotel delicatessen and bakery. Pool, gym, tennis, bowling and billiards. Ballroom and conference facilities equipped for simultaneous interpreting. A fleet of Mercedes Benz sedans as well as hotel cabs. Fully equipped business center and a ticketing office. Five minutes by car from railway station, 20 minutes from airport.

The Garden Hotel, 368 Huanshi Dong Lu, tel. 773388, telex 44788 GDHTL CN. (Hong Kong reservations through Peninsula Group, tel. 3–732–1321). Canton's newest hotel, now under the management of the Peninsula Group, which has gained much China experience running Beijing's Jianguo Hotel. The Garden has more than 1,000 rooms and 35 suites, including the Presidential Suite which occupies the entire 23rd Floor. Formal Chinese restaurant (**The Peach Blossom**) and the **Connoisseur**, an expensive Western restaurant. Both Chinese and Western food served in **The Carousel**, a revolving restaurant. Conference facilities include a banquet hall/ballroom that can hold 1400. Fully equipped business center, including computers and word processors. Gym (being built), pool, tennis and squash. Ten minutes drive from railway station, 20 minutes from airport.

The White Swan Hotel, Shamian Island, tel. 886–968, telex 44688 WSH CN. (Reservations also through Hong Kong tel. 5–240192, Beijing tel. 557–496, Shanghai tel. 582–582 ext. 3337). The first Hong Kong-China joint venture hotel in Canton, the White Swan is near the city's center, on a Pearl River island linked by bridges to the city. More than 1,000 rooms and 30 dining areas, including the grill where China leader Deng Xiaoping has twice indulged his fondness for Western steaks. Also: three Chinese restaurants, a Japanese restaurant and Tex-Mex food in the **Songbird**. Full conference facilities and business center. Gym, pool, tennis. Its location in the former Franco-British concession area (see **Sights and Sounds**, below) is five minutes by taxi from the Hoverferry pier and half an hour from the railway station and the airport.

Restaurants

Cuisine at Canton's leading hotels tends to be very good, largely because managers have noticed that their long-staying business residents (of which there are many) eat nearly all their meals at their hotels.

That said, however, Cantonese food deserves exploration. Those who favor hot and spicy dishes like those from Sichuan may need time to appreciate the delicate quality of Cantonese cooking. In winter, look for filling soups and casseroles; in summer try the fresh seafood and vegetables. Crab, abalone, prawn, shrimp and squid are favored ingredients of any dinner. And the quantity and quality of fresh fruit in summertime is spectacular, especially lichee, mango and watermelon.

Make a point of trying at least one 'dim sum' meal, preferably for breakfast or lunch. There are dozens of small, tasty dishes to be tried: if your Chinese isn't what it might be, just point. If you're too shy to try a public restaurant, the Garden Hotel's 'dim sum' lunches are recommended.

● A selection:

Ban Xi Restaurant, 151 Xiangyang Yi Lu, tel. 889–318. Hours: 06:30–10:30, 11:00–14:00, 17:00–21:00. A favorite with foreign visitors for many years, it may now have gotten a bit blasé. The main dining room is a classic Chinese setting with a view over a lake; private dining rooms as well. Specialties include chicken in tea leaves, roast pork and 'dim sum' wrapped in the shape of birds and animals. Reservations advised.

North Garden (Bei Yuan), 439 Dengfeng Road, tel. 333–365. Elegant court-style furnishings, bamboo groves and an inner courtyard lend a tranquil effect that disguises the fact this veteran restaurant can serve up to 8000 guests a day. Roast suckling pig is a favorite, and so is sweet-and-sour goose. Fish with pine-nut sauce is also recommended.

Guangzhou, South Wenchang Road, tel. 887–136. Stays open until the horrendously late hour of 21:30, which may account for its popularity with foreign tour-groups. Good: shark's fin soup with shredded chicken, steamed chicken in fiery maotai liquor, and simple fried seafood.

● For the adventurous:

There are two wildlife restaurants in Canton and both offer unusual dishes. Not recommended for a surprise banquet honoring a visiting executive vice president, but a broadening experience.

The Delicious Wild Game Restaurant, (Yeweixiang), 249 Beijing Road, tel. 330–997. Turtles and pangolins and dogs and cats and wild boars and bears and, for all we know, lions and tigers and elephants.

The Snake Restaurant, 41 Jianglan Road, tel. 883–811. All the local snakes, cooked any way you wish, skinned before your eyes to prove their freshness. And of course snake wine, a favorite winter tonic, made by dripping snake gall bladders into a glass of rice wine or (bring your own) Dom Perignon.

After hours

There's no truth to the report that there's no nightlife in Canton—if your idea of nightlife means stretching out with the latest paperback spy novel. Yes, there are bars and discos in the leading hotels, and their hours are a bit longer than counterparts out in the city. (The China Hotel's disco is worth a whirl.) Overseas Chinese sometimes can stir up a bit of excitement, but their Western counterparts will find more action in Hong Kong.

Sights and sounds

Modernization is beginning, and visitors are advised to see as much of the old city as they can before the wreckers start work. Perhaps the single most interesting sample of old Canton, for the foreigner, is the island to which foreign traders were limited a century ago.

Shamian Island: Known as Shameen in its years as a foreign enclave, the island is now something of a ghost town, save for the busy White Swan Hotel on its western end. Late in the last century Wesleyan missionary J.A. Turner described it as 'a paradise, with its shady avenues, princely houses, cooing doves and an atmosphere of peace and quiet as contrasted with the hooting of native crowds.'

Now the British Consulate has become the Canton office of the province's foreign ministry. The French Consulate was on the eastern tip of the half-mile-long island.

Sacred Heart of Jesus Cathedral: A few minutes walk northeast from Shamian Island on Yi De Road, this impressive cathedral (finished in 1863) is open for services again. Two morning masses daily; three on Sunday.

Xi Mi Road Market; then to Huifu Road. Xi Mi Road Market is a moment away. A lively spot, it offers an idea of the variety of food available since agricultural reforms began in 1979.

Huai-Sheng Mosque: Five minutes walk past the market, along Xi Mi Road, leads to this 7th Century building situated in what long ago was the Tartar Quarter. Reputedly built by an uncle of the Prophet Mohammed, buried north of the city.

Temple of the Six Banyan Trees: A few blocks north of the Mosque, headquarters of the province's Buddhist organization. Built originally in 479 A.D. and renovated several times. The Banyan trees vanished long ago.

Another Muslim relict is the 1300-year-old tomb of **Abbey Wangus**, built by the Moslems of Canton to honor a prophet who according to legend came here at the orders of Mohammed himself. This is located just north of Canton Gymnasium, near the Lanhua Orchid Exhibition Gardens. A cluster of Ming Dynasty buildings is nearby.

Chen Clan Classical Learning Academy, off Liwan Lu: Built late in the Ching Dynasty and finished in 1894, this complex of colorfully decorated halls and courtyards now houses the Guangdong Folk Arts Exhibition Hall. Handicraft items are on sale.

Liurong Temple, Liurong Lu: A seven-story pagoda which can be climbed, large Buddhist temple just behind it, all carefully restored and crowded.

Visitors with political leanings might be interested in the following:

Sun Yat-sen Memorial Hall, just south of Yuexiu Park: Completed in 1931, it is used for mass meetings and cultural events.

Peasant Movement Institute, 42 Zhongshan Road, Section 4: Students were trained in Marxist theory and military tactics. Mao Tse-tung and Chou En-lai lectured here.

Memorial Park to Martyrs of the Canton Uprising, on Zhongshan Road, Section 3: A large tomb contains the remains of 5,000 who died in the December

47

1927 rebellion. Nearby is the Pavillion of Blood-cemented Friendship between the Chinese and Korean Peoples, as well as the Pavillion of Blood-cemented Friendship between the Chinese and Soviet Peoples. Chrysanthemum shows are held here in the autumn.

Weekends

Determined weekenders have been known to fly to Hong Kong. For those who prefer to stay in China, there are a few alternatives.

Conghua Hot Springs: 80 kilometers north of Canton, two hours by car. A riversite dotted with villas and bamboo groves, the spa offers hot mineral water baths in large private bathing rooms. Enthusiasts claim that the waters are good therapy for tension, arthritis and general aches and pains. Three hotels, none luxurious: Hot Springs Hotel, Pine Garden Hotel and the Hubin Guesthouse.

Foshan: thirty minutes by car west of Canton, this is one of China's most important folk-craft centers and has been one for 4,500 years. Ceramics, silk and metal goods. The 134-room **Overseas Chinese Mansion** is known for fine food.

Chung Shan Hot Springs, in Zhongshan, tel. 22311: Three hours south of Canton by car, near Macau. There's a hot spring resort with many sports, as well as an Arnold Palmer-designed 18-hole golf course.

Shenzhen

Welcome to China's version of the Wild West. Not as wild as Tombstone, Arizona, perhaps, nor Deadwood City, South Dakota. But Shenzhen is a lot more hardcharging than, say, Tuotuo Heyan, out in Qinghai, or Bingzhongluo, in Yunnan. Quite simply, Shenzhen is the cutting edge of China's very intense modernization program; it's a pilot project for tomorrow'a China.

Or so visionaries say. But back in 1979, when China's leadership announced that the sleepy little Hong Kong border village was to become a Special Economic Zone, a rash of headscratching spread across South China. In those days, the town was noted only for its rickety wooden bridge, across which most China-bound travelers teetered in the years after the Communist government took power in 1949.

Foreign investment was slow to start, but by 1985 it had reached US$600 million. The boom has seen Shenzhen's population increase ten times from its pre-1979 level of 30,000. Within its sprawling 327-square kilometer city limits are 500 new firms producing everything from plastic shoes to integral circuits—and the skyscraper, at 53 storeys, is China's tallest.

With this running growth have come the inevitable problems: slapdash city planning, intermittent electricity failures and regularly overloaded phone systems. Local currency is, for all practical purposes, the Hong Kong dollar, despite the best efforts of Beijing authorities to push its own Foreign Exchanges Certificates (FECs).

Shenzhen, in fact, is much more freewheeling than the mainland. Hong Kong's go-for-it influence is common, fanned by the enclave's ready access to the territory's television and radio output. Hong Kong businessmen permeate Shenzhen: some conmen have been derisively nicknamed the 'briefcase businessmen'.

Shenzhen's officials will impress those foreigners who've endured agonizingly long bargaining sessions with cadres in Shangai or Peking. Their backgrounds vary: some are farmboys from the local area, with recent business training—and some are recent Beijing University graduates who've turned down a post-graduate course in the States for a crack at Shenzhen's opportunities. And Shenzhen's younger set is going its own way too: with flashy Hong Kong fashions and the 'Shenzhen slipper'—a high-heeled sandal for men only.

With all deliberate speed, in fact, Shenzhen is developing its own characteristic style. There are a pair of good world-class hotels in operation now, and an unbelievable 20 more in various stages of negotiation. A Club Mediterranée is in the works as well. So is an amusement park, aimed at Hong Kong's mass market. But Shenzhen itself is the best show of all: watching an economic revolution gather speed can be a heady experience.

● Arriving

Most will arrive by train: Shenzhen is just 45 minutes away from Hong Kong's Hung Hom Railway Station in Kowloon. (The option is to drive up in the company car or van). Smart travelers will take the 09:30 express, which enables them to clear Hong Kong immigration formalities before departure. Otherwise, you'll face a 45-minute slog through the border barriers on arrival. There are plenty of daily trains.

> Note: Travelers headed for Shenzhen's port area of Shekou, about 30 kilometers from Shenzhen itself, should take the hydrofoil service run by the Hong Kong and Yaumati Ferry Co. It takes 50 minutes to get from Taikoktsui, in Mongkok, Kowloon, to Shekou.
>
> Note: Visas for Shenzhen are available in Hong Kong through China Travel Service, in 48 hours, though for an extra fee a visa can be obtained overnight.

● Orientation

Shenzhen is the fastest growing of China's four major Special Economic Zones (the others are Xiamen, Shantou and Zhuhai), established in 1979–80 as part of the government's campaign to bring in foreign investment. Local officials can conclude deals on their own, without waiting for Beijing's approval. The zone is on Hong Kong's northern border, and is 113 kilometers from Canton.

● Transportation

Metered and inexpensive taxis are available at the left of the railway station exit. Drivers speak little English: have your destination written out in Chinese. Shuttle bus services are offered by the Shenzhen International Hotel and the East Lake Hotel. Cars can be rented at hotels.

● Money

Officially, foreign business travelers are expected to use the Foreign Exchange Certificates (FECs) they get in exchange for their cash or travelers checks at the frontier. In practice, the Hong Kong dollar is preferred.

● Tipping

Not necessary.

● Communications

Major hotels offer direct dialling to Canton and Hong Kong, and phone communications within the SEZ itself are usually adequate. Telex facilities are available only at the Cable and Wireless Co. Ltd. office in the Shenzhen Telegram building, in the town's center. Some hotels hope to have their own telex and facsimile services soon. Postal service is adequate.

● What to wear

Weather patterns here are similar to those in Canton and Hong Kong, and thus light cottons are the rule. While Shenzhen remains in its growth stage— and this is likely to last for several years—heavy shoes and safari suits will be more useful than high heels and dinner jackets. Umbrellas will be handy during the April–September rainy season. Trousers are fine for women.

● Languages

English and Mandarin are widely spoken by local officials and hotel personnel. Cantonese is the local dialect.

● Doing business

*Business hours from 08:00 to noon, with an hour's break for lunch, and conclude at 17:00 or 18:00. (The long South China siesta was banned by reformers in 1984).

*Evening meals begin at 18:00—the mainland custom.

*Many foreign firms have offices in the north and east blocks of the Shenzhen International Commercial Complex.

*Business cards should have Chinese translations in the simplified characters taught on the mainland, and your name should be translated into Mandarin, not Cantonese.

*Shenzhen's hotels offer only limited business services. There are rarely secretaries available, for instance, or translators, or telex and facsimile services. Nonetheless, your hotel sometimes can help out. Ask.

*Hotels can charge for long-distance calls from the first ring onward: *be warned*.

Shopping

Save your money for Hong Kong's shops.

Hotels

East Lake Hotel (Donghu Binguan), tel. 22727/8. Reservations via office in Hong Kong, 5861–0504. A quiet, resort-like hotel with 136 rooms, the joint-venture East Lake is used as a combination home and office by many resident foreigners. Pool, tennis, European and Chinese restaurants. Shuttle bus every half an hour (07:00 to midnight) to railway station.

Shenzhen International Hotel (Ya Yuen Binguang), Tung Mun Road, tel. 22763 or 22773. Reservations via office in Hong Kong, 3/699121, telex 54228 ITD HX. A joint venture between Shenzhen's Forestry Department and Hong Kong businessmen, this 96-room hotel is located close to the town's center. It has its own car fleet, a good Cantonese restaurant, and a European coffee shop and restaurant. Can provide business services at times if alerted in advance.

Nanhai Hotel (Nanhai Jiudian), Shekou, tel. 91991. Reservations in Hong Kong via Miramar Hotel, tel. 3–681111. Good location for contacts in this coastal enclave. Pool and gym, tennis, minigolf and a sauna.

Restaurants

(Ask your hotel to reserve a table).

Ban Xi Restaurant, Jian Sheh Lu. Cantonese food.

Hong Kong Restaurant, Wai Yun Lu. Cantonese food.

Wa Yuan Seafood Restaurant, Ren Min Nan Lu. Good seafood.

After hours

Valentino's, Shenzhen Bay Resort Hotel, 25 minutes by car from central Shenzhen. Some foreign businessmen say this is the place to see Shenzhen's 'mods' in action, but remember that those outgoing local ladies are merely curious about foreign devils and nothing more.

Sights and sounds

Hong Kong is an hour south by train, Canton two hours north. For those who might wish to investigate Shenzhen's admittedly paler delights, consider the following:

Honey Lake Hotel: an amusement park of sorts.

Xi Li Lake Resort: camping.

Xiaomeisha Holiday Resort: basic cottages and an ice-skating rink.

Hong Kong

Higher, Faster, Richer

Stand at the corner of Queens Road Central and Pedder Street at noon. Try to avoid being run down by the packs of Jaguars and Mercedes Benzes. In ten minutes, on any working day, every sort of financial shark that ever swam will shimmer past.

So at least goes the legend, and like most legends it has at least a tinge of truth. Certainly Hong Kong Island's Central District harbors the big operators. Ever since its founding in 1842, the colony has lured seekers of quick fortunes as readily as Reno draws crapshooters. Now that Britain has agreed to return control to China when treaties run out in 1997, much of the deep uncertainty of recent years has ended. Once again, business can concentrate singlemindedly on the Fast Buck.

Suitably, this is a very fast track. Nowhere else in the world does turnover turn over quite so rapidly. The Hong Kong investor matter-of-factly expects his money back in two years, and what looms a decade down the road concerns him much less. Banks here accept risks unthinkable elsewhere. So do businessmen. This is Asia's top financial market—and its flashiest. It is third largest in the world and wants to go higher.

For winners, there are spectacular rewards. Flashy homes, swift racehorses, superb cars and all the other symbols of affluence one could ask for. The great marques are all here: from St. Laurent to Gucci to Hermes to Cartier; from Rolls to Mercedes to Ferrari to Daimler. Great clothes, great gems, great furs. Nowhere is status so relentlessly sought, so blatantly bought.

And the food: all the world's great cuisines are represented—some much more resplendently than others. But it's still difficult to go wrong on Chinese food. Most ranking restaurants will be happy to steer neophytes toward their better offerings. (But surprisingly, perhaps, wines in many well-regarded restaurants are barely adequate: a few respectable offerings amid much overpriced rubbish.)

This is a city of visual impact, of surface spendor. The rushing crowds, the huge new skyscrapers, the shattering neon signs of Kowloon, Central and Causeway Bay all combine to kick adrenalin glands into permanent high gear. The beautiful apartments on the Peak, the stunning Asian women, unforgettable sunsets at Repulse Bay, lovely yachts and luxurious junks: Hong Kong is a treat. Thoughtful it isn't.

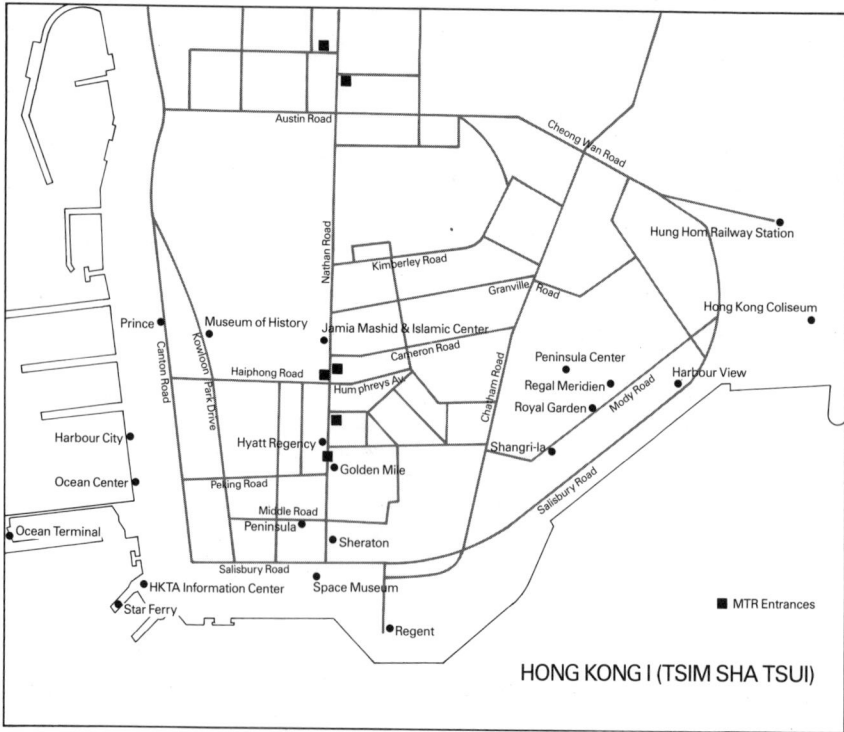

HONG KONG I (TSIM SHA TSUI)

The mood is up, the pace frantic, the fortune there to be made. Will the vitality last through 1997? These days no one knows. But one thing is sure: the colony's final decade is going to be a thriller.

Spotlight

Even in high-tech Central Hong Kong, this building is astounding: 52 levels, its floors slung like so many steel plates from eight steel masts. Its resemblance to the rocket launchers of Cape Canaveral is striking, and the speed with which this new headquarters of the Hong Kong and Shanghai Banking Corp. shot up once its predecessor was demolished makes the Canaveral comparison even more apt. The basic technology, however, is much more closely related to the latest in suspension bridge technology.

Why the, er, bridgework? In one word, flexibility. British architect Norman Foster, holder of a 1983 gold medal for architecture, faced three major challenges:

*The new building needed to be much larger than the old, though built on the same small site.

*It needed to be rapidly modifiable as banking and computer technology evolved.

*And it was needed yesterday.

Foster's solution met those requirements neatly and at the same time won quick international recognition for the beauty and efficiency of the design. The use of the mast opens up floorspace that ordinarily would have been usurped by massively thick traditional support columns. Floors here are wide open to light; they are almost totally unobstructed.

The finished product is a triumph of international prefabrication. The masts themselves were made in Britain and brought in by ship. The aluminum cladding was made in the United States. And from Japan came ingeniously packed modules containing air conditioning units, electrical services and even toilets, prefabricated right down to toilet paper holders and ashtrays. On the day, everything clicked together perfectly.

But not cheaply. Though exact figures are being kept confidential, most estimates are that total cost was about US$640 million. Be it remembered, however, that all that money bought beauty as well as utility.

Foster likes to show technology in operation. Thus, for example, the pair of huge escalators that lift customers to the banking floors have transparent sides, putting the working intricacies fully on view. The 23 passenger lifts are out in the open as well. The stunning central atrium (52 meters high) evokes comparisons with the great cathedrals of Europe. And in truth the building does inspire feelings of awe.

But for all the high-tech involved, a fair amount of Chinese tradition went into the effort as well. At several important stages of construction, local geomancers were called in as consultants to ensure that mystic orientations were properly observed. Opening day was set in consultation with the geomancers, who saw it as a day of good auguries.

Nor was tradition ignored. The famous Shanghai-cast bronze lions, Stitt and Stephen (Stephen is the one that growls), were carefully moved from the portals of the old building and then, just as carefully, moved back to the doors of the new. And as usual, the bank's chairman has a very posh apartment indeed atop the building—with, of course, a helicopter pad.

Why put all this effort—and all this money—into a building that as of 1997 will stand on Communist Chinese soil? Bank officials say it's a vote of confidence in the city—capitalist or communist. Others believe, oracularly, that the bank wouldn't have gone ahead with the project without certain guarantees from the Beijing government.

There is, of course, no question at all about China's commitment to Hong Kong. Not far from the Hong Kong Bank's new building, work already is under way on the new offices of the Bank of China. Designed by US architect I.M. Pei, this ultramodern, 70-story structure will tower far above Foster's building. It will in fact dominate Hong Kong's skyline, and symbol manipulators can make of that what they will.

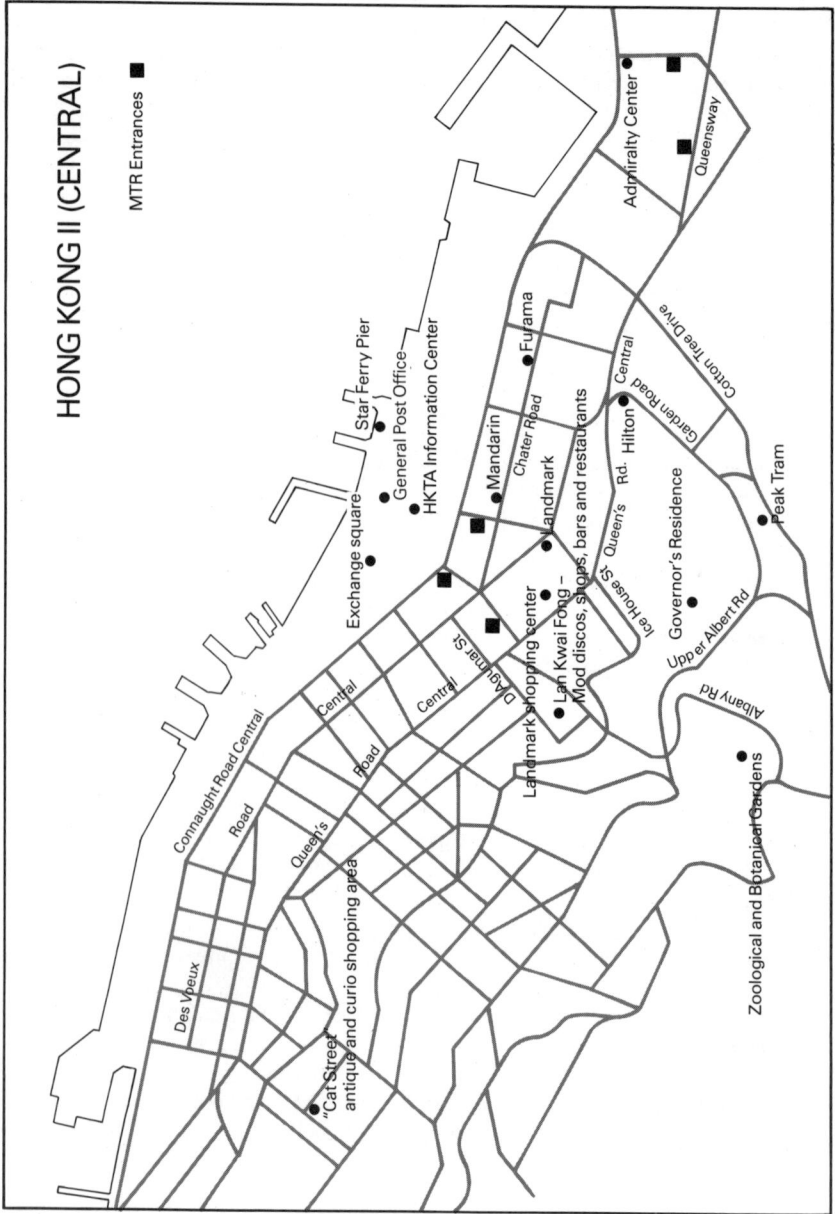

HONG KONG II (CENTRAL)

■ MTR Entrances

Star Ferry Pier
General Post Office
HKTA Information Center
Exchange square
Mandarin
Chater Road
Landmark
Furama
Central
Hilton
Queen's Rd.
Garden Road
Cotton Tree Drive
Admiralty Center
Queensway
Peak Tram
Governor's Residence
Ice House St.
Queen's St.
Upper Albert Rd
Albany Rd
Lan Kwai Fong –
Mod discos, shops, bars and restaurants
Landmark shopping center
D'aguilar St.
Central
Road
Central
Connaught Road Central
Queen's
Road
Des Voeux
"Cat Street"
antique and curio shopping area
Zoological and Botanical Gardens

● Arriving

Flying into Hong Kong, as 90% of its visitors do, lands one smack in the middle of the action. One of the two major approaches to Kai Tak leads the big jets low over the rooftops of jampacked Kowloon, and the terminal's somewhat antiquated processing facilities reinforce the impression: too many people and not enough coping. This is particularly true about Hong Kong's hotels at most times of year: capacity has not kept up with demand. *Never* arrive without a confirmed reservation.

Once through the often-interminable lines, look for the hotel's representative. He'll summon a hotel car (average cost $20) and make sure the luggage goes too. Other transport includes: cabs, cheap and usually plentiful; and a public bus service that runs near most major hotels in Kowloon and Hong Kong Island. (Fare: under US$1).

● Orientation

Many visitors see only one or two portions of this British (until 1997) territory. (Major hotels are located on the tip of Kowloon peninsula, in an area called Tsim Sha Tsui, or on Hong Kong Island, in the Central and Causeway Bay districts.) The island and Kowloon are linked by subway, tunnel and the beloved Star Ferries.

● Transportation

Taxis are usually easy to find, and inexpensive, but tend to vanish during rainstorms and between 16:00 and 18:00, when shifts change. Public buses are frequent and, at fares ranging from HK$1 to HK$5, are reasonable, but consult locals about routes. There's a nostalgia-buff tramway along the island's north rim, at a fare of about 10 US cents.

The colony has a fine new subway system which now links the island with Kowloon and outlying suburbs and the island's north coast. Fares depend on distance traveled. Trains move fast and are icily air-conditioned, but can be jammed during rush hours.

A broad selection of ferries also helps speed transport. Besides the Star Ferry route between Kowloon and the island's Central district, others crisscross the harbor and extend to much of the archipelago. Fares vary, but are low.

> Note: Because most office buildings are clustered in Central, Causeway Bay and the tip of Kowloon Peninsula, only minimal planning is necessary to link up several appointments in a short time.

● Money

The Hong Kong dollar, worth about 12 US cents and pegged to the US dollar, breaks down into 50, 20 and 10 cent pieces. Coins: HK$1, HK$2 and HK$5. Bills: HK$10, HK$50, HK$100, HK$500 and HK$1000. Banks are open 09:00–16:00 Mondays through Fridays and 09:00–12:00 Saturdays.

Exchange offices are open on Sundays and holidays at the airport, Star Ferry Piers, hotels and many major retailers too.

● Tipping

Built into most bills are 10% service charges. Most Hong Kong residents usually leave a bit on top, from small change on up to an extra 5% if service has been particularly good.

To get a good table in a top restaurant, the discreet offer of HK$50 or HK$100 may smooth your way. This is rarely necessary, save at absolute peak weeks in the fall and spring, or over the year-end holidays.

● Communications

International direct dialling is possible from major hotels and most residences.

(Call 5–2891 for specifics). Circuits are plentiful and quality high. Local calls (HK$1) can be perplexing: prefixes (think of them as area codes) must be used for calls *outside* the immediate area but are not needed inside it. Example: to call Kowloon from Hong Kong island, dial a 3 before the actual number. Other prefixes: 5 for Hong Kong numbers, 0 for New Territories numbers. Oddity: directories are scarce. Instead, phone 108 for information.

Hong Kong is a leading world communications center. Cable and Wireless (HK) Ltd. offers the following: telex, telephone, telegram, leased circuits, Bureaufax, IDAS (International Database Access Service) and international facsimile. The Post Office has two mail deliveries every weekday to main commercial and industrial areas. 'Speedpost' offers high-speed assured delivery to many overseas addresses within 48 hours.

● What to wear

Either it's hot or it's not. During summer (May–October) wear lightweight suits and ties for business; there are occasional rainstorms and a typhoon now and then. During winter (November–March) it's cool enough for fall-weight clothes, with woolens and even furs useful in January and February when the temperatures dip into the 40s(F). Most offices and shopping areas are air-conditioned, as is the subway.

● Languages

Cantonese, a dialect of standard Mandarin, is spoken by 95% of local Chinese. English is widely used in central areas but facility in it drops sharply on the outlands. Only a bit of Mandarin is spoken.

● Doing business

*A basic resource is the Hong Kong Tourist Association, located at the Star Ferry concourse in Kowloon and on the 35th Floor, Connaught Center, Hong Kong Island. Phone: 3–671111. Office Hours: generally, from 09:00 to 17:30, on weekdays, and 09:00 to 12:00 Saturdays. Very efficient.

*All major hotels offer facilities for business travelers, including secretaries, translators and general local business advice. The Furama Hotel has office suites. Interlingua (tel. 5–430188) offers a full range of technical translation, production services and interpretation. And there is a 24-hour full-range business center at Riggs, Ocean Center, Kowloon, tel. 3–696607.

*Most businessmen find it useful to print a Chinese translation of their name and company on the back of their business cards.

*Don't forget to put cash aside for the outrageous Hong Kong departure tax, payable at the airport: HK$120 for adults, HK$60 for children under 12.

*Trade Development Council, 31st Floor, Great Eagle Center, 23 Harbor Road, Hong Kong, 5–833–4333, telex 73595 CONHK HX: responsible for developing markets for Hong Kong products. A quasi-government unit with 25 offices overseas, it can put foreign businessmen quickly in touch with local opportunities.

*Trade and Industry Departments, Hong Kong Government, Ocean Center, 5 Canton Road, Kowloon, 3–722 2573, telex 50151 INDIK IN. The Trade Department is responsible for certificates of origin, import and export licensing and general trade controls. The Industry Department is responsible for development of local industry and promotion of industrial investment.

*General Chamber of Commerce, 9th Floor, Swire House, Chater Road, Hong Kong, 5–237177, telex 83535 TRIND HX. A wide-ranging organization providing a variety of services in trade and industrial promotion. The oldest organization of its type, it has more than

2800 members and is linked to the International Chamber of Commerce.

*American Chamber of Commerce, 10th Floor, Swire House, Chater Road, Hong Kong, 5–260165, telex 83664 AMCC HX. Established in 1969, it has more than 1700 members (American and non-American) and runs a top-rated business briefing service for US firms interested in the Hong Kong and China markets.

*Chinese Manufacturers Association, third and fourth floors, CMA Building, 64–66 Connaught Road Central, Hong Kong, 5–456166, telex 63526 MAFTS HX. Promotes trade and industrial development, organizes annual new products award competition, presses for quality improvement.

Useful phone numbers

● Airlines:

Air France, 5–248145, 3–684902.
Air India, 5–214321–4, 3–829558.
Air New Zealand, 5–640123, 3–7236938.
Air Niugini, 5–242151–2.
Alitalia, 5–237041, 3–829448.
All Nippon, 5–251306, 3–8297595.
British, 5–775023, 3–689255.
British Caledonian, 5–260062, 3–8298225.
Canadian Pacific, 5–227001, 3–8298225.
Cathay Pacific, 5–640123, 3–7236938.
China Airlines, 5–218431, 3–674181.
Garuda, 5–235181, 3–829689.
Gulf, 3–8298337, 3–8293347.
Japan Airlines, 5–230081, 3–829524.
KLM, 5–251255, 3–8298111.
Korean Airlines, 5–235177, 3–686221.
Lufthansa, 5–212311, 3–665201.
Malaysian, 5–218181, 3–8297967.
Northwest Orient, 5–217477, 3–8297346.
Pan American, 5–231111, 3–8297155.

Philippine Airlines, 5–227018, 3–694521.
Qantas, 5–242101, 3–8298792.
Royal Brunei, 5–223799.
Royal Nepal, 3–699151/2.
Singapore Airlines, 5–201313.
South African, 5–775023, 3–689255.
Swissair, 5–293670, 3–8297355.
Thai, 5–295601, 3–8297421.

● Emergencies:

Police, Fire, Ambulance dial 999.

● Hospitals:

Queen Mary Hospital (island side), 5–8192111.
Adventist Hospital (island side), 5–746211.
Queen Elizabeth Hospital (Kowloon), 3–7102111.

● Churches:

Church of England: St. John's Cathedral, 5–234157 and St. Andrew's Church, 3–671478.
Roman Catholic: St. Joseph's Church, 5–252629 and Rosary Church, 3–685731.
Methodist Church, 5–757817.
Baptist Church, 3–692237.
Union Church, 5–237247.
Quaker Services, 5–435123.
Jewish Services, 5–594821.

● Diplomatic Representatives:

Australia, 5–731881.
Austria, 5–239716.
Bangladesh, 5–728278.
Belgium, 5–243111.
Brazil, 5–257002.
Burma, 5–8913329.
Colombia, 5–458547.
Costa Rica, 5–665181.
Cuba, 5–760226.
Denmark, 5–8936265.
Dominican Republic, 3–7231836.
Ecuador, 3–692235.
Egypt, 5–244174.

France, 5–294351.
Germany (West), 5–298885.
Haiti, 5–244306.
India, 5–284029.
Indonesia, 5–7904421.
Iran, 5–414745.
Israel, 5–220177.
Italy, 5–220033.
Japan, 5–221184.
Korea (South), 5–430224.
Malaysia, 5–270921.
Mexico, 5–214365.
Netherlands, 5–227710.
New Zealand, 5–255044.
Nigeria, 5–8939444.

Norway, 5–749253.
Pakistan, 5–274623.
Panama, 5–452166.
Peru, 3–803698.
Philippines, 5–7908823.
Portugal, 5–225789.
Singapore, 5–272212.
South Africa, 5–773279.
Spain, 5–253041.
Sweden, 5–211212.
Switzerland, 5–227147.
Thailand, 5–742201.
United Kingdom, 5–230176.
USA, 5–239011.
Venezuela, 3–678099.

HONG KONG III (WANCHAI)

■ MTR Entrances

Royal Hong Kong Yacht Club
Entry to Cross-Harbour Tunnel (vehicles only)
Wanchai Ferry Pier
Causeway Bay Typhoon Shelter
Noon Day Gun
Harbour Road
Hong Kong Arts Center
Hong Kong Exhibition Center
Excelsior Hotel
Food Street
World Trade Center
Kingston St
Gloucester Road
Gloucester Road
Jaffe Road
Jaffe Road
Lockhart Road
Lockhart Road
Hennessy Road
Hennessy Road
Lee Garden Rd.
Johnston Road
Wanchai Road
Hopewell Center
Football Stadium
Wong Nei Chung Road
Wong Nei Chung Road
Happy Valley Race Course
Aberdeen Tunnel
Hong Kong Stadium

Shopping

Call it the world's largest toystore for adults, call it Baghdad-on-the-South-Chinese-Sea, call it superBloomies: by any name you like, Hong Kong is the most spectacular shopping scene in the world. Because it's a duty-free port, most products are cheaper here than in their lands of origin. Quality is high and prices are low—it's a great place to go broke saving money. Other cities have their specialties: silk in Bangkok, batik in Jakarta, precious stones in Rangoon. But Hong Kong has pretty much everything, and it's tax-free.

Don't be afraid to bargain. Aside from major department stores, where prices are pretty much immovable, bargaining is part of the shopping routine here. Ask the merchant for his best price, cut it politely by a third—or half—and negotiate from there. 'Gweilos' (foreign devils) who pay the asking price are regarded as fools. They are.

Major shopping areas are located both on Hong Kong island and on the Kowloon peninsula. Very roughly, Kowloon offers a wider choice of cameras, electronic goods and gems, but the island's Central District has higher quality, and prices to match. Shop around. Compare prices. And bargain, haggle, bargain.

For antiques, look at Charlotte Horstmann/Gerald Godfrey, in the Sea Terminal, for the top-of-the-line items. Ada Lum, in the Mandarin Hotel, is also top-notch. For less-expensive items, try the Hollywood Road area of Central: though bargains aren't as plentiful here as they were in the Forties and Fifties, there's plenty of good, authentic material. Be cautious. It helps to know a bit about jade, for instance, or Sung Dynasty figures. Fakes abound. There's nothing wrong with buying a Ching Dynasty copy of a Tang Dynasty camel, for example, but be sure to pay the proper price.

There's a jade market on Kansu Street in the northern section of the Kowloon peninsula. Hundreds of dealers offer thousands of items. Some is the real stuff: Sung, Ming or Ching. Some is real enough, but modern. And some is dross. *Caveat emptor.*

For clothes, there are fine tailors for both men and women, but prices are steeper these days than in the Fifties. Bangkok, for men's clothes at least, offers fair quality at lower prices than Hong Kong. And forget those stories about 24-hour suits: most responsible tailors these days ask at least a week and two fittings to do a decent job.

Among the best for men: Baromon and A Man Hing Chong, both on island side. For women: Betty Clemo (Kowloon) and Peer, in Central.

Hotels

● Hong Kong Island

Mandarin, 5 Connaught Road, Central, tel. 5–220111, telex 73653 MANDA HX. One of the great hotels of the world and by many believed to be Hong Kong's best. Built two decades ago and regularly renovated, its suites are superb, regular rooms pleasant, restaurants and bars tops (though the staff can be a bit distant).

Hilton, 2 Queens Road Central, tel. 5–255111, telex 73355 HILTL HX. Another in the fine Asian Hilton group, this was built in the early Sixties and gets better with age. Efficient staff. Bars and restaurants topnotch. Outdoor pool and fitness center.

Furama, 1 Connaught Road, Central, tel. 5–255111, telex 73081 FURAM HX. An Intercontinental group member, service is cheerful, and its La Rotisserie restaurant is very good indeed. Alone in Hong Kong, this hotel offers business suites, which combine a functioning office with separate sleeping quarters, located next to the hotel's business center. New health center.

Excelsior, 281 Gloucester Road, Causeway Bay, tel. 5–767365, telex 74550 Excon HX. Well located near the World Trade Center in the fast-growing Causeway Bay area.

Victoria, Shun Tak Centre, 200 Connaught Road, Central, tel. 5–407228, telex 86608 HTLVT HX. Five restaurants, floodlit tennis courts, pool.

● Kowloon

Peninsula, Salisbury Road, Kowloon, tel. 3–666251, telex 43821 PEN HX. Almost like a private club, intractably rococo, superbly comfortable, the Pen is regularly listed among the top 20 hotels in the world. Fine rooms, fine food, fine shops in the arcade.

Regent, 18 Salisbury Road, Kowloon, tel. 3–7211211, Telex 37134 HX. Wonderful harborside location with a memorable view of Victoria. Nicely furnished rooms, good restaurants. Headquarters for the garment trade.

Shangri-La, 64 Mody Road, Kowloon, tel. 3–7215215. Among the newer grand-luxe hotels, in a new area (Tsim Sha Tsui East) and near good shops. Large, comfortable rooms.

Royal Garden, 69 Mody Road, Kowloon, tel. 3–7215215. Another winner

in the Tsim Sha Tsui East area, with a superb French restaurant in La Lalique and an excellent Chinese restaurant as well.

Kowloon, 19–21 Nathan Road, tel. 3–698698, telex 47604 KLNHL HX. Managed by the Peninsula group, Telecenter computer terminals in every room, compact and comfortable.

Prince, Harbour City, Canton Road, tel. 3–7237788. Recently opened in a huge new shopping area.

Hong Kong Hotel, 3 Canton Road, Kowloon, tel. 3–676011. Good restaurants, well-located in the Harbour City-Ocean Terminal area.

Sheraton, 20 Nathan Road, Kowloon, tel. 3–691111, telex 45813 HX. Flagship of the group's Asian hotels; well managed and well located. Deluxe tower floors, business center, rooftop pool. Sky Lounge perfect for a romantic cocktail.

Hyatt Regency, 67 Nathan Road, Kowloon, tel. 3–662321, telex 43127 HX. Renovated in 1985. Hugo's restaurant is always good value. Regency Club for business travelers. Polaris Bar, 16th floor, offers a great view.

Holiday Inn Golden Mile, 46–52 Nathan Road, Kowloon, tel. 3–693111. Good shopping, good entertainment area. Group tours.

Holiday Inn Harbour View, 70 Mody Road, Kowloon, tel. 3–7215161. Quieter than its sister inn, most of its rooms have good views of, what else, the harbour. Pool, health club.

Royal Meridien, 71 Mody Road, Kowloon, tel. 3–7221818. New and very French, with plenty of chic *boutiques* and a health club.

Regal Meridien Airport, San Po Road, Kowloon, tel. 3–7180333. Stroll across an enclosed bridge from Kai Tak to this new French-run hotel. Soundproofed. A China Traders Center specializes in service for businesspeople with an eye on China.

Restaurants

● European

Gaddi's, Peninsula Hotel, Kowloon, tel. 3–666251. Still—probably—the colony's best: superb food, good wines and elegant decor.

Pierrot, Mandarin Hotel (25th Floor), Central, tel. 3–220111. The island's answer to Gaddi's, with a great view of the harbor thrown in. Superb, innovative *cuisine nouvelle*.

Mozart Stub'n, 8 Glenealy, Central, tel. 5–221763. A little bit of Salzburg, fittingly perched on the hillside just above the Central district. Classic Austrian cuisine, including the inevitable Wiener Schnitzel, good national wines and some fetching Cantonese waitresses kitted out in dirndls.

Jimmy's Kitchen, 1–3 Wyndham Street, Central, tel. 5–265293. A China Coast standby for more than 50 years. Good Western food and a few tasty Asian dishes, including a fiery dry Madras curry. (In Causeway Bay, there's a related restaurant named Landau's (tel. 5–7902901) that's almost as good. And there's a branch in Kowloon that needs work.)

Grills. There are three superb grillrooms, all on the Hong Kong side, all located in top hotels (Mandarin, Hilton, Excelsior) and each with its partisans. There's little to choose between them, frankly, but those with a feeling for journalism might lean a bit to the Hilton entry. It features a corner dedicated to the late Richard Hughes, dean of Far East journalists. All have topnotch staffers, good wines and great steaks.

● Chinese

Cantonese Fat Siu Lau Seafood, 3rd floor, Houston Center, Mody Road, Kowloon, tel. 3–686291. Fine Cantonese-style seafood (there are those who say there's nothing better) in a handsome South China-style room.

Luk Yu Tea House, 24–26 Stanley Street, Central, tel. 5--235463. A gourmet's temple for generations, now rebuilt exactly in its old style, that features marvellous food. Two cautions: it's better enjoyed with a Cantonese-speaking friend—and the service can be grudging.

Eagle's Nest, Hilton, Central, tel. 5–233111. Perhaps the best *dim-sum* in town, improbably located atop the Hilton Hotel. Quick service, splendid views.

Szechuan Red Pepper, 7 Lan Fong Road, Causeway Bay, tel. 5–768046. Simple decor, complicated tastes, mostly garlic and pepper and other nerve-tingling spices favored by those who love this superb cuisine. Try crispy rice dishes, garlic prawns and pepper soup—and then experiment.

Pep'N Chilli, 12–22 Blue Poll Road, Happy Valley, tel. 5–738251–4. A cool, grey-green, upscale version of the Red Pepper. Fancier decor, fancier clothes, fancier staff—but the same incandescent food. Try their camphor-smoked duck. Co-owned by a son of the Red Pepper folks.

Sichuan Garden, 3rd Floor, The Landmark, Des Voeux Road, Central, tel. 5–214433. Huge, noisy, good hot food at reasonable prices. Not quite so fiery as the restaurants cited above, but very good. Tops: lobster balls with hot chili sauce.

Beijing American, 20 Lockhart Road, Wanchai, tel. 5–277277. Unpretentious, noisy, crowded, no-nonsense style and menu and staff. Fine hotpots, dumplings, roast chicken and barbecued beef.

Pine and Bamboo, 30 Leighton Road, Causeway Bay, tel. 5–773567. Famous for good hotpots and a generally fine Peking-style menu. Try quick-fried vegetables, sesame-seed bread, dumplings, Peking duck. Service sometimes off-hand.

Tien Hung Lau, 18–C Austin Avenue, Kowloon, tel. 3–662414. An oldtimer, famed for its beggar's chicken (wrapped in lotus leaves, then baked in clay). One must be absolutely sure to understand the prices of each dish before ordering: bills have a way of multiplying here.

Beijing Garden: there are at least four restaurants in this chain, located in Central, Causeway Bay and Kowloon. Good food, moderate prices, efficient service. All recommended.

● Shanghai

Shanghai Garden Restaurant, Hutchinson House, Central, tel. 5–248181. Good solid Shanghai-style seafood, 'drunken chicken' (marinated in wine) and the omnipresent fried noodles—along with representative dishes from other areas of China. Handsome room, good service.

Japanese Ginza, Regent Hotel arcade, Kowloon, tel. 3–696138. Expensive, but worth it. Classic decor, fine *sushi*, *tempura* and *teppanyaki*.

Okahan, Lee Gardens Hotel, Hysan Avenue, Causeway Bay, tel. 5–7954040. Small, expensive, noted particularly for incredible beef, but its other dishes are all top-quality.

● Indian

Ashoka, 57 Wyndham Street, Central, tel. 5–249623. North Indian cooking, all prepared to order, and delicious. Tandoori specialties. Hot-curry enthusiasts should be sure to say so: they tend to underplay their chillies for folks they don't know.

Gaylord, 6 Hart Avenue, Kowloon, tel. 3–7241001. Consistently good Indian classics, including the inevitable Tandoori chicken, many types of kebabs and curries, curries, curries.

● Indonesian

Indonesian, 26 Leighton Road, Causeway Bay, tel. 5–779981. One of several suspiciously similarly named restaurants (New Indonesian, etc.), but this one is favored by Indonesian expatriates. Great *satay*, *gado-gado* (salad), beef *rendang* and assorted Indonesian curries, and splendid *nasi goreng*. Oddity: after 22:00 most nights, young Cantonese singers drop in, warble a few songs, then prettily yield to the next in line. Curiously charming.

● Vietnamese

Yin Ping, 24 Cannon Street, Causeway Bay, tel. 5–8329038. There are those who argue that Vietnamese cooking is Asia's best. Yin Ping's food helps bear out that argument, though the simplicity of the decor may be deceiving. Go early: they close at 22:00.

● Korean

Arirang, 19 Canton Road, Kowloon, tel. 3–692667; and two other locations: Hyatt Regency, Nathan Road, Kowloon, tel. 3–665551, and 76 Morrison Hill Road, Island side, tel. 5–723027. Good Korean barbecue with all the trimmings, efficient service, moderate.

◢■■■■▶ After hours

Hong Kong's once rowdy nightlife scene has gone upmarket. The bars are still plentiful but the Suzie Wongs are scarce: glossy discos have replaced the storied Wanchai dives. And like discos everywhere, today's favorite is tomorrow's forget-it.

But action abounds. Though Wanchai's now passé, the island's Central and Causeway Bay districts, and Kowloon's Tsim Sha Tsui offer all sorts of entertainment. Noteworthy is the ongoing popularity of the disco craze, particularly in Tsim Sha Tsui (TST, as it's known to the locals).

Hot Gossip, 160 Canton Road, tel. 3–724–028, which has a long bar topside and a packed dance floor below. Up-market Cantonese and European crowd.

The Cavern, 35 Hankow Road, tel. 3–683829. Has a certain reputation as a place to meet fellow adventure seekers. Lots of pretty Filipinas.

Canton, 19 Canton Road, tel. 3–721–0209, very new, very loud, very futuristic and very full of young locals.

Hollywood East, 71 Mody Road, tel. 3–722–5597. Wondrous decor, plenty of action.

Zodiac Disco, in Bar City located below the New World Trade Center on Salisbury Road, tel. 3–698571. Hong Kong's first Japanese disco, and as might be expected, madly mod. Huge dance floor and—wait for it—a *sushi* bar.

Other Kowloon spots that might be worth a visit:

Bottoms Up, 14 Hankow Road, tel. 3–675–696. A long-established topless bar with an interesting twist or two.

Red Lips, 1A Lock Road, tel. 3–684511. One of the favorites during Vietnam War R&R days—and the girls haven't changed.

Rick's Cafe, 4 Hart Avenue, tel. 3–672939. Yes, named after that Rick's. No Bogarts or Dooley Wilsons, but okay food and drinks.

● **Island Side**

Godown, Basement of Sutherland House, Chater Road, Central, tel. 5–221608. Good jazz, avoidable food, pleasant crowd.

Bull and Bear, Hutchison House, 10 Harcourt Road, Central, tel. 5–257436, a good solid English pub, complete with darts and starchy pub food. Lively clientele.

Nineteen 97, Lan Kwai Fong (between Wyndham Street and D'Aguilar Street, Central), tel. 5–260303. The best of a friendly little group of bars and discos in a chic shopping and nightlife area. The name, of course, is a reference to the year that Hong Kong is scheduled to be taken over by China.

Mad Dogs, 33 Wyndham Street, Central, tel. 5–252383. Many residents swear this really is the colony's best pub. Two bars on two levels, with a pleasant little courtyard out back.

Pastel's, 12 Pedder Street, tel. 5–218421. A very cool crowd and sophisticated decor. Private, but one can often win entry by showing a passport.

Note: For the diehard pursuer of the Suzie Wong legend, it should be pointed out that it is indeed possible to find company for an evening. The shabbier bars will allow tourists to pour whisky-tinted tea down their hostesses all night, then sock them with an enormous bill—and finally be no help at all in curing your loneliness.

So: always ask about prices before ordering anything at all. Keep track of what's been ordered. Don't expect to find hearts of gold in the nightlife scene—that gold melted long ago. Hong Kong by night can be a very tough scene indeed.

Sights and sounds

The Peak: Since 1888, the Peak Tram has been shuttling residents and visitors up and down from Victoria Peak (397 meters) and it still provides one of Hong Kong's handsomest views. The 8-minute ride costs about 50 US cents. Once the scene has been admired, take an hour's stroll around the Peak area, via Lugard and Harlech Roads, then have a meal in one of the three passable restaurants topside.

Ocean Park: A great place for the kids—and many adults too. A stunning cable-car ride takes visitors out to a splendid, isolated headland on the south side of Hong Kong island. There are thrill rides and a splendid seal pool, an atoll life display and a porpoise and diver show that stars a killer whale. Next to the park is Water World, with some good water slides and many swimming pools—including one with waves. Crowded on warm-weather weekends.

Curios and antiques: The Island's Hollywood Road-Upper Lascar Row area, famed as a thieves' row called Cat Street years ago, offers a trove of antiques and curio shops. Probably the colony's best selection. Bargain and be cautious.

Space Museum: Located across the street from the Peninsula Hotel in Kowloon, the Space Museum has a regular planetarium show and free exhibitions on space science. (tel. 3-7212361).

Zoological and Botanical Gardens: Just up from the lower Peak Tram terminus are pleasant hillside gardens, with an interesting bird collection and a respectable zoo. In early mornings, locals practice Tai Chi Chuan (graceful Chinese setting-up exercises) here.

Bird Market: Hundreds of cage birds on sale daily in Kowloon's Hong Lok Street, near the subway's Argyle station. Cantonese, like most other Chinese, enjoy birds as pets, take them out in cages for daily strolls, pit songbirds against each other in trilling contests.

Stanley Market: A raffish market in the island village of Stanley where shoppers sometimes can find well-known labels at absurdly low prices. And respectable porcelain and china, rattan furniture and many other good buys. There's also a pleasant restaurant nearby, called—with startling originality—Stanley's. Good food. Reservations advised.

Horse Racing: Three times a week, during the September–May season, the Royal Hong Kong Jockey Club offers well-organized and wildly popular racing. There are two tracks: one at Happy Valley on Hong Kong Island, the other at Shatin in the New Terriories. Visitors, by producing HK$50 and their passports at the Island-side off-course betting office, can buy a ticket allowing entry to the members' enclosure (tel. 5-7904827).

Hong Kong Museum of Art: Regular exhibitions of Asian and Western art, including paintings, sculpture and ceramics, at City Hall on the island (tel. 5-224127). A branch of the Flagstaff House Tea Ware Museum, near Central, houses ancient Chinese tea ware in a nicely restored colonial mansion built in 1844 (tel. 5--299390).

Fung Ping Shan Museum: Chinese bronzes and ceramics, located on Hong Kong University on the island (tel. 5-8592114).

Han Tomb and Museum: An actual Han Dynasty (206–229 AD) tomb, restored as part of a small museum at Sham Shui Po, Kowloon (tel. 3-862863).

City Hall and Coliseum: Sites for most of Hong Kong's major spectacles—concerts, recitals and other entertainments. The Coliseum, at Hung Hom in Kowloon, is new, and is a major venue for both entertainment and sports. It can also be converted into an ice-skating rink. City Hall, on Island side, has a concert hall, theater and exhibition halls. It has been the center of the colony's cultural life since it opened in 1962 (tel. 5–228928).

Weekends

Many travelers with free time in the colony choose to spend it in the great outdoors. There's good tennis available, and hiking and sailing too. Windsurfing is also popular. For the less athletic, there are plenty of quick trips available: to Macau, or Canton, for instance (see separate chapter). It's also possible to go just across the China border on day trips. Some suggestions follow.

Charter a junk: A junk big enough to carry 20 persons can be rented for HK$1800 (US$230) per eight-hour day. Two crewmen are included in the cost of the junk, which has a head and galley (simple stove and fridge). Bring your own food and booze. There are plenty of quiet island beaches within easy reach. Phone The Boating Center, 5–223527 or 5–223529.

The Outer Islands: Hong Kong consists of much more than the island of Hong Kong itself and the Kowloon peninsula. There are 235 islands in the archipelago, though most are uninhabited (water shortages). One worth a visit is Po Toi, which has a couple of noisy but quite good seafood restaurants crammed with sunburnt daytrippers. For spy-novel buffs, Po Toi is the scene of the bloody denouement of John le Carre's *The Honorable Schoolboy*. It is best to borrow a friend's yacht for the trip, but it's reachable by ferry, too.

Sailing: The Royal Hong Kong Yacht Club is linked with clubs all over the world by reciprocal agreements. Call them at 5–7902187.

Golf: To play at the Royal Hong Kong Golf Club's top-ranked Fanling course (three 18-hole courses), the greens fee is HK$300 (US$38), weekdays only. At the club's nine-hole course on Hong Kong Island, greens fees are HK$100 (US$12.80), again only on weekdays.

Windsurfing: Three beach areas rent windsurfers (Sai Kung in the New Territories, Stanley on the Island, and Cheung Chau, one of the outlying islands).

New Territories: Hong Kong's not all shops, though many visitors won't believe it. But north of Kowloon is the land known as the New Territories—376 square miles of rolling green hills where rural Chinese life goes along quite peacefully. A six-hour bus tour takes visitors through the farmlands to old villages and country markets and on up near the China frontier. Price: HK$150 (US$19), which includes lunch.

Shenzhen: For a quick glance at the other side of the border, there's a one-day tour of the town of Shenzhen that includes a visit to an agricultural commune, an arts and crafts center, a kindergarten and even a guided walking tour of the town itself. Price: about HK$450 (US$58), which includes lunch. (For additional description, see Shenzhen chapter.)

Zhongshan: Another one-day tour of transborder China, this one by way of

Macao. Tourists take a jetfoil from Hong Kong to Macau, then board a bus that rolls through tiny Macau (see below) and across the border into Zhongshan County. After a visit to a former residence of Sun Yat-sen, founder of the Chinese republic, there's a lunch at Shiqi and a visit to a commune before the voyage back to Hong Kong via Macau. Price: about HK$450 (US$58).

Macau

Macau, only an hour away by boat from Hong Kong, is three centuries older in time and a strongly recommended antidote for anyone suddenly afflicted by the dread 'Hong Kong hustle'. The tiny Portuguese territory offers much that fast-modernizing Hong Kong has lost: winding cobblestoned streets, faded pink, green and blue buildings, pedicabs, and a quiet and generally relaxed style of life. In a very pleasant way, this tiny Oriental Portugal (one peninsula, two islands, 6 square miles) constitutes a living museum.

Then there's the other Macau: bright lights, discos and night clubs, fast-paced gambling casinos (both Western and Chinese games), *jai-alai* and trotters and dogracing—and if that's not enough, every November there's a frantic week of Grand Prix auto and motorcycle racing.

Something for everyone? Well, pretty much. There are some good and reasonable restaurants (Portuguese, Chinese, Italian, Korean and Japanese) and browsable coffee shops. There are gold and jewellery shops, and some buyable Chinese curios mixed in with the worst glitz ever. Antique shopping, once rewarding, is better done in Hong Kong or Taipei. There are a couple of fair beaches on the outer island of Coloane, and interesting churches and temples everywhere.

The half-day usually budgeted for Macau by Hong Kong visitors is not enough. Much better is to take a full day—or three. There is nothing like Macau anywhere in the world, and it isn't going to last much longer in its present form. Historically, Macau is a gem, the only well-preserved example of the treaty ports that speckled the China coast a century ago. Its old buildings, crowded market alleys, incense-reeking temples and ancient churches stand now as they've stood for centuries.

The city came into existence early in the 16th Century, when Portuguese traders first arrived in China. After the Portuguese came the Dutch, the French and the English, and eventually the Americans, all long before British victory over China in the Opium Wars put Hong Kong on the map as well.

From Macau, missionaries spread Christianity to Japan, China and even Vietnam; and the evidence of that civilizing mission still abounds today in Macau's churches, schools and cemeteries.

It's all quite a sight: *real* living museums aren't all that common in our world of Disneylands. Macau today is in the sunset of an illustrious past, and it's a sunset very much worth seeing.

MACAU

Barrier Gate

Canidrome

Avenida do Almirante Lacerda

Avenida do Coronel Mesquita

Rua do Pe. Antonio Roliz

Rua da Ribeira do Patane

Estrada do Repouso

Museum and Old Protestant Cemetery

Ruins of St. Paul's Cathedral

Old Monte Fortress

Avenida do Conselheiro

Estrada da Vitoria

Jai Alai Stadium

Ferry Pier

Floating Casino

Avenida de Almeida Ribeiro

Rua do Campo

Loyal Senate

Excelsior Hotel and Casino

Teatro Dom Pedro

Rua Central

Rua da Praia Grande

Rua da P.E. Antonio S. Lourenco

Avenida do Infante

Avenida da Amizade

Lisboa Hotel and Casino

Calcada da Barra

Estrada da Penha

Bella Vista Hotel

Pousada Sao Tiago

● Arriving

Macau is 40 miles by sea from Hong Kong, and a fleet of high-speed ferryboats is the only direct link between two ports. Ask the hotel to make boat and hotel reservations, or join one of the many tours. Or buy the tickets at Hong Kong's brand-new Macau ferry pier.

Visas are available on landing in Macau for most nationalities. To check, call the Macau Tourist Information Bureau, Hong Kong tel. 3–677747.

There's a broad selection of ferries: fastest are jetfoils (50 minutes), while hydrofoils and jetcats are only a bit slower. High-speed ferries make the trip in 100 minutes and are far more comfortable than the faster craft. For nostalgia buffs, two of the old three-hour ferry boats still run—and offer private cabins.

During the week, tickets are easy to buy, but beware of weekends. On Fridays, hordes of Hong Kong gamblers flood from their offices to the ferries, spend the weekend in Macau's casinos and trickle back exhausted on Sunday nights. Reserve early, in both directions.

● Orientation

Macau is a self-governing Portuguese territory on the southeast coast of China. Its 6-square mile area consists of a peninsula, on which the city is located, plus the islands of Taipa and Coloane, linked by causeway and bridge to the city. The population is about 400,000, of which 95% are Chinese and 3% Portuguese.

● Transportation

Taxis are cheap and plentiful, though many drivers speak only fragmentary English. There are lots of pedicabs, but remember to settle a price for the trip before starting off. Bikes can be rented. So can Mokes, which are strange-looking but very practical little British cars which make Macau touring a lot more fun.

● Money

The Macau *pataca* and the Hong Kong dollar look much alike and are almost equal in value (HK$100 equals about *patacas* 103). Remember that while Hong Kong money is readily accepted in Macau, *patacas* are worthless in Hong Kong. There are 100 *avos* in a *pataca*, should anyone ask about *centavos*.

● Tipping

Minimal, as in Hong Kong. Service charges are included in most restaurant bills.

● Communications

Telephone and telex systems are adequate, but direct dialling is only now being installed. Mails are slow.

● What to wear

Macau is subtropical, as is Hong Kong, so cottons are good news. Neckties and business suits are very rare. Woolens in winter.

● Languages

Cantonese is spoken by just about everyone here, including the resident Portuguese. English is spoken adequately if not elegantly at hotels, restaurants and of course the casinos.

Hotels

There are three truly first-class hotels—the tiny Pousada Sao Tiago, the larger and superbly run Oriental and the Hyatt Regency on Taipa Island. There are several more just a notch or two below.

The Oriental, Avenida da Amizade, tel. 567888, telex 88588 OMA OM, reservations in Hong Kong, tel. 5–268888. Known as the Excelsior until it changed its name in 1985, the Oriental is a representative member of the toprank Oriental Mandarin group. Its 483 rooms have pleasant views (there are two suites), there is a fine grill, casino and a well-equipped health center and pool. One of Asia's nicest hotels.

Pousada de Sao Tiago, Avenida da Republica, tel. 78111, telex 88376 TIAGO OM, reservations in Hong Kong tel. 5–891–0366. Only 23 rooms but every one is a gem and most have balconies. Good formal restaurant (La Fortaleza), friendly bar, tiny pool and well-trained staff. An old-style inn built into a cliff and an architectural triumph.

Hyatt Regency, Taipa Island, tel. 27000, telex 88152 HTMCU HX OM, Hong Kong reservations number tel. 3–661311. A typical Hyatt operation, located a bit inconveniently on Taipa island across the bridge from the city, but there's a fine restaurant and a disco. A new resort area next to hotel features a sport clubhouse and recreation complex.

Bela Vista, Rua do Boa Vista, tel. 783821. A must for nostalgia buffs, this turn-of-the-century hotel offers a splendid view of the harbor from its perch on the bluffs in the old part of town, but it's not as comfortable as the newer inns.

Estoril, Avenida Sidonio Pais, tel. 572081, Hong Kong reservations tel. 5–457021. Small (89 rooms), located near many historic sites, nightclubs, pool and sauna.

Lisboa, Avenida da Amizade, tel. 77666, telex 88203 HOTEL OM, Hong Kong reservations tel. 5–415680. Perhaps Asia's oddest-looking hotel, with a huge double-tiered casino at its heart. Its just-completed new wing makes it Macau's biggest. Several restaurants, shopping arcade for casino winners.

Presidente, Avenida da Amizade, tel. 71822, telex 88440 HPM OM, Hong Kong reservations tel. 5–416056. New, with harbor views, Korean restaurant and Skylight Disco, with hostesses and escorts. Sauna.

Royal, Estrada da Vitoria, tel. 78822, telex 88154 ROYAL OM, Hong Kong reservations tel. 5–422033. Member of Japan's Dai-Ichi hotel group, three restaurants, bars, pool and disco.

Sintra, Avenida Dom Joao IV, tel. 85111, telex 88321 SINTA OM, Hong Kong reservations tel. 3–807193. Small but comfortable rooms, close to casino and shopping areas.

Pousada de Coloane, Praia de Cheoc Van, Coloane, tel. 28143, Hong Kong reservations tel. 5–455626. Tiny (22 rooms) and far away from the city, good food and wine and perched just above a pleasant beach.

Restaurants

The food is good and the prices fair—and the assortment of flavors is fascinating. Standard Portuguese fare has been much modified by its contact with Asia: there are apt to be exotic spices folded into one's *bacalhau* or *feijoada*. There are a few special Macanese dishes that must be tried: African chicken, for instance, and the spicy prawns, both guaranteed to light up sluggish taste buds. Seafood is splendid: Macau sole is delicious, and so are the freshwater crabs and yellowfish and even steaks and chops. Portugal's love affair with the codfish is much in evidence: diners can try cod baked, broiled, grilled or fried, and the traditional *caldo verde* soup is always good. Don't neglect Portuguese wines: The so-called Vinho Verde (a full-flavored white) is good, and so are the red and white

Daos. There's an astonishing selection of Port available, and brandy as well.

There are fine restaurants at many hotels: The Grill at the Oriental is a favorite, as is O Pescador at the Hyatt and La Fortaleza at the Pousada de Sao Tiago.

Henri's Galley (4 Avenida da Republica, tel. 76207) has probably the best African chicken in town, and the spicy shrimps are excellent. The decor is simple but the tastes complex, and Henri is a great host.

There's good Chinese food at the **456**, a Shanghai-style restaurant at the Lisboa Hotel, and the Oriental Hotel's **Dynasty**. **Fat Siu Lau** (64 Rua da Felicidade, tel. 57385) offers good Macanese food and its squab has a high reputation.

Farther afield, there's **Pinocchio** in Paipa village for sardines, quail and good wine, and the Portuguese restaurant at **Pousada de Coloane** for excellent sole. Macau's only **Korean** restaurant is in the Presidente Hotel.

After hours

For most of Macau's visitors, nights are spent in the casinos—at least while cash reserves hold out. The pawnshops on nearby streets display sad artifacts (fancy watches and jewellery, expensive cameras) left behind by gamblers who couldn't quit.

For winners, and non-gamblers, there's a lively and sexy cabaret show called the Crazy Paris, located in a comfortable theater at the Hotel Lisboa.

And then there are the discos—the Green Parrot at the Hyatt, and the Skylight at the Presidente. The latter offers a nightly floorshow. Hostesses are available at most of Macau's nightclubs, including the Mermaid (at the Lisboa), the Paris (at the Estoril) and the San Fa Un (also at the Estoril). The latter has Mandarin singers and Cantonese food. The Chu Seng nightclub, out at Macau's Raceway on Taipa, offers Thai and Filipino singers and dancers.

Sights and sounds

Camoes Museum, Praca Luis de Camoes. A small but worthwhile collection of early Chinese (Han, Tang and Ching) bronzes and pottery including two poorly restored Tang horses. Downstairs are some excellent China coast paintings including several works by George Chinnery and Auguste Borget. The buiding itself is a good example of colonial architecture and was from 1733 to 1833 the headquarters of British East India's Company Select Committee.

Camoes Gardens, Praca Luis de Camoes. A public park dedicated to the famed Portuguese poet, whose bronze bust stands in a hilltop grotto surrounded by verses from his poems engraved on stone slabs.

Old Protestant Cemetery, next to Camoes Museum. Buried here are British and American naval officers and seamen, traders and missionaries from most of Europe and North America, and their wives and children, who died more often of war and disease than simple old age. The Irish painter George Chinnery lies buried here, as well as Robert Morrison, who compiled the first English/Chinese dictionary and translated the Bible into Chinese. Nearby is the old Morrison Chapel, where Anglican services are still held every Sunday morning.

Ruins of St. Paul's Church, Rua da Sao Paulo. Destroyed by fire in 1835, this baroque church built by Japanese and Chinese craftsmen under Jesuit supervision is Macau's best-known monument. Only the superb façade remains on the hilltop, but its carvings are interesting.

Old Monte Fort, near St. Paul's ruins. Built by Jesuits in the 1620s, its cannons helped repel Dutch attackers even before the fortress was finished, and its buildings served as a seminary for Jesuit missionaries who were assigned to China, Vietnam, Korea and Japan. Superb views of the city.

Kun Yam Temple, Avenida do Coronel Mesquita. This Buddhist temple dates back to the 1620s and is reputed to be the site of the signature in 1844 of the first treaty of trade and friendship between the United States and China. Kun Yam is Cantonese for Kwan Yin, the Chinese goddess of mercy.

Leal Senado: The town hall, located on Avenida Almeida Ribeira in the center of the city, dates back to 1784 and has been renovated several times since. With its beautiful blue-and-white Portuguese tiles and fine wood carvings and statues, it is the city's finest example of Portuguese colonial architecture. A new art gallery is on the second floor.

● China Trips

Several tourist agencies here run regular trips into China. On most itineraries are the new golf course and hot springs resort at Chung Shan, Sun Yat Sen's birthplace, and the inevitable collective farms, crèches and schools.

Jakarta

The first and most lasting impression of Jakarta is one of 7 million people in constant motion. Day and night, weekdays and weekends, the capital's streets are crammed with thousands of smiling Indonesians on the move. Jammed into battered buses, bouncing in sputtering three-wheeled 'helicacks', perched on snarling motorcycles or clinging to suburban trains that must date back to colonial days, the people of Jakarta circulate in what any scientist would see as classic Brownian Movement.

And as they move, Jakarta expands, by at least a quarter of a million people a year. The city is huge. At 650 square kilometers, it is already two-and-a-half times the size of the republic of Singapore and in another decade or two the city will engulf most of Java's northwest elbow. Jakarta is Indonesia's sprawling great magnet: from all 13,600 islands of the archipelago, people swarm to the capital, seeking jobs, fortunes or just a marginally better chance to improve their lives.

Two decades ago, Jakarta boasted just one top-class hotel, the city's taxi fleet consisted mostly of *betcaks* (pedicabs) with a few just-arrived diesel Mercedes for visitors to quarrel over. Streets were impossible, good restaurants almost nonexistent, politics unstable and electricity uncertain. Today's Jakarta, with its skyscrapers, many good hotels, plentiful (though maltreated) cabs and squadrons of fancy imported sedans, has burst the bonds of the urban slums of the Sixties. Though the oil-fuelled economic boom of the Seventies has eased, the city remains a more attractive and livable place. And though foreigners, particularly first-timers, still grouse bitterly about Jakarta's hassles, the city has a way of growing on one. There are once-unrelenting Jakarta haters who have come to have an almost unexplainable fondness for the place.

It is, even more so than other Asian capitals, a city of enormous contrasts. Next to a flashy new skyscraper will be a carefully tended little plot of vegetables or rice or even flowers, or a rundown stall selling clove-scented kretek cigarettes or the local version of fast foods. Going home from a restaurant at night, your taxi may find itself hemmed in by pedicab drivers unwilling to give an inch to your driver. Just outside the lovely home of your host in Menteng or Kebayoran, you may encounter the unlovely smell of a distinctly ripe drainage ditch.

But for Indonesians, there's nothing like Jakarta. They call it Ibu Kota, the 'mother city', and in truth there is an implicit degree of maternal fertility. Its rich red earth is wildly rich: orchids, jasmine, bougainvillea and banyans flourish here despite and between the lush encroachment of concrete.

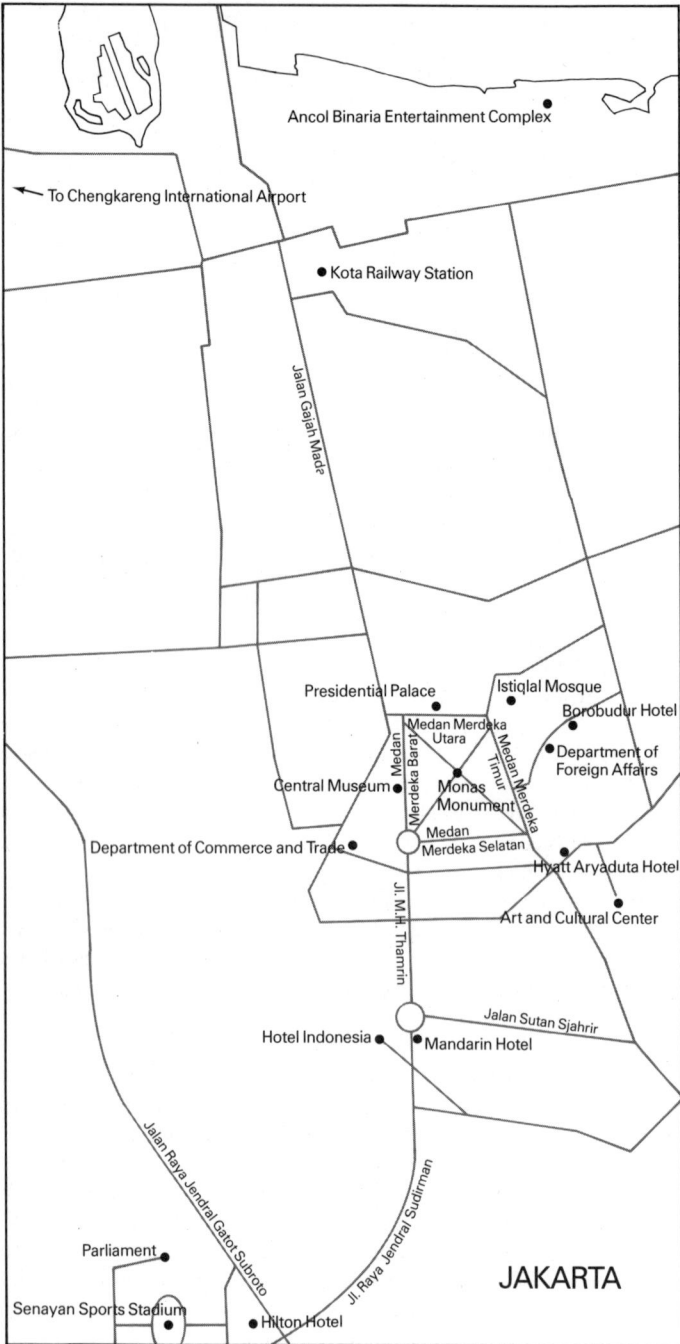

Ancol Binaria Entertainment Complex

← To Chengkareng International Airport

Kota Railway Station

Jalan Gajah Mada

Presidential Palace

Istiqlal Mosque

Borobudur Hotel

Medan Merdeka Utara

Medan Merdeka Timur

Central Museum

Monas Monument

Department of Foreign Affairs

Merdeka Barat

Medan Merdeka

Department of Commerce and Trade

Medan Merdeka Selatan

Hyatt Aryaduta Hotel

Art and Cultural Center

Jl. M.H. Thamrin

Jalan Sutan Sjahrir

Hotel Indonesia

Mandarin Hotel

Jalan Raya Jendral Gatot Subroto

Jl. Raya Jendral Sudirman

Parliament

JAKARTA

Senayan Sports Stadium

Hilton Hotel

And Jakarta is just as fertile a ground for ideas: it's the national center for art, education entertainment and society, as well as the country's political heart. Testifying to its vitality is the decision of ASEAN (the Association of Southeast Asian Nations) to establish its headquarters here.

ASEAN's choice was in its way a tribute to the fact that Jakarta is by far Southeast Asia's oldest capital city. About 1500 years ago, a Hindu king named Purnawarman made his capital here. The Portuguese arrived in 1522 and were thrown out five years later by a local Muslim potentate named Fatahillah, who gave the city the first form, Jayakarta, of its present name. But it wasn't until the Dutch seized the port in 1619 (and named the city Batavia) that Jakarta began to grow to international fame.

The Dutch ruled for more than 300 years, until they were thrown out by the mercurial dictator Sukarno after World War II. Traces of their legacy persist, as do the distinctly unlovely monuments of the Sukarno era. But those days ended in 1966, when now-president Suharto took control, ended quarrels with neighbouring nations and began a careful building program.

Jakarta still has a long way to go. If the city planners have their way, the Indonesian capital could become one of Southeast Asia's more distinguished capitals by the time the century turns. But however well controlled that growth may be, odds are that Jakarta's happy pandemonium will never be much muted.

▶ Spotlight

It's not for nothing that the Spice Islands are Indonesian. There's a spice to life here that even foreigners quickly taste: it's in the food, of course, but in the way or ways of life as well. Perhaps it's because Jakarta is the lodestone for Indonesians of so many different cultures, religions and lifestyles. Whatever the reason, the life of the senses thrives here: in films, literature, design and—perhaps most spectacularly—in music.

The sounds of Jakarta are manifold: all through the day, the street vendors who rove residential sections signal their passing with a wonderful variety of whistles, rattles and bongs, each with its own special meaning. The listening housekeeper knows immediately whether it's Ali the spice-seller or Achmed the rice-seller who's passing by. And from the hundreds of transistor radios comes the ancient lilting melodies of *gamelan* orchestras, the xylophonic sounds of the *angklun* and the inevitable punk rock. Consider also the avant-garde music of Guntur Sukarno, son of the late president, or the haunting tunes of national favorite Ebiet G. Ade. On Indonesian television, new music stars blossom every night. They may never appear again, but there are times that everyone in Jakarta seems to be either rehearsing, performing or remembering their night in the spotlight.

One current rage is *dangdut*, especially as interpreted by Jakarta's own version of Elvis Presley, Roma Irama. *Dangdut* is heavily amplified rock with Mideast undertones, an odd fusion of fundamental Islamic verse and raw, hip-grinding rhythms that local Moslem authorities seem to approve but which government at times heartily dislikes. Irama's performances in Jakarta regularly attract crowds of

50,000 and up. He starts his shows with the Arabic greeting Salaam Aleikum, shouts his songs and trots out vivacious dancing girls, intones passages from the Koran and in general works his audience into frenzies.

In total contrast are the sounds that emanate from the Bird Market (Pasar Burung) behind a shopping plaza on Jalan Pramunka. Here men young and old coax and cajole their feathered pets into performing their arias. It is another testament to the creative urge here that some trainers dye and paint their birds to enhance nature's already spectacular colors. Others attach wooden whistles to the tails of their pigeons. Why? Sit back at dusk on some mellow Javanese evening and listen as the birds swoop overhead, their bamboo whistles trilling wonderful crescendoes.

● **Arriving**

Jakarta's new international airport at Cenkareng opened in mid-1985 and its teething pains did not last long. Immigration and customs barriers have been lowered substantially in recent years, and entry into Indonesia these days is much simpler than it used to be. Visitors from nearly 30 nations can expect to receive a two-month stay permit with little difficulty, and customs checks are usually minimal.

Business travelers, by the way, can use the tourist pass for low-profile visits, but those planning high-level negotiations might consider obtaining a five-week business visa before arriving.

> Note: Jakarta collects an airport departure tax. Check your hotel for amounts.
>
> Cengkareng is about 25 kilometers from central Jakarta, and public transport should be avoided. Take your hotel's limousine or minibus: cost is minimal and will be added to your bill. Second choice is a taxi. The blue or yellow cabs are the better bets, but make sure the driver turns his meter on. Some cabs are in nearly new condition; some look as if they lost a demolition derby. Be prepared.

● **Orientation**

Jakarta is the capital of the Republic of Indonesia, an enormous string of 13,600 large and small islands stretching 5120 kilometers from east to west. It is the fifth most populous nation in the world. Jakarta is located at the western end of the island of Java, the smallest but most heavily populated of the republic's five major islands. About 85% of the population are Moslems: other faiths include Hinduism, Buddhism and Christianity.

● **Transportation**

Taxis are cheap and plentiful, but as noted above they can be dauntingly decrepit at times. If you find a serviceable cab and an agreeable driver, consider hiring him by the day. You might also want to rent a chauffeured car for a day or week: most business travelers set this up through their hotel, or with the aid of business contacts. Costs depend on the size (and condition!) of the car and run from about US$5 to US$9 an hour. Do *not* attempt to drive yourself in Jakarta until your Indonesian is adequate and your nerves steely. (Recommended: Bluebird Taxis, tel. 325607).

For trips out of town, a car with driver can be pleasant, but remember that the road networks are still not much more than basic.

> Note: In no other Asian country can a smile do so much for you. Arrogance is guaranteed to get you nowhere at all. Let your cabbie keep the small change; give your driver Rup. 1000 or Rup. 2000 for a snack and smokes if the workday runs long.

● Money

The basic unit is the *rupiah*, which in recent years has settled down to about 1100 per US dollar. Bills are printed in denominations of 100, 500, 1000, 5000 and 10,000; coins 5, 10, 25, 50, and 100. Best change rates are at the city's moneychanging offices. One good one is P.T. Sinar Iriawan, Jalan Iriawan 3, Menteng (near the city's center), tel. 351115.

When changing money, be sure to get plenty of Rup. 1000 notes: cabbies, for instance, are given to claiming they cannot change Rup. 10,000 or Rup. 5000 notes.

● Tipping

Generosity pays in Indonesia. While most hotels and upmarket restaurants add 10% service charges, a bit more on top will be welcomed. Slipping Rup. 5000 to a headwaiter at a fancy nightspot may be useful but not always necessary.

● Communications

Major hotels have business centers and nearly all have IDD (international direct dialling) as well. It's often easier to call London or New York than to reach an office five blocks away. Though local service has improved significantly in the past decade, it's still not perfect, and numbers have a way of changing almost without notice. If you have difficulties, ask the hotel operators for help. Telexes and cables are most easily sent through your hotel. To avoid the high hotel

surcharges on international calls, use the government office in the Jakarta Theater Building, Jalan Thamrin (across the street from the Green Pub.) The postal system works adequately in Jakarta but slows radically away from the capital. Courier services are preferable.

● What to wear

Jakarta is tropical; cottons are the rule. For business meetings, a tie and short-sleeved shirt are routine. Just as acceptable are the so-called 'safari' suits, which are practical throughout Southeast Asia. Evening invitations may specify 'batik', which means that long-sleeved batik shirts may be worn by male guests. Light cotton dresses are fine for women.

> Note: Shorts, sandals and singlets are acceptable for beach resorts but are best avoided in Jakarta.

● Languages

In Jakarta, just about everyone speaks Bahasa Indonesia, the standard form of local Malay. English is spoken by many in the capital, while educated people over 40 also may speak Dutch. Carry a phrase book: some of that spoken English is pretty poor.

Hotel bookshops stock a fair selection of books and newspapers in English. Don't be surprised by inky splotches in foreign newspapers and magazines: the government routinely censors stories it considers politically sensitive photos it considers lewd and just about anything printed in Chinese characters, no matter how innocuous.

● Doing business

*Doing business here can be frustrating. Schedules are at best elastic and at worst non-existent, and direct answers are scarce (Indonesians share the Asian inability to say 'no', even though they mean it). And yes, you may encounter what Westerners call 'corruption', though to Asians this is simply the way things get done.

*Thus a newly arrived businessman or businesswoman should seek out all the advice available. The Australian and US embassies have good commercial libraries. The American Chamber of Commerce (tel. 354993) has members representing many countries and can be very helpful.

*The Indonesian government's principal office dealing with foreign investors is BKPM, the Investment Coordinating Board. (Jalan Gatot Subroto 6, tel. 512008 and 512769, telex 4561 BKPM IA, about 5 minutes by cab from the Hilton). This office publishes a 'Guide for Investors' that can be obtained by writing them at Box 3186 in Jakarta or by contacting their offices in Paris, Frankfurt or New York.

*Entertaining one's business contacts is very much the thing to do: business luncheons and suppers are frequent. Western businesswomen, however, will find it difficult if not impossible to pay for dinners with Indonesian males. Fending off advances is easily enough done with a smile: it's not necessary to employ judo or tae kwan do.

*Business hours vary. Some offices start work at 07:00; banks often open as early as 08:00. Government offices shut down by 14:00 on weekdays and 11:00 on Saturdays. Businesses stay open no later than 16:00 or 17:00. On Fridays, the Islamic holy day, many offices close by 11:00. Almost all major religious holidays (Moslem, Buddhist, Hindu and Christian) are celebrated.

*Jakarta runs on what locals ruefully call *jam karet* or 'rubber time'. Traffic is sticky and so is the weather. Your contacts may be late for appointments quite often—so be prepared. Carry a book or magazine to read while waiting. Or study *bahasa*.

Government offices
Agricultural Department, tel. 591135.

Communication Department, tel. 366705.
Finance Department, tel. 365079.
Industry Department, tel. 515509.
Information Department, tel. 377408.
Trade and Cooperatives Department, tel. 341403.

Business phones
KADIN (Indonesian Chamber of Commerce and Industry), tel. 367096.
Pertamina (Indonesian State Oil Enterprise), tel. 347246.
Central Bureau of Statistics, tel. 372808.

Tourist Promotion Board, tel. 364093

*Cosmetics, shaving creams and even deodorants are scarce and expensive. Bring a supply along.

*Though office space is abundant these days, rents remain high and two-to-three-year leases (with all rent payable in advance) are usual.

*Business cards printed in English are sufficient. It's not necessary to include a *bahasa* translation.

*Don't drink tap water. The local bottled water, Aqua, is safe.

■ Useful phone numbers

● Embassies:

Afghanistan, 333169.
Algeria, 349310.
Argentina, 338088.
Australia, 323109.
Austria, 345811.
Bangladesh, 324850.
Belgium, 348719.
Bolivia, 425139.
Brazil, 368380.
Brunei, 510576.
Bulgaria, 346725.
Burma, 340440.
Canada, 584031.
Chile, 587611.
Colombia, 370108.
Czechoslovakia, 346480.

Denmark, 346615.
Finland, 334126.
France, 332807.
Germany (East), 349547.
Germany (West), 323908.
Great Britain, 330904.
Hungary, 587521.
India, 518150.
Iran, 330623.
Iraq, 355016.
Italy, 348339.
Japan, 324308.
Korea (North), 346457.
Korea (South), 512309.
Malaysia, 332170.
Mexico, 348974.
Netherlands, 511515.
New Zealand, 357924.
Nigeria, 345484.
Norway, 354556.
Pakistan, 350676.
Papua New Guinea, 583568.
Philippines, 343745.
Poland, 320509.
Romania, 349524.
Saudi Arabia, 346342.
Singapore, 348761.
Spain, 325996.
Sri Lanka, 321018.
Sweden, 333061.
Syria, 344272.
Switzerland, 347921.
Thailand, 343762.
Turkey, 516250.
USSR, 327007.
USA, 360360.
Vatican, 341142.
Venezuela, 583051.

Vietnam, 347325.
Yugoslavia, 333673.

● **Airlines:**

Air India, 323707.
British, 333207.
Cathay Pacific, 326807.
China Airlines, 354448.
Garuda, 370108.
Japan, 322207.
KLM, 320708.
Lufthansa, 710247.
Malaysian, 320909.
Pakistan, 332351.
Philippines, 370108.
Qantas, 327707.
Royal Brunei, 377409.
Sabena, 372039.
SAS, 584110.
Singapore, 584011.
Swissair, 373608.
Thai, 320607.
UTA, 323507.

● **Emergencies:**

Medical: The Medical Scheme, Setiabudi Building, Jalan H. Rasuna Said, Kuningan, 515481, 515367, 515597.

Dental: Metropolitan Medical Center, Wisata Office Tower, (west of Hotel Indonesia), 320408.

Hospital: Rumah Sakit Pertamina, Jalan Kyai Maja 29, Kebayoran, 707214, 707211.

Pharmacy: Apotik Melawai, Jalan Melawai Raya 191, Kebayoran Baru, 716019. (Open 08:00 to 21:00.)

Shopping

Jakarta's shops and department stores have lots to offer, but do not bother with anything imported unless you've just run out of toothpaste or razor blades. Instead, concentrate on wares made locally, particularly the splendid dyed fabric known as *batik*. The process is long and intricate, the fabrics vary from many grades of cotton on up to silk, and the colors are richly superb.

Batik is available in the traditional lengths and patterns, and in contemporary styles as well. One of Indonesia's best known designers, Iwan Tirta, has two shops in Jakarta; one at the Hotel Borobudur and another in Menteng, at Jalan Panarukan 25, which sells fabrics by the yard and in readymade shirts, dresses and blouses. Other good spots for batik include the Sarinah Department Store at Jalan Thamrin 11; Batik Danar Hadi at Jalan Raden Saleh 1A and Toko Batik, G.K.B.I., Jalan Jendral Sudirman 28.

Other traditional crafts include woodcarving, painting, silver, leather, jewelry and basketweaving. For a good look at them all, spend an evening at Pasar Seni, Taman Impian Ancol Complex, where you can watch the craftsmen at work. The Sarinah Department Store also has a good selection of handicrafts.

One can spend happy afternoons browsing in the antique shops of Jalan Surabaya, but be wary: fakes abound. A general rule is that genuine articles will be expensive. Reliable antique dealers include Lee Cheong, Jalan Majapahit 32; Johan's Art and Curio, Jalan H.A. Salim 59A; and Djody Art and Curio, Jalan Kebon Sirih Tamar Dalam 22.

Bargaining is essential, except at the modern shopping centers and department stores. Paying the first price quoted in the stalls along Jalan Surabaya, for instance, means that you're paying about twice what the object is worth. Cut any asking price by 80% and bargain from there.

Hotels

Jakarta's best hotels are regularly full, or nearly so. Never arrive without a confirmed reservation unless you have resident friends with extra bedrooms.

Borobodur Intercontinental, Jalan Lapangan, Banteng Selatan, tel. 370108, telex BDO JKT 44156. Renovations in 1985 brought this aging, oddly designed hotel back to top levels. Set in a huge park (with tennis and squash, a fine pool and a jogging trail leading through its 23 acres of tropical gardens), it's close to key government offices and Pertamina headquarters.

Hilton, Jalan Jendral Gatot Subroto, Senayan, tel. 583051, telex 46673. Probably Jakarta's best, set in 32 acres of gardens with a dozen tennis courts, two pools, seven restaurants and its own big shopping area. Beautiful lobby patterned on the Sultan's palace in Yogyakarta. Splendid new Garden Wing (1985) topped with an elaborate penthouse featuring its own pool and admirable antiques.

Located south of the city's center.

Hyatt Aryaduta, Jalan Prapatan 44–46, tel. 376008, telex 46220 JKT. A centrally located veteran. Three restaurants, pool. Regency Club floor, business center.

Indonesia, Jalan Thamrin 58, tel. 320008. Jakarta's first international-class hotel, now 20 years old. Pool, tennis courts, three restaurants.

Mandarin, Jalan Thamrin, tel. 321307, telex 61755 MANDA JKT. Elegant, quiet, centrally located, fine service. Pleasant bar, good restaurants, small pool.

Sari Pacific, Jalan Thamrin 6, tel. 323707. Somewhat less expensive but well-run, with good restaurants, one of Jakarta's top discos (Pitstop) and a most amiable staff.

Restaurants

Jakarta's hotels offer a fine array of good restaurants, but the prices are on the high side. Most business clients, you'll find, will enjoy a steak at the grill of your hotel perhaps even more than dining out at one of the capital's few good 'outside' restaurants.

Indonesian food, however, should very definitely be sampled—whether in a good hotel restaurant or out in the city.

Perhaps the best way to get the broadest sample is to order (with several friends, please) the *rijstaffel* (Dutch for rice table), which consists of a dozen or more dishes of individual delicacies—chicken, beef, vegetables, eggs, all cooked with a rainbow of spices—served with rice. Top it off, if there's room, with some of the superb local fruits (rambutan, a cousin of the lychee, is one favorite) and perhaps a glass of chendol (a creamy drink containing a variety of sweet jelly) or kachang, chopped ice on a base of crushed red beans and covered with sweet syrups.

> Note: avoid roadside stands, no matter how good the odors. Your Indonesian friends will guide you to safe spots.

Oasis, Jalan Raden Saleh 47, tel. 326397. Elegant, lively, set in an old Dutch mansion decorated with an interesting collection of Indonesian art objects, good continental and Indonesian food. Superb *rijstaffel*. About 21:00 each evening, Batak singers put on a show that's worth seeing. Reservations required. Expensive.

D'Jit Pochana Thai restaurant, Complex Kehutanan, Jalan Gatot Subroto, tel. 581784. Bizzarely located in the Ministry of Forestry, excellent Thai food typical of this Bangkok-based chain, private Thai-style dining room available. Reservations recommended. Expensive.

Satay House Senayan, Jalan Kebon Sirih 31A, tel. 326238 and at least three other branches around town. Jakarta's best liked chain features *satay* (meat grilled kebab-style over charcoal) of chicken, beef and lamb (no pork, in deference to Islamic standards) and tasty fried squid. Moderate prices.

Salera Bagindo, Jalan Melawai 8, Kebayoran Baru, tel. 733571. and several other branches. A new chain that serves excellent rice and local specialties, simple, clean, air-conditioned locations. Fine for a quick meal, inexpensive.

Taman Sari Grill, Hilton, Jalan Jendral Gatot Subroto, Senayan, tel. 583051. One of the top hotel restaurants, continental cuisine, large wine list, fine service. Expensive.

Pizza Ria, Hilton, Jalan Jendral Gatot Subroto, Senayan, tel. 583051. Outdoor, next to lake in Hilton's huge park, good pizza and pasta and cappucino, strolling singers. Moderate prices.

Spice Garden, Mandarin Hotel, tel. 321307. Probably the best Chinese food in town. Specializes in Sichuan food, including abalone soup with fresh asparagus and camphor-smoked duck. Very expensive.

Summer Palace, Jalan Menteng Raya 29, Tedja Buana Building, 7th Floor, tel. 332989. Cantonese and Sichuan food. Beijing duck and sharkskin soup readily available. Expensive.

Tokyo Garden, Lippo Life Building, Jalan Rasuna Said Kaveling B10-11, tel. 517828. Very tasty and very expensive food. Extraordinary homegrown dishes as well as the usual *shabu-shabu* and *sushi*. Superb decor, *tatami* rooms.

Nippon Kan, Indonesian Bazaar, Hilton grounds, atmospheric tea-house style restaurant on a quiet pond, with gardens and a waterfall. Three private dining rooms, specializes in *shabu-shabu*. Expensive.

George's Curry House, Jalan Teluk Betung 32 (in the lane between the Indonesia Hotel and the Kartika Plaza), tel. 325625. Indian, Sri Lankan and Sumatran curries in this easygoing annex to the George and Dragon Pub. Specialties include Tandoori Murk, charcoal-roasted chicken marinated in a blend of herbs and spices. Moderate.

▶ After hours

Jakarta's nightlife scene is one of Southeast Asia's best-kept secrets, but word has leaked out somehow. There's something for every taste, from the grotty to the flashy, from massage parlors to poetry readings. But beyond the major hotels (which offer good bars and some very fair but pricy discos), it's best to sally out with a local friend as guide.

At some of the local clubs, young ladies known as *kupu kupu* (butterflies) will dance and drink with you free of charge. Lots of other things are negotiable, but health standards leave something to be desired. The same problem afflicts the Bangkok-style massage parlors (mostly in Glodok or Chinatown).

By all means visit Taman Impian Jaya Ancol (Dreamland Park), a $20 million entertainment complex which is one of Asia's largest. There are many hostess clubs here, along with seafood restaurants, bowling alleys, drive-in movies, an interesting art and entertainment area called Pasar Seni (Art Market) and an area called Dunia Fantasie in which supermod robots portray scenes from Indonesian legends. The center of attraction is the Giant Wheel, 33 meters high, which offers terrific views of Jakarta from up top.

Further up-market, intellectually at least, is Taman Ismail Marzuki (TIM) where local artists and writers gather for plays, poetry readings, ballets and concerts. And films.

Note: Watch out for *bancis*, the local transvestites, who parade along Jalan Latuharhary in the posh Menteng district. At least a few bewildered foreign businessmen have found out 'the girls' aren't what they seem.

The Jaya Pub, upstairs in a small building behind the Jaya Building on Jalan Thamrin, tel. 327508. Indonesia's best jazz, best vocalists. Fair food. Popular with foreign residents. Inexpensive.

The Green Pub, Jakarta Theater Building, Jakarta Thamrin 9, tel. 359332. Jazz and Country & Western alternate here; fair Tex-Mex food; moderate prices.

The Oriental Club, Hilton, Jalan Jendral Gatot Subroto, tel. 583051. Top-of-the-line disco, wealthy local designers and entertainers. Expensive.

Blue Ocean Restaurant and Nite (cq) Club, Jalan Hayam Wuruk 5, tel. 361134. A classic Chinese hostess club, room for 2,000, live shows at 21:30 and 23:00 every night featuring magicians, singers, dancers and even acrobats. Cantonese and Hakka menu, hundreds of hostesses from which to choose. Can be expensive.

Ebony, Kuningan Plaza, Kav. 11–14, Jalan Rasuna Said, tel. 513700. A plush members-only club, but foreigners can buy entree for Rup. 10,000, which includes the first drink.

Stardust, Jayakarta Hotel Tower

Arcade, Jalan Hayan Wuruk 126, tel. 624408. A former movie theater transformed into what must be one of Asia's larger discos. A huge dance floor, giant videos constantly displayed on the screen, laser beams and even a tame flying saucer.

Tanamur, Jalan Tanah Abang Timor 14, tel. 353947. One of the more amusing of lower-brow discos, usually warms up after midnight, sweet and non-pushy *kupu kupu*. Moderately priced.

● **Cinemas**

There are several movie houses but tickets are expensive (up to US$5 a ticket) and US and European films are often crudely censored.

Ratu Plaza Theaters, Ratu Plaza Shopping Center, Jalan Jendral Sudirman.

Gajah Mada Theaters, Gajah Mada Plaza.

Sights and sounds

If you can find the right Indonesian friend, ask for a tour of one of Jakarta's *kampongs*, the self-contained villages which make up the city. Stroll the narrow lanes, don't be too quick to reject an invitation to have a glass of tea, keep your eyes open. For the most part, the locals will enjoy your visit as much as you do.

Museum Nasional, Jalan Merdeka Barat 12, tel. 360976. The exhibits tend to be a bit dusty, but this museum offers a large collection of Indonesian cultural artifacts ranging from prehistoric days up to the present. Good collection of Chinese ceramics. Guided tour in English on occasion.

Jakarta City Museum, Jalan Fatahillah 1, tel. 679101. Housed in an old Dutch building, this museum has a good collection of paintings, furniture and exhibits on the city's growth. Undergoing renovation: phone before visiting.

Fine Arts Museum (Balai Seni Rupa), Jalan Taman Fatahillah 2, tel. 676090. Indonesian paintings and sculpture, plus a superb collection of porcelains donated by the late Vice President Adam Malik.

Wayang (Puppet) Museum, Jalan Pintu Besar Utara 27, tel. 679560. Originally a Protestant church, this museum contains a large collection of finely carved wooden puppets and shadow puppets, many of which are valuable antiques. Occasional performances. Call before visiting.

Monuman Pancasila Sakti, Lubang Buaya, Pondok Gede. Located just south of the city, this impressive monument commemorates the deaths of six army generals in the abortive communist coup of 1965—a watershed in modern Indonesian history.

Gereja Sion, (Portuguese Church), Jalan Pangeran Jayakarta 1, the city's oldest church, begun in 1639. Still in use. Fine 17th Century baroque pulpit and canopy.

Sunda Kelapa, Pasar Iran, northwest Jakarta. Interesting view of Dutch colonial history and contemporary squalor. Drive through the port area for a close look at the splendid *pinisi* schooners still used by Buginese seamen to ferry timber and spices around the islands. Pasar Ikan (Fish Market) is most colorful in early morning: technicolor stench. **Museum Bahari** (open 09:00 to 14:00, tel. 660518) has exhibits of maritime history.

Taman Anggrek Indonesia Permai, Slipi. A flower park with hundreds of varieties of orchids. Some for sale. Open 08:00–18:00.

Taman Mini Indonesia, Pondok Gede,

Kramat Jedi, tel. 849524. A showcase of the diverse peoples and places of the Indonesian archipelago. Full-size and scale models of houses and temples from all parts of the country, huge domed aviary, cultural performances and craft demonstrations.

Weekends

Bali is one of the all-time great weekend destinations, with one *caveat*: your weekend may stretch to a week or two. It's just that pleasant. In 1597, after all, two Dutch sailors named Emmanuel Roodenburg and Jacob Claaszoon set the pattern for many later European arrivals by abandoning their Dutch expedition and staying for the rest of their lives.

Today's Bali has changed from the isle of simple beauty that lured Roodenburg and Claaszoon, and some old hands say that the coming of the jumbo jets in the early Seventies turned it into a tourist zoo. In part (a very small part), the claim is accurate: there are beach areas that are swamped by drunken tourists, and the Kuta area in general is best enjoyed by the hedonist young.

But 90% of Bali is as lovely and unspoiled as ever. There are superb landscapes that spill in a cascade of padi fields from the heights of cloud-shrouded volcanic Gunung Agung. There are festivals and ritual dances and haunting gamelan music at at least one and often at many of the island's 20,000 temples every day. Bali is Hindu, not Moslem, and there is a joyously pantheistic spirit that lingers everywhere on the island.

● Basics

Arriving: Unless you're flying in from Australia, you will clear immigration and customs in Jakarta. Ngurah Rai International Airport, on the southern tip of the island, is small and reasonably well organized. If you haven't arranged a hotel bus to meet you, bargain a bit with one of the many cabbies at the airport exit.

Orientation: Bali's capital is Den Pasar, but most visitors stay either at the southern beach resorts of Sanur or Kuta, or north in the hills at Ubud. There's also a new hotel complex at Nusa Dua. The beach hotels can be reached by cab for US$5 to US$8, Ubud for about US$15 to US$20.

Transportation: If you like your airport cabbie, bargain with him for a day rate to tour the island's many lovely sites. Hotel desk clerks can be helpful in arranging a car and driver.

Communications: Phones work reasonably well, and the post office does its best to get those postcards on their way. A few hotels have telexes (there's one in Ubud's new post office)—but remember that Bali is not exactly a hive of business activity. Den Pasar central post office is useful for telexes and international calls.

What to wear: Bring along shorts, a bathing suit or two, some t-shirts and polo shirts, and perhaps a sweater or jacket for the mountains. Try the batik sarongs; they're unisex. The dress code—if there is one—is very relaxed indeed.

● Shopping

There are a lot of lovely things for sale in Bali, and lots of junk as well. Bali has been a volcano of art for centuries—batik (not as good here as the Javanese variety), woodcarving, painting, silverwork and jewelry. Avoid most shops in the beach areas; instead, drive north from Den Pasar to Batubulan, Mas, and Peliatan to Ubud. Along the road, you'll see studio after studio. Park and browse. Prices tend to be high: bargain mercilessly. Don't buy in a hurry. Look carefully for flaws. There are lovely things to be bought in Bali, but be sure you're getting good value.

● Hotels

Tanjung Sari, Sanur Beach, tel. 8441. Comfortable bungalows, pleasant small pool, good food and lovely landscaping.

Bali Hyatt, Sanur Beach, tel. 8271, telex 35127. Big, nicely laid out gardens, large pool, tennis courts, fine restaurant (the Spice Islander). Well managed.

> Note: Sanur Beach offers a great view of Gunung Agung but is not as pleasant for swimming as Kuta, down the isthmus.

Bali Oberoi, Seminyak (west of Kuta), tel. 5581. Bungalows with lovely gardens, good pool, very quiet.

Three Brothers, Legian Beach (near Kuta), no phone. All sorts of bungalows (at low prices), 15-minute walk to beach.

Poppie's Cottage, Kuta Beach, no phone: run by the restaurant of the same name, air-conditioned, moderate prices.

Nusa Dua Beach Hotel, Nusa Dua, tel. 71210. The first of a group of huge new hotels being built in the Nusa Dua area, a pleasant tropical park on the island's southern extremity. Big pool with swim-in bar, lots of handicraft shops, large rooms with sea views, group tours.

Bali Handara Country Club, in the mountains near Bedugul, tel. 6419. Mainly for golfers, the club is considered world-class. Beautiful vistas when the clouds roll away, cool, quiet and expensive.

Han Snel Cottages, Ubud. Pleasant cottages in the garden of a Dutch painter's compound. Fine food (see below) pleasant bar and great tranquility.

● Restaurants and nightlife

Balinese food is much like that of Java—*nasi goreng*, various subtle and not-at-all subtle curries, and good seafood. The exception is the superb *babi guling* (roast pig) which is awfully good but may be a tad too rich for Westerners. Most restaurants here double as night spots.

Made's Warung, Jalan Pantai Kuta, Kuta beach: home-made pate, grilled tiger prawns, and lobster are among the favorites at this restaurant favored by many in Bali's expatriate colony. Run by a Balinese and her Dutch husband.

Poppie's, in the lane behind Made's in Kuta: frozen banana daiquiris, good tuna, another expat favorite.

Chez Gado-Gado, on the beach near Seminyak: a Franco-Balinese effort, set on the beach under a big Balinese Bale Banjar pavilion. Saturday night disco.

Blue Ocean, on the beach just behond Legian. Good seafood, regular discos and parties. Inexpensive.

Murni's Warung, Ubud. Murni is Balinese but makes the best Upper Elk Valley all-American hamburger you ever tasted. Great cookies and apple pie—and the *satay* is delicious too. So is the *Nasi Campur*—fried rice with all sorts of oddments added.

Cafe Lotus, Ubud. Like Murni's, a popular spot for local artists and writers. Good pasta, fine breakfasts and Balinese smoked salmon.

The Griya, Ubud. Bali's best barbecued chicken.

Han Snel, Ubud. Excellent food, nice bar, set in a lovely Balinese garden. The owner, a Dutch painter and long-time resident, has a gallery of his own works.

● Sights and sounds

Bali, quite simply, is beautiful: it is difficult to find a vista that is offensive to the eye. For full impact, ask your hotel where the nearest festival is going on (there seems to be at least one a day, and they're all good fun). Or attend a village dance—they're just as frequent. There are 'kulchur' nights at the big hotels, but there's more spontaneity in the villages.

Bali Museum, Puputan Square, Den Pasar. A valuable collection of early Balinese artifacts, housed in traditional style buildings.

Museum Puri Lukisan, Ubud. Attractive collection of local painting, some of which is for sale. Traditional and modern styles.

Besakih Temple, Gunung Agung. This is the 'mother temple' of the island. Its three main edifices—dedicated to the Hindu trinity of Shiva, Brahma and Vishnu—contain 18 sanctuaries. It's worth noting that Besakih has survived numerous eruptions of tempermental Gunung Agung, including the one that killed thousands of villagers in 1963.

Goa Gajah, Bedulu. The Elephant Cave, as it's called in English, may date back beyond the 11th Century. The entrance (and highlight) is a splendidly carved witches mouth which is surrounded by carvings of monsters, demons and animals. Inside, at the end of the cave's left branch, is a statue of Ganesh, the elephant god.

Goa Lawah, outside Klungklung. This is the bat cave. It stinks, and the walls of the cave are covered by hundreds of most repellent bats. A curiosity.

Kintamani, Mt. Batur. A scenic ride up the terraces to a superb view of Batur (still active) and its lovely crater lake. Beware of the souvenir sellers.

Klungklung, 40 kilometers from Den Pasar. The Kerta Gosa (Hall of Justice), built in the 18th Century, has ceilings covered with spectacular murals depicting the laws of the land—and the horrid punishments that await those who break them. This was the site of the last *puputan*, or mass suicide, of the Balinese protesting the Dutch conquest.

Sangeh, 22 kilometers north of Den Pasar. A nutmeg forest and small temple (Pura Bukit Sari), infested by hundreds of extremely nasty monkeys who rifle pockets, purses and camera bags in search of peanuts but are willing to steal anything else they find. Charmless.

Tampak Siring, 36 kilometers northeast of Den Pasar. The sacred spring of the Balinese, overlooked by a presidential palace built by the late President Sukarno.

Tanah Lot, 15 kilometers northwest of Den Pasar. A small but handsome temple atop a rocky seaside islet. Reachable on foot at low tide. Caves at its base contain sea snakes, which are best avoided. At sunset, a beautiful view...but overtouristed.

Kuala Lumpur

Up From Slumber

Much of Kuala Lumpur's drive springs from the synergy of three major ethnic groups working and competing in a city that only two decades ago was one of Southeast Asia's sleepiest. Chinese still predominate in business, but Malays—encouraged by government policies that give them preference in some areas—have taken to wheeling and dealing in a most untraditional manner. And the Indians, brought to the peninsula a century ago to work on plantations, are not far behind.

In KL's many new housing estates, the ethnic differences are blurred. But in older parts of this wildly scattered city, contrasts are clearer. Just three blocks from the Hilton, for example, the mosques and night market of the Malay Kampong Baru district offer a vivid contrast to the Chinese shops and houses in Jalan Chow Kit a block away. The Indian core of KL is on Jalan Brickfields, where there are Hindu temples, curry restaurants and even academies for teaching Bharatanatyam classical dance. And all around the city, smaller pieces of the Malaysian mosaic appear: Thais, Punjabis, Indonesians, Gujeratis and various Arab nationalities all have their specific areas.

Religious variety, accordingly, is striking. The Chinese immigrants brought with them Buddhism and Taoism, while the Tamils of South India (who comprise 80% of Malaysia's Indian population) have set up many temples to Subramaniam. And there are of course a wide variety of Christian churches, as well as Thai and Sri Lankan Buddhist edifices and occasional flag-sporting Sikh temples as well. And all these are overshadowed by the scale of the state-supported religion, Islam, reflected in the multitude of mosques all over town.

The ethnic diversity has other consequences, perhaps most notably in eating opportunities. KL's inhabitants love their food, and they observe few cultural boundaries when it comes to their palates. In recent decades, the *satay* (broiled meat and fish kebabs) and *mee hon* (noodle) stands have been supplemented by a broad array of Japanese, Thai, Indian, Indonesian, Korean and Mideast restaurants. Chinese food ranges from Cantonese to Szechuanese, Hainan, Fukienese and Beijing styles. And Western food is growing in popularity too: fast foods predominate, but Italian restaurants are starting to show up in very unlikely places, and there are several good French bistros.

Despite diversity, however, the basic culture is Malay. Less apparent in KL, the Malay influence becomes much more obvious in the countryside. And most

KUALA LUMPUR

Ampang Shopping Complex ●
Ming Court Hotel ●
Coq D'or Restaurant ●

Jalan Sultan Ismail

Selangor Race Course ●

Jalan Ampang

Jalan Tun Perak

Hilton Hotel ●

Jalan Raja

Jalan Bukit Bintang

Jalan Sultan

Jalan Cheng Lock

●Chinatown

Jalan Pudu

Regent Hotel ●

J. Sul Mohamed

● Mandarin Hotel

Railway Station ●

Jalan Kinabalu

Stadium Negara ●

Jalan Stadium

Jalan Hang Tuah

● Masjid Negara (National Mosque)
● National Museum

● Merdeka Stadium

● Istana Negara

Malays, Westernized though they may seem at first acquaintance, observe Islam's basic religious prohibitions. Discrimination against women lingers, though in the past 15 years much progress has been made. In the mid-Eighties, for example, there were four women cabinet members, and women hold a growing percentage of senior jobs in the rapidly expanding corporate and government sectors.

Spotlight

Just 125 years ago, a shabby band of Chinese miners pushed their flat-bottomed boats up the syrupy Klang River from the mangrove swamps where the Klang melts into the Straits of Malacca. Thirty miles upstream, the miners found the Gombak tributary, and along its jungled banks staked out tin mine claims at what soon became known as Kuala Lumpur—'muddy estuary.'

Nowadays, KL has grown into the capital of a Malaysian federation that spans the South China Sea, politically linking peninsular Malaya to the East Malaysian states of Sabah and Sarawak. The rivers are just as muddy, however, and traffic (on water or land) doesn't move much more quickly than those boats that inched upstream so long ago.

Equally unchanged is the basic premise that led to KL's founding so long ago: a fast profit. Though a century of growth has softened the rigors of life here, the drive for profit still rules the city. KL's rough pioneer origins still show through its affluence. This is no haven for the arts: few cities of its wealth and size (about 1 million residents) have no professional theater, no dance troupe, no orchestra. Art galleries are few and offerings uninspired. Even indigenous crafts, such as batik cloth or wood-carvings, are often poor in quality and hard to find.

The city has grown remarkably since the sleepy Fifties and Sixties, but an upgrading of roadways and main boulevards finished only a few years back has been overtaken by a motormania afflicting every aspirant to the still-forming middle class. As a result, traffic jams are awe-inspiring and motoring manners perhaps Asia's worst.

But despite the traffic, KL deserves its reputation as one of Southeast Asia's most livable cities. Some newcomers sneer at it as the 'Dallas of Southeast Asia'; others acknowledge it as a leafy green relief from the noise and dirt of Bangkok and Jakarta. Though the high-ceilinged bungalows that attracted Somerset Maugham have gone, there are still pleasant contemporary villas surrounded by orchids and hibiscus, all round the city.

For the foreigner, KL's ethnic mix (Malays, Chinese and Indians) can be confusing at first. Relax. The locals are used to outsiders, and ceremony and protocol are not as important here as in some other Asian cities. But don't order *pork* when dining with Malays, avoid *beef* with Hindus, keep your voice down and your liquor intake low. If you're thinking of opening an office here, pay close attention to the Malays you'll meet: Malaysian law generally requires new companies to have at least one Malay partner (not Chinese, or Indian, but *Malay*) and your choice of a 'bumiputra' (son of the soil, as Malays are known) can be important.

All this because KL is driven: the city thinks of growth rather than management, of money to be gained rather than redistributed, of jam today and never jam tomorrow. Car, television and home ownership here outpace most other Asian cities. It should come as no surprise to find there's an absence of civility in many business dealings. There's no lack of push in Kuala Lumpur—those hard-working miners a century ago laid down a pattern that still persists.

● Arriving

Subang International Airport went through a thorough renovation in the mid-Eighties and is among Asia's better organized. It's best to take a taxi from the airport to your hotel. Depending on location, fares will average about US$10. Some travelers prefer the white air-conditioned limos. If you're one, pay in advance at the well-marked counter at the airport exit. If you arrive by train at KL's splendid old central station, taxis will take you on to your hotel. (Sadly, the old Station Hotel has been closed.)

● Orientation

Kuala Lumpur is the capital of the Federation of Malaysia, which became independent from Britain on August 31, 1957. The nation includes the old Malay peninsula states and sultanates, as well as the British Borneo colonies of Sabah and Sarawak, which joined the federation in 1963. The population of Malaysia is about 15 million; broken down racially as follows: Malay 50%, Chinese 36%, Indian 10% and smaller units 4%.

● Transportation

Traffic is thick and public transportation scanty: take taxis. And because these can be elusive, particularly during rush hours and at around 15:00, when shifts change, consider hiring a car with driver if you have several calls to make during the day. Cabbies aren't exactly gracious, but most speak enough English to get you around efficiently. Self-drive cars are available but are best avoided for in-city travel: these are more useful for trips out of town. Roads are generally good.

● Money

The basic unit of currency is the *ringgit*, or Malaysian dollar (M$), which is divided into 100 cents. There are bills of $1, $5, $10, $50. $100 and $1000. Coins of 1, 5, 10, 20, 50 and $1 are circulated. The *ringgit* is worth slightly less than the Singapore or Brunei dollar.

● Tipping

Tipping is generally unnecessary: a 10% charge is added to most bills.

● Communications

KL is not one of Asia's most efficient communications centers, though the government is making a serious effort to bring its systems up to international standards. A few hotels now have direct-dial facilities. The postal system is adequate.

● What to wear

KL is hot throughout the year, and humidity is regularly over 80%. Wear cottons. Shirt-and-tie is the usual business uniform, but wear a jacket when meeting a contact for the first time. Remember that air-conditioning is usual in most offices, hotels and homes.

● Languages

Malay is the national language, but English is widely spoken, even outside major cities, Several dialects of Chinese are used, including Fukienese, Chiuchow and Cantonese. Most Indians speak Tamil.

● Doing business

Business hours run from 09:00 to 17:00, though banks and shops open at

10:00. Saturday hours—less frequently worked now—are from 09:00 to about 11:30. On Friday, the Islamic day of prayer, government offices close at noon, but shops remain open.

*Top-rated hotels have business centers with telex facilities, temporary secretarial and translation help, and photocopiers.

*Business cards are essential, but English is sufficient. Avoid Malay or Chinese translations—which might be counterproductive.

*Business luncheons, dinners and full evenings are usual. The host pays: don't offer.

Useful phone numbers

● Airlines:

Aeroflot, 423231.
Air India, 420166.
Bangladesh Biman, 483765.
British Airways, 426177.
Cathay Pacific, 433755.
China, 427344.
Czechoslovak, 280176.
Japan, 225102.
KLM, 427011.
Korean, 428311.
Lufthansa, 425555.
Malaysian, 206633.
Pakistan International, 425444.
Philippine, 429040.
SAS, 426044.
Sabena, 425244.
Singapore, 923122.
Thai, 937133.
UTA, 226952.

● Embassies and High Commissions:

Australia, 423122.
Austria, 484277 (Trade Commission, 424727).
Bangladesh, 423252.
Belgium, 485733.
Bolivia, 425146.
Burma, 423863.

Canada, 89722.
China, 428495.
Czechoslovakia, 427185.
Denmark, 225357.
Egypt, 468184.
Finland, 413011.
France, 484122 (Trade Commisssion, 429444).
Germany (East), 462894.
Germany (West), 429666.
India, 221766.
Indonesia, 421022.
Iraq, 480555.
Italy, 465122 (Trade Office, 486115).
Japan, 221533 (Trade Organization, 427872).
Korea (South), 482177 (Trade Center, 429930).
Korea (North), 420650.
Libya, 464656.
Netherlands, 431143.
New Zealand, 486422.
Pakistan, 483822.
Philippines, 484233.
Poland (Commerce Office), 460940.
Romania (Trade Office), 482065.
Saudi Arabia, 479433.
Singapore, 486377.
Sri Lanka, 423094.
Sweden, 485981.
Switzerland, 480622.
Thailand, 488222 (Commerce Office, 424601).
Turkey, 429832.
United Kingdom, 941533.
USA, 469011.
USSR, 467252.
Vietnam, 484036.
Yugoslavia, 464561 (Trade Commission, 945141).

● Chambers of commerce:

Associated Chinese Chambers of Commerce and Industry, 280278.
Associated Indian Chambers of Commerce, 920255.
Federation of Malaysian Manufacturers, 484011.
Malay Chamber of Commerce and Industry, 433090.

Malaysian International Chamber of Commerce and Industry, 942177.

National Chamber of Commerce and Industry.

● Government offices:

Agricultural Ministry, 982011.

Energy, Telecommunications and Posts Ministry, 946677.

Finance Ministry, 946066.

Housing and Local Government Ministry, 947615.

Information Ministry, 445333.

Labor and Manpower Ministry, 424088.

Land and Regional Development Ministry, 921566.

Malaysian Industrial Development Authority, 943633.

Primary Industries Ministry, 986133.

Public Enterprises Ministry, 985022.

Science, Technology and Environment Ministry, 420044.

Trade and Industry Ministry, 940033.

Transport Ministry, 948122.

Works and Utilities Ministry, 919011.

Sabah Chamber of Commerce, 088/54913 (Kota Kinabalu).

Chinese Chamber of Commerce, 088/52312 (Kota Kinabalu).

Sarawak United Chamber of Commerce of Sarawak (Kuching).

▶ Shopping

Don't expect to find much treasure in KL. Prices and selection are far better in Singapore, Bangkok or Hong Kong. That said, there are a few spots worth a browse.

You should look for Malaccan-style furniture, often engraved or inlaid with shells. Traditional brasswork is occasionally interesting. Selangor pewter is well made and handsome.

Karyaneka Handicraft Center, Jalan Raja Chulan 186–88, tel. 431686. This government-backed center promotes Malaysian handicrafts in a beautifully designed traditional building. Handicrafts from all the nation's 14 states.

Batek Malaysia Bhd., Wisma Batek, Jalan Tun Perak, tel. 923233. A good selection of locally made batik in a variety of fabrics, as well as woven textiles, brass, silver and even kites.

Jadi Batek Center, 59 Jalan Ismail, tel. 424575. More batik, mostly from Kelantan, in many different fabrics. Dresses, skirts and men's shirts as well.

Pasar Malam, Kampong Bahru, a night market which offers a wide variety of food and interesting antiques, some of which may be genuine. A great place to stroll for an hour or two—and don't forget to bargain.

Selangor Pewter, 231 Jalan Tunku

Abdul Rahman, tel. 986244. A wide range of Malaysian-made pewter objects, all top quality.

Rupa Art Gallery, 15 Jalan 8/7, Petaling Jaya. One of the few interesting art galleries in the capital area, run by artist Victor Chin.

UAL Art Gallery, Lobby, Kompleks Antarabangsa, Jalan Sultan Ismail, (next to Hilton Hotel.) Good watercolors of Kuala Lumpur and Malaysian scenes.

▶ Hotels

Equatorial, Jalan Sultan Ismail, tel. 242–2022. A favorite meeting place for leading government and business officials, with very good Chinese and Japanese restaurants. Rooms pleasant enough.

Federal, 35 Jalan Bukit Bintang, tel. 248–9166, telex MA 30429 FEDTEL.

Renovation is bringing it back into shape. Located in an interesting and lively area of KL.

Hilton Kuala Lumpur, Jalan Sultan Ismail, tel. 242–2122, telex 30495 HILTELS MA. Fine hilltop location and a favorite conference venue, a good grillroom (expensive) and an Italian restaurant beside the pool.

Hilton Petaling Jaya, 2 Jalan Sultan, Petaling Jaya, tel. 553533, telex 36008. Close to Sebang Airport, it's sited in a business-industrial area which makes it a natural for the quick business visit to the capital area.

Holiday Inn, Jalan Pinang, tel. 481066. Reliable quality, located near the race track.

Hyatt Saujana, Open May 1987, tel. 248–3377. telex MA 30290 PREMBA. Close to Subang airport, fitness center and pool, executive club floors, private chalets, near golf courses.

Malaya, 162 Jalan Cecil, tel. 227722, renovating, located in the lively, old central area.

Merlin, Jalan Sultan Ismail, tel. 480033. Under renovation after a decline from its days at the top.

Ming Court, Jalan Ampang, tel. 439066. One of KL's best. Good French and Japanese restaurants, pleasant pool and comfortable rooms. A bit far from city center but close to key embassies.

Regent, Jalan Sultan Ismail, tel. 425588, telex MA 30486. Another top-ranked hotel, with a good European restaurant (Suasa). Nice pool and gym.

Shangri-La, 11 Jalan Sultan Ismail, tel. 232–2388, telex SHNGKL MA 30021. New and swanky, this opened-in-1985 hotel is part of an office and apartment complex. Chinese, Japanese and French restaurants, health club and pool, tennis and squash.

Restaurants

KL offers a reasonably broad choice of good restaurants. Malay food is spicy, built on rice, and delicious. Specialties include *satay* (meat or fish grilled kebab-style over charcoal); rice cooked in coconut milk; *gado gado*, a salad of vegetables and eggs covered in hot peanut sauce, and all sorts of seafood. Indonesian cuisine resembles Malay style cooking so closely that only experts can distinguish the dishes.

Sidewalk stalls offer a great way to sample the specialties of the area, but restaurants are a bit more hygienic.

● Malayan and Indonesian

Kampung Restoran, 10 Jalan Perak, tel. 437113. Outdoors style under *atap* roofs, daily lunch buffet, seafood specialties, modest prices.

Yazmin, Ampang Shopping Center, Jalan Ampang, tel. 487490. Buffet style, wide choices, cultural shows (Malay dances) at both lunch and dinner.

Kwali Indonesian Restaurant, Plaza Yow Chuan, Jalan Pekeliling, tel. 420580. Inexpensive, named for the Malay version

of the Chinese wok. Two branches in Petaling Jaya, one other in KL.

● Chinese

Country Kitchen, 21 Jalan Barat, Petaling Jaya (accross from the P.J. Hilton), tel. 566312. Specializes in Hakka food, a variety rarely encountered and which is less spicy than other styles. Good steamed carp.

● Indian

Akbar, Jalan Medan Tuanku, tel.
920366. Good fish-head curry, crab
masala, reasonable prices and large
portions.

Bangles, 600 Jalan Tun Abdul Rahman,
tel. 983780. The unassuming decor and
address conceals one of the best Indian
restaurants in Southeast Asia. Full range
of *kuftas, biryanis* and just about
everything else.

Jothy's, 21B and C, Jalan Barat,
Petaling Jaya, (opposite P.J. Hilton), tel.
575819. Huge variety of north and south
Indian food, reasonably priced.

● Korean

Koryo-won, Kempleks Antarabangsa,
Jalan Sultan Ismail, tel. 427655. Nice
decor, barbecue specialties.

● Japanese

Daikoku, Wisma Antarabangsa, a local
favorite.

● Western

Copper Grill, Menara Promet, Jalan
Sultan Ismail, tel. 438057. Has something
of a reputation locally for its lobster
thermidor.

Coliseum, near railway station. A
favorite from colonial days, this
unprepossessing restaurant offers a good
steak and fried rice and more than an
echo of KL's rugged past.

Coq d'Or, 121 Jalan Ampang, tel.
429732. Located in the mansion of a
departed millionaire whose will specified
his heirs could not sell the house, the Coq
d'Or is a landmark. The surroundings are
elegant, but the quality slips a bit now
and then.

Rive Gauche, 34 Jalan Ampang, tel.
201609. Some say this is KL's best
European restaurant. Not cheap.

Suasa, Regent Hotel, tel. 422–022.
Very popular, very expensive and
excellent service. Reservations advised.

Troika, Kompleks Kewangan, Jalan
Raja Chulan, tel. 416735. Good Russian
dishes and a favorite of the diplomatic and
business community. Prices steepish.

◀▶ After hours

Late-evening fun is available in KL, but the scene is a lot less lively than
Bangkok's. And some of it is private, such as the disco at the new Raintree Club,
or the basement bar at the Selangor Club. Women should note that the bars of the
better hotels make sure that female guests won't be annoyed by would-be romeos.
Boring comings-on to foreigners—either female or male--are extremely rare in
KL.

Bacchus, 7 Jalan Rajah Abdullah, tel.
915898. Good food, an excellent pianist
and a friendly atmosphere.

Peppers, Ampang Park Kompleks,
Jalan Ampang. Guitar music, up-market
Malay crowd.

Pertama Night Club, Pertama
Kompleks, Jalan Tuanku Abdul Rahman,
tel. 982533. The classic Chinese
nightclub, huge and noisy and superbly

run. Worth a visit just to see the
spectacle.

Regine's, Plaza Atrium, tel. 230–6020.
Comfortable, a little less blatant than
other discos in town, and though it's a
membership club, guest cards are
available from most hotels.

Tin Mine, Hilton Hotel, tel. 422122.
Lively and popular disco in—you guessed
it—a tin mine decor.

⬤▬▬▶ Sights and sounds

Batu Caves, 14 kilometers north of the city, on the Ipoh road. A Hindu shrine built into a huge cave that once a year becomes the site of the festival of Thaipusam. The day-long ceremony, a rite of penitence, involves a surprising amount of self-mutilation and is not recommended to the sensitive.

Jalan Bandar Section. There are several interesting sites in this area of old Kuala Lumpur, notably the Chan See Shu Yuen Temple. Built in 1906, this elaborately carved Taoist temple is KL's most ornate. Just down the road is the Shri Mahamariamman Temple, an almost equally elaborate Hindu place of worship. And further along is the Central Market, a quintessential Southeast Asian food market and a fascinating experience.

Lake Gardens. Pleasant green parklands and gardens, with boats for rent and picnic areas. A huge bronze monument commemorates Malaysia's victory over a Communist insurrection (1948–60). Parliament House is nearby, as is a memorial to the late Tun Abdul Razak. (He was the nation's second prime minister and was a leading figure in Malaysian development.)

National Art Gallery (Balai Seni Rupa Negara), in the former Majestic Hotel just opposite the central railway station, Jalan Sultan Hishamuddin. Works by local artists.

National Mosque, near city center. One of Southeast Asia's largest, the architecture is contemporary Islamic. Visitors are allowed, but shoes must be removed; women must cover their heads.

National Museum (Muzium Negara), Jalan Bangsar. Housed in a modern building constructed on traditional Malay lines, the museum offers interesting collections of the native arts of both Malays and the aboriginal Orang Asli peoples of East and West Malaysia. Valuable collection of Straits Chinese (Nonja) artifacts. Worth a detour.

Railway Station, Central district. Built at the turn of the century in an inimitable Moorish rococo style, it is at heart a vintage English train shed. The exterior is unforgettable.

Selangor Turf Club, Jalan Ampang. Its history dates back to 1896, but the current plant is modern. Part of a circuit that offers racing, alternating between Singapore, KL and smaller tracks in other cities. When the horses are running elsewhere, crowds still show up here to bet and watch the races on television. Hearing the fans cheer an empty track is mildly hallucinatory.

◀▬▬▶ Weekends

Getting away from KL for a weekend is reasonably painless. There are flights to the lovely island of Penang and to the unspoiled east coast beaches near Kuantan. Several hill resorts are within reasonable driving distance of KL, as are the Malacca Straits cities of Port Dickson and Malacca.

Genting Highlands: An hour's drive from KL, on good roads, with modern hotels, a casino, boating on an artificial lake and an 18-hole golf course. For bungalows, book in advance through Fraser's Hill Development Corp., tel. 093/382201, or in KL at tel. 480033. Beautiful gardens, superb jungle views.

Cameron Highlands: Perhaps the loveliest of all the highlands resorts. Its gardens produce fine flowers, fruits, vegetables and tea. There's an 18-hole golf course, and tennis and badminton courts, and swimming in a natural jungle pool. Fine selection of small, cozy hotels and bungalows. Bring sweaters: nights are cool.

Penang: Less than an hour by plane north from KL, Penang island has fair beaches, fine shopping areas and a mixture of classic old hotels and modern beach resorts. Fast becoming one of Southeast Asia's favorite resorts.

Port Dickson: About 90 minutes away, this is KL's most popular beach resort despite the fact that its beaches are sometimes not as clean as they might be. Several good resort hotels here, with their own pools and tennis courts.

Malacca: A fine old relic of the colonial past, Malacca offers a selection of well-preserved old buildings and churches dating back 200 or so years. A few good hotels.

● Eastern Malaysia

Further off, but worth a journey if time permits, are the East Malaysian states of **Sabah** and **Sarawak**. A few suggestions: Sabah Sepilok Forest Reserve, near Sandakan. A carefully preserved 4,000-hectare tract of rich tropical rain forest, full of Bornean wild life. Its single greatest attraction is the Orangutan Rehabilitation Center, where young orangutans illegally captured or orphaned in the jungle are trained to resume life in the wild. The young orangutans are enormously attractive, the center's staff impressively devoted to their tasks, and the sole bad feature are the leeches which infest the jungle. Be warned. Sandakan can be reached easily by air from Kota Kinabalu. The Sabah Hotel, in Sandakan, is highly recommended (tel. 213822).

Tanjung Aru, beach resort just outside Kota Kinabalu, tel. 58711. Comfortably balconied rooms, a huge pool and a respectable selection of restaurants. Easy access to the lovely islands of the offshore national park, and a full range of sports.

Kinabalu National Park: About two hours by good roads from Kota Kinabalu. The park, which includes the highest mountain in Southeast Asia in 4,101-meter (13,455-foot) Mt. Kinabalu, is a beautiful nature preserve. There is a well-organized program for visitors, and a comfortable group of hotels intended mostly for those who come to climb the mountain. That climb, a tough one and a half-day hike, draws thousands every year. Good Hyatt hotel in Kota Kinabalu.

● Sarawak

The central government is putting a great deal of money into building up Sarawak's tourist attractions, but so far the capital of Kuching is about the only magnet for visitors. Take a look at the palace of the 'White Rajah' Brooke family, who ruled Sarawak for more than a century. Trips to Iban Longhouses can be arranged by travel agents. The Sarawak Museum is worth an hour's visit.

Manila

Up From Adversity?

Years ago, Manila was a great city; years from now, it may be one again. But for the moment, shabbiness permeates this faded beauty by the bay. The sunsets are as stunning as ever, the Manilans are friendly, the humor as quick. But the long economic slump has cost the city dearly. One hopes the new Aquino government will find the money, for instance, to repair the burnt-out high-rises along bay-front Roxas Boulevard—these tend to depress first-time arrivals. In the Fifties and early Sixties, Manila was top of the Asian League, but those times are long past.

Ah, the boosters say, look at Makati. And at first glance, this business heart of Manila glistens in comparison to the aging downtown area. There are swanky hotels and smart restaurants and drop-dead boutiques out here. But look again: potholed streets and cracked sidewalks and not-quite-finished buildings.

That said, the city is far from moribund. Filipino business people are as active as ever and so is much of the business world. The women are perhaps even lovelier: at top levels, this is an extremely cosmopolitan society and Manila's beauties are testimony to it. There are extraordinarily fine hotels and restaurants, and halting efforts are being made to restore those parts of old Manila, devastated by World War II, that made this city one of the beauties of the world.

It's worth remembering, in fact, that this is one of Asia's older capitals. Some historians trace its beginnings back to the Fifth Century, when the first traders settled here. As the centuries passed, merchants visited 'Maynilad' from as far away as Arabia, bartering for the gold and pearls of the islands. In 1571, the Spanish conquistador Miguel Lopez de Legaspi arrived to crush the Muslim sultanate and replace it with a Spanish colonial administration. The Spanish rule lasted until 1898, (with a brief English interlude, 1763–1764) when the United States captured Manila in the Spanish-American war. In 1946, Manila became the capital of the newly independent Republic of the Philippines.

During the Spanish centuries, Manila's growth was slow. Not until the 19th Century did the colonial rulers allow trade to blossom, and it was not until independence in 1946 that a boom began. When it came, it came with a rush that slowed finally only in the early Seventies. Hurt by soaring oil prices and crumbling demand for key raw materials such as sugar and coconuts, the economy went into a swoon that still continues.

MANILA

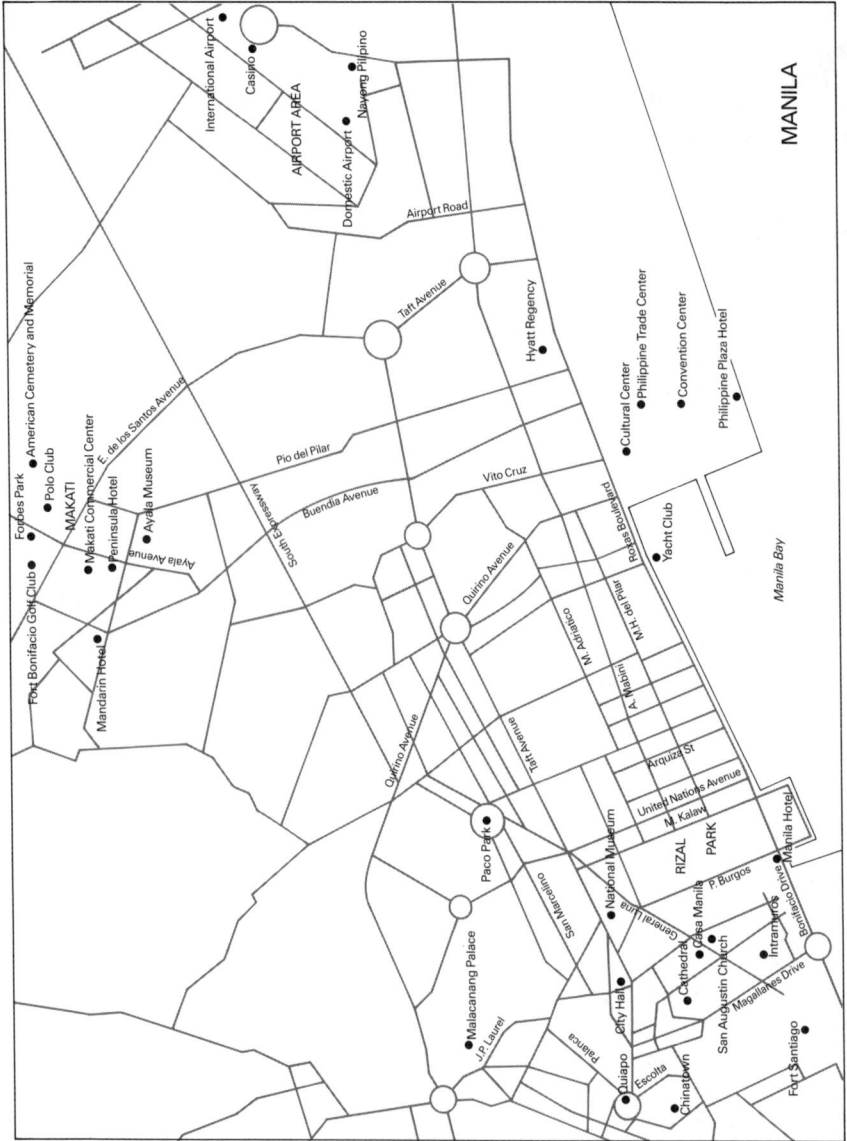

But the charm of Manila continues to work its spell. For Americans, the version of English spoken here is evocative—the slang of the Thirties and Forties is alive and well here. For business travelers from the United States and Europe as well, personal contacts are all-important. The pace of business is slower here than in Hong Kong, say, or Osaka, and a deal is as likely to be firmed up over the coffee table as over the conference board. Life is patterned on the politenesses of a time perhaps past in Europe or the States: one rises when a lady enters the room, one lights her cigarette. Never offer to split a check: let your host pay—or pay it all yourself. There is graciousness to life here that is all Manila's own, and it will almost certainly outlast current uncertainties.

▶ Spotlight

What do the following have in common?:
*A Manila debutante cotillion of the Twenties.
*A Shanghai dive of the Thirties.
*A Tokyo hostess restaurant of the Forties.
*A Danang NCO club in the Sixties.
*A Singapore dinner dance in the Seventies.
*A Bangkok nightclub of the Eighties.
The answer's easy: a Filipino band.

For reasons endlessly debated, Filipinos have provided the musical talent for Asia's evening entertainments for a long time, and there is no sign their vogue is ending. One of the few tenable explanations is that somehow the arrival of the Americans—and American jazz and popular music—found something very *simpatico* in the Filipino soul.

But the Filipinos long ago went far beyond simply playing US tunes. That they still do, and do superbly. But from the hundreds of Filipino bands scattered from Los Angeles to Abu Dhabi one hears pop, rock, salsa, punk, reggae from every musical nation in the world. And it's just as possible to hear some peculiarly Filipino twists to this myriad of songs—not only translations into Tagalog or Taglish, but musical adaptations as well. You haven't lived until you've heard the Sound of Music sung by a Filipino star. (It's almost as much fun as The Yellow Rose of Texas in Cantonese).

In Manila, there'll be good Filipino music in the lounges of just about all the major hotels, most playing top-of-the-charts material that might as well be the real thing. And the absurdly active night-life scene is very musical indeed. Try to catch Jaqui Magno, perhaps Manila's best jazz singer. If she's not around, drop in at the Hyatt Regency's Calesa Bar, a starting point for many young singers.

There's folksinging as well, notably the Hobbit in Malate which is staffed by dwarves and stars a 3-foot-5 clone of Elvis Presley named Egoy the Playboy. His version of Blue Christmas will wring your heart. The Hobbit is also home to Freddie Aguilar, the nation's major protest singer. One needn't speak Tagalog to be moved by his version of Bayan Ko (My Country).

101

Music is so pervasive here, and so popular, that more often than not a Manila party will turn into a singalong. In years past at the Malacanang, a presidential birthday party often produced singing tributes from cabinet ministers, then a band of generals and the palace staff too.

Nor are journalists immune. Former First Lady Imelda Marcos used to finish off an evening interview with foreign journalists by kicking off her shoes and launching into a romantic ballad—and then coaxing her listeners to sound off too.

● **Arriving**

Manila International Airport, built only a few years ago as a showcase, either has aged dismayingly quickly or has not yet shaken down. For whatever reason, both incoming and outgoing processing can be infuriatingly slow, and the mobs of wellwishers only add to the sense of brainless disorganization. But corrupt? Not for the ordinary traveler—though smalltime smugglers are pounced upon by inspectors.

Once past the barriers, push the luggage cart to the exit and seek your hotel's representative. He'll take over the chores, pop you into a car or minibus, see that the charge (about US$10) goes on your hotel bill and accept a tip (US$1 or US$2) cheerfully. Fallback: find a Golden Taxicab (the sole cabs authorized at the airport), which charges under US$5 for the trip into town. Avoid the helpful lad with the unmarked sedan: he'll certainly overcharge and perhaps mug you as well.

● **Orientation**

Manila (technically, Metro Manila) is the capital of the Republic of the Philippines, a nation of 53 million scattered over more than 7,000 islands. Manila is the heart of the urban conglomeration of Metro Manila, which has a population of 8.3 million in 17 contiguous municipalities (four cities and 17 towns). The official capital, Quezon City, is part of Metro Manila.

For the business traveler, a choice must be made between staying in Makati, the city's financial heart, or in Manila proper, closer to many government offices and the bay—and considerably livelier. There are fine hotels in both areas. Because daytime traffic jams are frequent, it's best to avoid traveling from one area to the other during business hours.

● **Transportation**

Manila's taxis are among Asia's least expensive, the drivers friendly and reasonably honest, and at least 25% of cabs are in fair shape. (Be wary). Your hotel doorman will get a good cab from the queue outside and tell you what the fare ought to be. On the street look for golden cabs (black and gold) or R & E cabs (yellow, with a green stripe on the hood).

To avoid enervating cab-flagging, consider hiring a cab by the hour: charges are about US$4 to US$5 an hour, for a minimum of US$2. Bargain. Or get a chauffeured sedan for still more: Avis (tel. 741–0907), Hertz (tel. 818–0257) and National (tel. 852–820) can tell you how much. Self-drives are not advised unless you're used to Asian traffic habits.

Do not take public buses.

Take those baroque Jeepneys only with a local friend as guide.

Try the newish Light Rail Transit system for the experience, but it's not terribly useful for the foreign visitor.

● **Money**

The ailing Philippine *peso* trades at about 20 to the US dollar. There are notes of 2, 5, 10, 50 and 100 *pesos*, and coins of 5, 2 and 1 *pesos* and 50, 25, 10, 5 and 1 *centavos*. The best place to change money is the government regulated grey market along Mabini Street in Ermita (between Padre Faura and Pedro Gil streets). Banks offer a better rate than hotels. Do *not* change money on the streets with local sharpies—they have awfully fast hands.

● Tipping

Most good restaurants add a 10% service charge to their bills, and another 5% is appreciated. In the hotel, small services should be rewarded with 5 or 10 or even 20 *pesos*. Give those kids who open up cab doors a *peso* or three. Bribing headwaiters for good tables is usually unnecessary.

● Communications

Manila's phones do not work well. International calls go through reasonably quickly, but direct dialling is rare. Local calls can take a long, long time. Telex communications are reliable: most hotels have efficient business centers which handle telexes. The postal system has its ups and downs but is now on an uptrend. Check with the hotel desk.

● What to wear

For 95% of the year, Manila is either hot (dry season, December–May) or hot and wet (rainy season, June–November), so lightweight cottons are the rule. For men, the *barong tagalog*, a lightweight formal shirt of Filipino design, is acceptable for business wear (short sleeves) or social occasions (long sleeves). Avoid readymade *barongs*: your hotel, or a friend, should be able to steer you to one of the many good—and reasonable—tailors. Women wear lightweight Western styles—and should be aware that Filipinas are perhaps the smartest dressers in Asia.

● Languages

The national language is Pilipinas (Tagalog), a Malay language with elements of Spanish and English mixed in. English is the standard language of business, and is spoken fluently by many in Manila and the provinces as well. Spanish, once prevalent, is fading.

● Doing business

After Houston or Frankfurt, the pace of business here is apt to seem slow. There is an absence of pressure: things don't happen here; instead they eventuate. Expect long conversations over coffee—but don't be surprised by the occasional hard charger. Socializing is the rule. With luck, you'll meet wives and families and uncles and cousins too. Filipinos have a tradition of gracious hospitality that permeates restaurants and hotels as well as private homes. But don't abuse that hospitality. Tempers can be short and retaliation sharp.

*Business hours: 09:00 to 17:00, with lunch between 12:00 and 14:00; and plenty of morning coffeehousing.

*Business centers exist in the top hotels. The best are in the Manila hotel (open 24 hours), Mandarin and Peninsula.

*Telex facilities are at major hotels and the following: Eastern Telecoms. 815–8921; Philcom, 891–861, and Globe Mackay/ITT, 521–8052.

*Anserfone, tel. 867–946, offers efficient telephone answering service.

*Travel: let the hotel concierge handle any problems. Airline offices feature long, long lines.

*Business cards: English is sufficient.

*Many embassies have useful commercial sections and business libraries as well. They are good sources for advice and facts.

*A useful annual publication is 'Doing Business in the Philippines', published by Sycip, Gorres, Velayo and Co. P.O. Box 589, Manila 2800 and P.O. Box 256, Makati 3117, tel. 893–011.

*The government-sponsored Foreign Investments Assistance Center, at 385 Senator Gil. J. Puyat Avenue, Makati, is described as a 'one-stop shop' for foreign investors. Tel. 818–1831.

▶ Useful phone numbers

● Chambers of commerce:

American Chamber of Commerce, Corinthian Plaza, Makati, 818–7911.

Australian Chamber of Commerce, Vernida Building, Makati, 884–563.

European Chamber of Commerce, Jardine Davies Building, Makati, 854–747.

Japanese Chamber of Commerce, Architectural Center Building, Makati, 883–233.

Philippine Chamber of Commerce, Chamber of Commerce Building, tel. 404–572.

● Government offices:

Board of Investments, 818–1831.
Bureau of Domestic Trade, 818–5701.
Foreign Affairs Ministry, 502–081.
Foreign Investments Assistance Center, 818–1831.
Securities and Exchange Commission, 780-931.
Tourism Industry, 599-031.

● Airlines:

Aeroflot, 867–756.
Air Canada, 868–551.
Air France, 509–111.
Air India, 815–2441.
Air Nauru, 595–395.
Air Niugini, 871–071.
Alitalia, 582–091.
American, 593–504.
British, 817–0361.
British Caledonian, 505–402.
Brunei, 817–1631.
CAAC (China), 608–111.
Canadian Pacific, 898–531.
Cathay Pacific, 598–061.
China (Taipei), 590–086.
Delta, 868–051.
Eastern, 506–444.
Egypt Air, 815–8476.
Garuda, 862–458.
Gulf, 816–4121.

Iberia, 817–9269.
Japan, 590–946.
KLM, 815–4790.
Korean, 815–8911.
Kuwait, 599–181.
Lufthansa, 815–9271.
Malaysian, 575–761.
Northwest, 582–776.
Olympic, 583–355.
Pakistan, 818–3711.
Pan American, 818–5421.
Philippine, 818–0111.
Qantas, 815–9491.
Sabena, 508–636.
SAS, 815–8421.
Singapore, 818–9951.
Swissair, 507–641.
Thai, 815–8421.
United, 868–051.
Western, 815–4944.

● Embassies:

Argentina, 875–655.
Australia, 874–961.
Austria, 817–9191.
Belgium, 876–571.
Bangladesh, 892–810.
Brazil, 817–9654.
Bulgaria, 817–7054.
Burma, 817–2373.
Canada, 815–9536.
Chile, 866–371.
China (PRC), 572–555.
Columbia, 817–7579.
Cuba, 817–1192.
Czechoslovakia, 700–582.
Denmark, 856–756.
Ecuador, 898–511.
Egypt, 880–396.
Finland, 898–934.
France, 876–561.
Gabon, 887–109.
Germany (East), 891–046.
Germany (West), 864–906.
India, 872–445.
Indonesia, 855–061.
Iran, 871–561.
Israel, 885–329.
Italy, 874–531.
Japan, 818–9011.

Korea (South), 817–5705.
Libya, 817–3461.
Malaysia, 817–4581.
Malta, 878–280.
Mexico, 815–2566.
Netherlands, 887–753.
New Zealand, 818–0910.
Nigeria, 817–3836.
Norway, 881–111.
Pakistan, 817–2760.
Papua New Guinea, 880–386.
Peru, 818–7209.
Poland, 861–863.
Romania, 817–6767.
Saudi Arabia, 817–3371.
Singapore, 816–1764.
Spain, 818–3581.
Sri Lanka, 857–372.
Sweden, 858–746.
Switzerland, 865–591.

Thailand, 815–4219.
United Kingdom, 891–051.
USA, 521–7116.
USSR, 817–9690.
Vatican, 593–515.
Vietnam, 500–364.
Yugoslavia, 816–4678.

● **Emergencies:**

Police (Manila), 599011.
Police (Makati), 886–920.
Fire (Manila), 581–176.
Fire (Makati), 880–058.
Manila Medical Center, 591–661.
Makati Medical Center, 853–311.
Manila Doctor's Hospital, 503–011.
Pharmacies (24-Hour Service) Botica
Metro, 880–464. (Makati)
University Drug, 593–857 (Manila).

Shopping

The best buys are Filipino handicrafts: woven cloth, shellcraft, woodcarvings, basket and mats of all kinds, even cigars. Forget antiques (lots of fakes) unless you're extremely knowledgeable and extremely rich—but keep an eye open for curios.

Western goods are everywhere. There are shopping centers all over Manila, offering the same sort of goods available in Munich or Manchester or Minneapolis, but prices are high and selection idiosyncratic. Besides, that sort of thing can be found back home.

Instead, prowl the markets, such as Quiapo, where Manilans hunt for bargains—a colorful and lively center in old Manila. Or try Cartimar, in Pasay City, which has some intriguing curio shops. Wherever you go, remember to bargain.

Look for cloth made of *jusi* (banana silk), *pina* (pineapple fibers), *ramie* or China grass (like linen). Mats made of *banig* (pandan leaves) can be interesting, and so can baskets woven of *nito* vine, bamboo strips, rattan, wicker, coconut leaves.

Probably the most typical handicraft product is the line of items made from capiz and other shells: lampshades, coasters, trays among many other items. Wood items can be lovely, though most are tasteless.

A few hunting grounds:

Pistang Pilipino: At the corner of Mabini and Pedro Gil Streets in Ermita. A sprawling flea market with dozens of stalls peddling hundreds of items, from basketware to beads to tee-shirts. Flexible prices.

Rustan's, Makati Commercial Center, Ayala Avenue, Makati, tel. 816–1786.

The capital's best department store, with a good selection of handicrafts and some very jazzy mod clothes as well. Prices on the high side; most credit cards accepted.

Susana Crafts, Makati Commercial Center, Ayala Avenue, Makati, tel. 879–161. A fine selection of handicraft products at moderate prices.

T'Boli Arts and Crafts, 1362 Mabini, Ermita, tel. 586–802. Unusual craft items from the outer islands, particularly from the big southern island of Mindanao.

Beautiful bags, arcane jewellery. Proceeds go to a church mission.

> Note: There are several antique shops along Mabini Street, in Ermita. In among the obvious fakes, a few pleasant curios can be spotted. There are a couple of very pricey shops on Calle Real, in Intramuros, in the Casa Manila complex.

Hotels

Manila hoteliers overbuilt in anticipation of a tourism boom that never quite happened. As a result: prices are flexible and discounts are readily available. The hotel fire scare, caused by the Regent of Manila fire disaster in late 1984, caused all leading hotels to improve their security regulations.

Century Park Sheraton, corner of Vito Cruz and M. Adriatico avenues, Malate, tel. 506–041, telex 40489 SHERMLA PN. Twenty-story high-rise, atrium lobby, pool and gym; near Harrison Plaza shopping center.

Hilton, United Nations Avenue, Ermita, tel. 573–711, telex 63387. One of the first Hiltons in Asia and past its prime. Pool and sauna, nice views.

Holiday Inn, 3001 Roxas Boulevard, Pasay City, Metro Manila, tel. 831–2621, telex 63344. Well located on Manila Bay, near convention center. Pool.

Hyatt Regency, 2702 Roxas Boulevard, tel. 831–2611, telex 63344 ETPHYA PN. On the bay and close to the airport, with the city's most popular hotel nightlife. The Calesa Bar offers fine jazz; the Louis Y Disco is popular with jetsetters. Good staff, good food.

Intercontinental, Makati Commercial Center, Ayala Avenue, Makati, tel. 894011, telex RCA 23314, ITT 45005, Eastern 64597. Well-located in center of businesslike Makati, efficiently run, recently renovated. Its Sunday Jazz Brunch is a hit. Pool. Check them for

advice on their provincial resorts.

Mandarin, Makati Avenue, corner of Paseo de Roxas, Makati, tel. 816–3601, telex 63756 MANDA PN. Quiet, elegant and efficient. Two fine restaurants. Pool and gym. First Manila hotel with International Direct dialling.

Manila Hotel, Rizal Park, tel. 470–011, telex ITT 40537, RCA22479, ETPI 63496. A favorite since 1912 of travelers and Manilans alike, its excellent restaurants, clubby bars and lovely lobby help explain its attraction. Topnotch management and staff, pleasant rooms, gym and pool.

Peninsula, corner of Ayala and Makati Avenues, Makati, tel. 819–3456, telex 22507 PENPH. Its huge lobby is one of Makati's favorite meeting places. Non-smoking floors. Large Presidential suite has its private helipad. Pool and gym.

Philippine Plaza, Cultural Center Complex, Roxas Boulevard, tel. 832–0701, telex 40443. This Westin hotel is the closest thing to a resort hotel that central Manila offers. A huge pool (with a bar at its heart), tennis courts and gym, and a convenient location next to convention center. All rooms with balconies and fine views and a large and lovely imperial suite.

> Note: Almost all hotels—with the exception of the Manila—will allow discreet overnight companions in rooms at a nominal charge.

▶ Restaurants

In a region famed for the diversity of its regional cuisines (Chinese, Japanese, Korean, Malay), Filipino food does not exactly stand out. The ingredients are fine: there's superb seafood, fresh vegetables and adequate meat at most good Manila restaurants. But what comes out of the kitchens does not measure up to the best in neighboring lands.

That said, try *adobo* pork and/or chicken stewed in vinegar and soy sauce and selected spices. Or *pata*: deep-fried spiced pig's knuckles. Or *kare-kare*: oxtail or knuckles, cooked in spicy peanut sauce and served with vegetables in a salty shrimp paste. For foreigners, the single most daunting delicacy is *balut*, duck embryo eaten from the shell and billed as an aphrodisiac, not an emetic.

Don't miss the fresh fruit, particularly the mango: the best in the world are produced here. Other native fruits are delicious too: papayas, bananas, pineapples, guavas, and even the disgusting-but-delicious durian.

● Western and Filipino

Bistro Burgos, 5007 Padre Burgos Avenue, Makati, tel. 880–411. Pleasant and quiet, European and local dishes. Moderate.

Evelyn's, 7 Concepcion Street, Roxas Boulevard, Pasay City, tel 50–51–30. Excellent local food, fresh grilled lobster and meat. Try the 'Bicol Express', a mixture of spicy meat and vegetables, or *Laing*, a coconut-and-yam-leaf concoction. Inexpensive.

Los Hidalgos, Gen. Luna Street, Intramuros, tel. 40–54–08. Elegant Filipino cuisine, served in an equally elegant colonial setting. Expensive.

Mario's, 7856 Makati Avenue, Makati, tel. 86–44–78. A longtime favorite for continental food. Flaming deserts. Moderately expensive.

Nielson Tower, 7929 Makati Avenue, Makati, tel. 817–8135. Improbably located in the old control tower of Manila's former airport, this fine restaurant is open to the public for supper only (lunch is reserved for its club members). Excellent continental and local dishes, good wines, good service and good taste. Expensive.

Patio de Guernica, 1856 J. Bocobo Street, tel. 521–4415. Located at Remedios Circle in Manila's arty district, it features steak, Spanish and Filipino dishes in an Iberian setting. Moderate.

Roma Ristorante Italiano, Manila Hotel, Rizal Park, tel. 470–011. Probably the best Italian food in town, attentively prepared and served. Good lunch buffet. Reservations recommended. Expensive.

La Taverna, 1682 M. Adriatico, tel. 58–53–72. Attentive service, good Italian food. Moderately expensive.

● Chinese

China Pearl, Makati Avenue, Makati, tel. 87–46–91. Good Cantonese food, moderate.

Shin Shin Garden Restaurant, 2126 A.

Mabini Street, Ermita, tel. 571–942.
Simple, tasty Chinese cooking with
splendid dumplings (jaudze).
Inexpensive.

Szechuan House, Aloha Hotel, 2150
Roxas Boulevard, tel. 59–90–61. Well-
spiced west China food. Moderate.

● **Japanese**

Ohtori-Ya, 808 Pasay Road, Makati,
tel. 89–32–11. Quiet and pleasant.

Standard fare. Moderate.

Furosato, 1712 Roxas Boulevard,
Pasay City, tel. 58–23–58. Grilled met and
fish, *sushi*. Private dining rooms.
Moderate.

● **Korean**

Korean Village, 1783 M. Adriatico,
tel. 50–49–48. Good barbecue, Korean
style, with the regular trimmings
including *kimchi*.

After hours

Manila's nightlife ranks right up there with Bangkok's and more often than not
Filipino friends are delighted to be guides. Cock an eye at the so-called 'tourist
belt' in Ermita, but watch wallets and avoid the many touts. Along M.H. de Pilar
Street, there's a broad selection of 'hostess bars'. Most are in the blocks between
United Nations Avenue and Pedro Gil Street: always ask about prices and don't be
hustled.

Clubs have a way of opening and closing without much notice. The following
selection of nightspots is offered with no particular guarantees: Check with a local
friend for the latest hits.

Cafe Alvarado, Glass Tower Building,
Alvarado Street, Legaspi Village, Makati,
tel. 818–5874. One of Makati's best bars
for jazz and pop music, tucked away in
the tower's basement. Good local
musicians.

Blackout Disco, 475 Padre Faura
Street, Ermita, tel. 594–007. A bit off the
beaten path; gogo dancers, video films in
the afternoons, fair food.

Blue Hawaii, 1427 M.H. del Pilar
Street, Ermita, tel. 595–482. Wild.
Usually jammed with girls and their
admirers, with a little bit of everything.

Calesa Bar, Hyatt Regency Hotel,
Roxas Boulevard, Pasay City, tel. 831–
2611. Good for jazz and quiet
conversations too, with an elite crowd.

Firehouse, M.H. del Pilar Street at the
corner of Santa Monica Street. Big,
brassy, clean and somewhat crazy, this is
the city's best known girlie bar.

Hobbit House, 1801 Mabini Street,

Malate, tel. 521–7604. Staffed entirely by
dwarves, this place has had a lot of
publicity and its fine folk music is as good
as advertised.

Playboy Club, Silahis Hotel, 1990
Roxas Boulevard, Malate, tel. 573–811. A
Playboy Club is a Playboy Club is a
Playboy Club.

Scotts/Anzac, 1407 M.H. del Pilar,
Ermita. A smaller version of the
Firehouse, with hostesses.

Spider's Web, 1337 M.H. del Pilar,
Ermita. A hangout for the foreign
correspondents who flood Manila from
time to time, it has no particular
ambiance but plenty of cheap beer and
hostesses.

Tavern on the Square, LPL Towers
Condominium, 112 Legaspi Street,
Legaspi Village, Makati, tel. 817–8244. A
favorite hangout for rising young
executives, it features top pop stars and
occasional revues and comedy acts.

Vintage, Pasay Road, Makati Avenue, Makati. Golden Oldie music on a fine sound system, friendly and lively crowd.

Weinstube, 1834 M.H. del Pilar Street, Ermita, tel. 500–167. Well away from the hostess spots is this oasis of good piano music and pleasant mood.

◣■■■■▶ Sights and sounds

American Memorial and Cemetery, McKinley Road, Fort Bonifacio, Makati (for information call the US Embassy, tel. 521–7116). Pacific war museum; more than 17,000 plain white crosses mark the graves of Allied war dead.

Ayala Museum, Makati Avenue (across from the Makati Commercial Center, Makati, tel. 899–866. Dioramas of Philippine history, artifacts, and a giant aviary out back.

Casa Manila, Aduana Street at Calle Real, Intramuros, tel. 487–734. A nicely rebuilt example of an elegant old 'Intramuros' home, well worth seeing. Antiques shops and restaurant nearby.

Casino, Imelda Avenue, Paranaque (near the international airport), tel. 831–2194. Showy, well-organized professional gambling in *pesos* or dollars; most popular games (craps, roulette, blackjack, etc.). Bring passports.

Corregidor Island, Manila Bay. Book tours via hotel concierge or direct at Sea Express Services, Hoverferry Terminal, Cultural Center Complex, Roxas Boulevard, tel. 832–3653. This somber island fortress was the scene of the last stand of US and Filipino troops against the Japanese in 1942. Recaptured in 1945. Museum, well-preserved ruins of fortifications and heavy artillery. Well-organized, informative tours.

Cultural Center of the Philippines, Roxas Boulevard, tel. 823–1125. Concerts, ballet, plays and lots more: telephone for information on current shows.

Fort Santiago, Intramuros. The heart of old Spanish Manila. Pleasant park, museum dedicated to National Hero Dr. Jose Rizal, executed by Spanish firing squad in 1896. The fortress has been partially restored.

Jai-Alai, Taft Avenue, Ermita (across from Rizal Park), tel. 574–002. Fast action and plenty of betting in this game imported from the Basque country.

Manila Cathedral, Aduana Street and Calle Real, Intramuros, tel. 481–243. The most recent of six cathedrals built on this spot: fires, typhoons, earthquakes and war destroyed its predecessors. Stained-glass windows by Filipino artists.

Metropolitan Museum, Roxas Boulevard. Regularly changing exhibitions of foreign paintings, prints and engravings.

Museum of Philippine Art, Roxas Boulevard at corner of T.M. Kalaw Street, tel. 587–365. Interesting collection of contemporary works by Filipino artists.

Nayong Pilipino, Pasay City (near international airport), tel. 832–3767. Basically, the Philippines in miniature, designed to give short-time visitors an impression of the enormous ethnic and scenic variety of the islands. On the grounds is the **Museum of Traditional Cultures**.

Paco Park, General Luna Street at the corner of Padre Faura Street, Paco. A national park that was once the old Spanish cemetery.

Rizal Park, between Roxas Boulevard and Taft Avenue. This huge parkland in central Manila is the site of the Rizal Monument, dedicated to the national hero executed here by a Spanish firing squad in 1896. Sentries maintain a 24-hour guard.

San Agustin Church, corner of General Luna Street and Calle Real, Intramuros. Manila's oldest church, spared by war, earthquakes and typhoons since the present building was completed in 1601. Exhibits of religious art.

▶ Weekends

A useful weekend package is offered by Philippine Airlines, under its PALakbayan program which packages three-day, two-night excursions at discounted prices. Book through hotel concierge or direct at 818–0111.

Staying closer to Manila? Take a day trip to verdant Tagaytay, an hour's drive south, to inspect the lovely lake Taal, with its live volcano nestled on an island in the lake. Two hours southeast of Manila is Pagsanjan Falls, in Laguna, where tourists shoot the rapids on rafts.

Also in the Manila area are the following less-well known destinations:

Hidden Valley Springs Resort, Alaminos, Laguna. Reservations via Manila phone 875–459. About 90 minutes from Manila by car, this is a former health spa turned tropical forest hideaway. Springs—some hot, some cold, all natural—bubble away beneath a cool green canopy of tropical vegetation. Great for romantics. Forest cottages, good swimming.

Puerto Azul Beach Hotel and resort, Ternate, Cavite. Reservations via Philippine Village Hotel, tel. 831–7011. About 90 minutes south of Manila by car, or by regular hotel bus from Silahis International Hotel, Roxas Boulevard, at 10:00. Golf (an 18-hole course), sailing (Hobie Cats), tennis, windsurfing and swimming.

Villa Escudero, at boundary of San Pablo City and Ciaong, Laguna. Reservations via Manila phone 521–0830. Pleasant rooms on a family coconut estate about 90 minutes by car from Manila. Swim in a forest river, eat native food and inspect treasures in a family museum.

● Further away

Cebu, the oldest city in the Philippines, is a major business center a little over an hour by air from Manila. (The trip can also be made by steamer in 24 hours.) There are fair hotels in the city, and pleasant beach resorts are not far away. There's also a casino, located in the Cebu Plaza Hotel, that offers all the usual action: roulette, blackjack, baccarat and lots of slot machines.

In a central plaza stands the cross supposedly planted by Magellan in 1521, when the Portuguese explorer first set foot on the island: the cross is protected by a larger casing. Not far away is San Agustin Church, inside which is an image of the Holy Child brought from Mexico three centuries ago. Also in Cebu is a monument to Lapu-Lapu, the chieftain who slew Magellan on nearby Mactan Island.

● Cebu hotels

Cebu Plaza, Nivel, Lahug, Cebu City,

tel. 73181. Restaurants, two pools, tennis.

Magellan International, Gorordo Avenue, Lahug, Cebu City, tel. 74611. Restaurants, 18-hole golf course, pleasant park.

Montebello Villa, Banilad, Cebu, tel. 77681. Small, resort-style hacienda, restaurants, bars, disco and pool.

● **Nearby resorts**

Coral Reef Hotel, Barrio Agus, Lapu-Lapu, Mactan Island. Reservations via Manila phone 815–4820. Quiet hideaway, offering scuba (with instructors), windsurfing, Hobie Cats, snorkeling and fishing. Thirty minutes from downtown Cebu.

Tambuli Beach Resort, Buyong Beach, Mactan Island. Reservations through 503–061 Manila phone. Similar facilities to Coral Reef (above), but catering to a younger crowd and offering slightly lower prices.

● **Other out-island destinations**

Baguio: The summer capital of the Philippines in the days before air-conditioning, and still a refuge when the hot weather strikes. Jammed at Easter. Lovely parks, good hotels, golf and tennis and blessedly cool weather most of the year.

Bohol: This island next to Cebu has white sand beaches, fine old Spanish churches and explorable caves. Several good new resorts.

Palawan: Perhaps the least-developed of the larger islands, fine beaches, interesting marine life and good diving.

● **...and still further away...**

Borocay Island, off the northern coast of Panay Island, has no airstrips, no nightclubs, no fancy hotels and no electricity. To get there, there's a short flight, a bus ride and finally a two-hour voyage in a motorized outrigger.

Once there, visitors stay in beach cottages, bake in the warm sand, eat simple foods bought from friendly locals. Bliss, or so one hears.

Philippines Airlines (tel. 818–0111) will help you get down there. Or call Pacific Airways, a small charter outfit, which flies three days a week to a nearby island. (tel. 832–2731.)

▶ Sports

Temporary memberships can usually be arranged with the following:

*Army and Navy Club, Luneta at Roxas Boulevard, tel. 573–861.

*Club Intramuros Golf Course, South Drive, Intramuros, tel. 588–171.

*Fort Bonifacio Golf Club, McKinley Road (inside Fort Bonifacio), Forbes Park, Makati, tel. 858–323.

*Las Rocas Tennis and Country Club, Limetkai Building, San Juan, tel. 704–461.

*Wack Wack Golf Club, Shaw Boulevard, Mandaluyong, tel. 784–021.

Osaka

The Second City

About the best thing that can be said for Osaka is that it's near Kyoto. Osaka is a fine old Japanese city with a long and important history. But aside from its major business and industrial community, the Osaka of the Eighties doesn't have much to recommend it. It isn't beautiful; and charm is not one of its strengths. A prominent Osaka architect recently described this boxy concrete-covered mass as a 'trash bin'. The city lacks the cozy neighborhoods, cultural riches, pockets of greenery and imaginative architecture that make Tokyo an appealing if unwieldy giant.

Osaka can also be a tough place for the foreigner. Though the city is making an effort to improve in this area, there's still a distinct shortage of bilingual signs. People who can speak English—or any other foreign language, for that matter—are scarce. Unlike Tokyo, which makes an effort to appear cosmopolitan, Osaka for all its cold modernity remains provincial. Attempts to court foreign guests remain clumsy at best.

Yet for all its gracelessness, Osaka is a decent place to do business. Hardware works, from telephones to telexes to computers. People are punctual. And Osaka, even more than Tokyo, is built around the business of doing business. In the 18th Century, after all, Osaka controlled about 70% of the nation's wealth. For years, Osakans were Japan's leading merchants. By Japanese standards, they are extremely direct in their business dealings. In Osaka, the traditional greeting among close friends is still '*mokari makka*' (how's business?).

These days, self-improvement is chic in Osaka. Long branded as the Chicago of Japan, the city is uneasy about its 'second-city' image and has begun a full-scale effort to shed its provincialism. Among the planned improvements are a huge new international airport ('the gateway to Asia') that will open in 1992, and a scheme to plant several million trees by 2001. Some large new hotels—designed to be a bit flossier than the current no-frills lot—are also going up.

For now, visitors can take comfort in the fact that while Osaka is severely short of style, the city is considerably easier to navigate than maze-like Tokyo. Osaka basically consists of two parts: *Kita* (north) and *Minami* (south). *Kita*, fanning out from Japan National Railways' Osaka Station, is the city's basic business and upscale amusement center: it's dotted with the newest department stores, office buildings, theaters and restaurants. *Minami*, centered on the Nankai Railway's

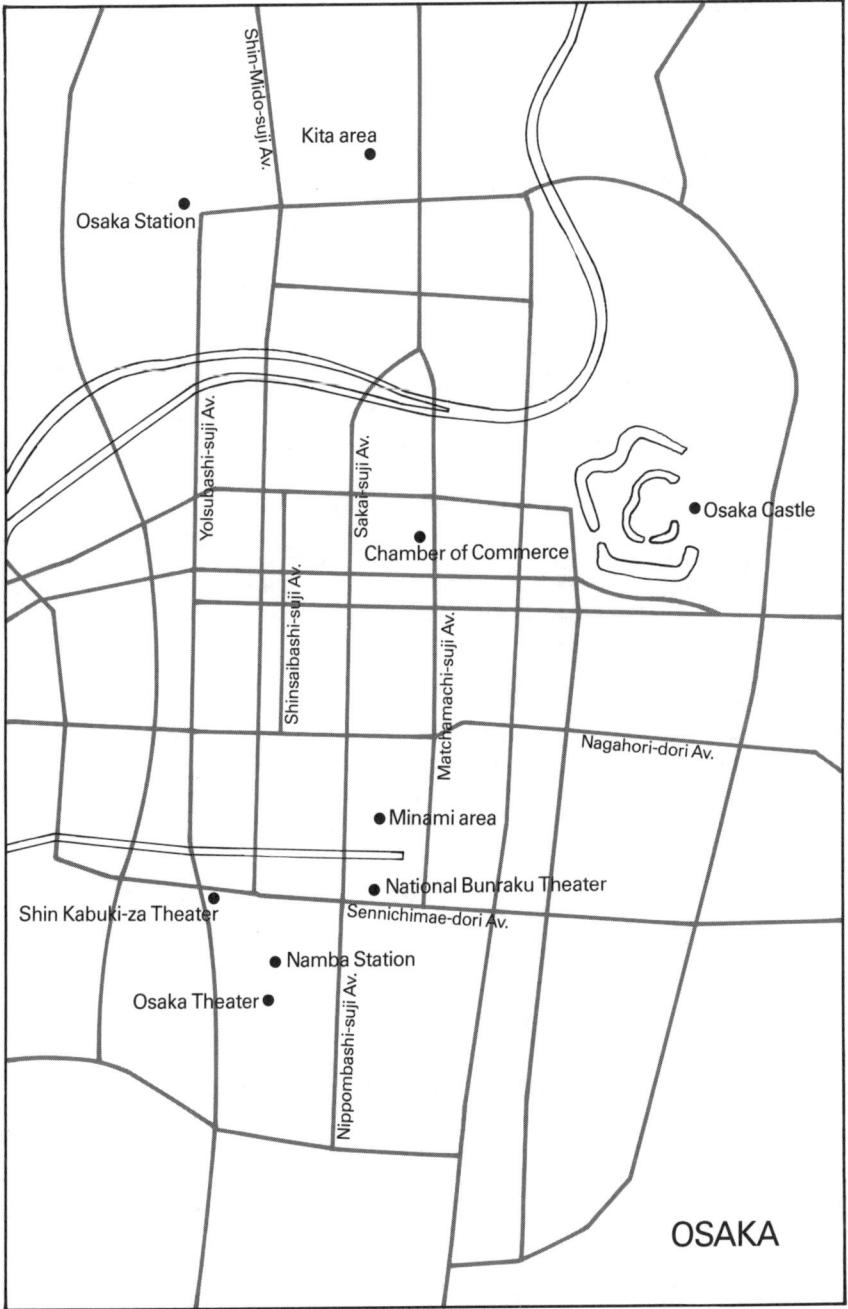

Kita area

Osaka Station

Shin-Mido-suji Av.

Yotsubashi-suji Av.

Sakai-suji Av.

Shinsaibashi-suji Av.

Chamber of Commerce

Osaka Castle

Matchamachi-suji Av.

Nagahori-dori Av.

Minami area

National Bunraku Theater

Shin Kabuki-za Theater

Sennichimae-dori Av.

Namba Station

Osaka Theater

Nippombashi-suji Av.

OSAKA

Namba Station, offers considerably livelier entertainments—both savory and less so—and much homier bars and restaurants.

From the two big rail centers one can go anywhere, and on weekends, or on days free of appointments, the best thing to do is to leave. Kyoto, Nara and Kobe are only short hops away: all three are superb Kansai cities, rich in tradition, charm and even natural beauty. The pleasures of life in this trio make Osaka bearable. Many of Osaka's most loyal businesspeople are those who commute from these places. Or, at the least, escape to them on weekends.

▶ Spotlight

In central Japan, not far from Osaka. is the sleepy hamlet of Rokko. Not much goes on there nowdays, but Rokko has already made its mark on Japanese history. On 1903, a British tea trader named Arthur Groom cleared a small patch of land and upon it built a three-hole golf course, the nation's first. Japan hasn't been the same since.

It takes the new arrival about five minutes to figure out that golf is the national obsession. Golf phrases punctuate the speech of industrialists and trade officials. Jack Nicklaus is a national hero. Golf clothes are wildly popular, even (or perhaps especially) among people who don't play the game. The most popular line of men's underwear is something called the Arnold Palmer white cotton brief.

Subway platforms are thronged by otherwise sane-looking men who can be seen flailing at the air with imaginary golf clubs—while others look on critically. These true believers are known as *kureji gorofua* (crazy golfers), a phrase uttered with affection. And as scores of business visitors from abroad have discovered, it's very good business to be a bit of a *kureji gorofua* themselves.

Not much business is conducted on the course. Instead, a match is an opportunity to spend some casual time with a business contact, and come to know him gradually, in the way most Japanese prefer. It's a chance to breathe some fresh air and get away from the stress-crammed office. It's also a chance to show off a bit, and perhaps catch an insight or two into an associate's personality. Businessmen agree that it's easier to deal with clients once they've played a round or two together.

Golf can in fact work wonders. A few years back, an American investment banking firm sent a woman officer to Japan, though not without a few misgivings about the huge all-male network that dominates the Japanese business world. She turned out to have a four handicap and quickly became the firm's most popular representative, courted by clients and colleagues alike who wanted to get her out on the course.

Golf's fashionable image here dates back to the turn of the century, when all uppercrust types played the game. In 1921, golf entered the public consciousness when the Emperor (then crown prince) was given lessons and a pair of plus-fours and sent off to Britain, where he played a gentlemanly match with the Prince of Wales. After the war, the US occupation forces's obsession with the game gave golf further impetus. And when the economy began to boom in the Sixties, and the heavy hitters began to find time for leisure activity, golf was an obvious answer.

Nowadays, for the fast-track folks, golf skill is part of the package, along with an attractive wife and a Tokyo University degree. One young banker says he learned golf at his father's behest, even though he personally cares little for the sport. 'You must learn golf to be a success in business', he explained.

● Arriving

Reaching (and thus leaving) Osaka is easy, whether you choose plane or train. Unlike Tokyo's Narita, Osaka International Airport is close to town. Comfortable buses leave every 15 minutes or so for four different areas of the city. The trip into town lasts about 30 minutes and costs Y360.

Taxis wait at the airport exits. By the expressway route, the trip downtown takes 20 minutes and the tab will be about Y5000. Bear in mind that Osaka airport serves many domestic points in Japan, as well as several international airports as well—including Seoul, Taipei and Hong Kong. From Osaka, Tokyo's 'city' airport, Haneda, can be reached by air in less than an hour.

Trains from Tokyo are all fast, but the *shinkansen* (bullet train) is a business favorite. The trip down is a comfortable 190-minute ride: passengers alight at Shin-Osaka and take a five-minute local ride into Osaka Umeda station, in the city's northern center. There are many major hotels nearby.

● Visas

Everyone must have a properly visa-stamped passport on arrival. Visas are issued at Japanese embassies and legations abroad, and multiple-entry visas are often available. *Do not expect* to be admitted to Japan without a visa.

● Orientation

Osaka, Japan's second-most-important business center (after Tokyo), lies 300 miles (500 kilometers) west of the capital, in the Kansai area, which also includes the compelling cities of Kyoto, Nara and Kobe. A major air and rail center, Osaka has a population of 2.65 million (but more than a million more during the day, when commuters flock to their offices) and is more notable for its entrepreneurial acumen than for its civic beauty.

● Transportation

The city's underground rapid transit system is clean, fast and easy to understand.

Buses are plentiful and routes are many, but one should use them only if absolutely sure of the destination and has the right change. Not many people speak English, or another foreign language.

For the business traveler, taxis are the best bet. Osaka doesn't have the maze-like quality of Tokyo. Still, ask the hotel clerks to write out the destination in Japanese—and always carry the hotel's card, or its matchbook, to show to a cabdriver on the return trip. Rush-hour traffic in Osaka is thick, but not quite as frustrating as Tokyo's.

● Money

Japanese money feels right. Notes are sized and color-coded in denominations of *Yen* 10,000, 5,000, 1,000 and 500. Coins: 500, 100, 50, 10, 5 and 1. The *yen* is one of the world's major currencies and is easily exchangable abroad. Most credit cards are accepted.

● Tipping

Do not tip. Most porters and waiters do not accept *pourboires* or *trinkgeld* or anything like it. Service charges are routinely added to bills at better restaurants and hotels (and a 10% luxury tax is added to bills for meals that cost more than Y2000). One exception: taxis, cruising after midnight. The usual tip is 20% of the fare...but few drivers will ask for it.

● Communications

Telephones and telexes are everywhere...and they *work*. Hotels offer business-center facilities as a matter of course: secretaries, translators and conference rooms are easily arranged. The public phones are color-coded: red, pink and blue for local calls, yellow for local and long-distance, and apple green for anywhere, including overseas. Local calls cost Y10 for three minutes, but it's wise to feed in a few more coins at the outset to avoid being cut off (surplus change is refunded).

Postal service is excellent.

● What to wear

Kansai weather isn't much different from Tokyo's: winters are a shade cooler and summers a touch warmer; but buildings are air-conditioned (and heated) as needed, though some buildings can be brutally drafty. For business meetings, coats and ties for men, and suits for women, are pretty much standard, though Osakans sometimes are not turned out as elegantly as their Tokyo counterparts. In general, dress in Osaka as in Frankfurt or Milan or Tokyo.

● Languages

Osaka's dialect is distinct from others in Japan: it's called 'Osaka-ben' and is spoken with pride. Many of its basic phrases are different from those used elsewhere, and even its rythyms strike

other Japanese as odd. English *may* be spoken by a business acquaintance, but don't count on it. Capable speakers of French, German or Italian are even rarer. Don't be fooled by shopsigns that promise that English is spoken: the speaker, one finds, is always mysteriously absent.

● Doing business

*When introduced to someone, try bowing, *à la Japonaise*. It'll be appreciated. Keep hands at sides, back and neck straight; *then* shake hands. (*Don't* hiss, however.)

*It is absolutely essential to have a business card (*meishi*), printed in Japanese on the reverse. Without such cards, foreigners are in immediate trouble. As the Japanese say, 'your *meishi* is your face.' And face is vitally important in Japan.

*Want to telephone a friend on the *shinkansen* (bullet train)? Dial the operator at (03) 248–9311 and tell her the contacts' name and train. Ships in port and near the coast can also be telephoned; ask the operator.

*Shoes are not worn inside traditional Japanese homes. Remove them at the door; slippers are provided.

*Yes, it's safe to drink the water.

*Most public toilets—as in other Asian countries—do not provide paper. Carry some.

*Electricity: 100 volts, 60 cycles.

*Working hours: 09:00 to 17:00 or 18:00, though many executives work later if only to prove their earnestness. Half-days on Saturdays are not uncommon.

*Private cars are available for hire with chauffeur through your hotel business center. Cost: about US$120 a day.

*Courier services such as DHL are readily available. Also, keep in mind the postoffice's International Business Mail service. Packets can be dropped off at most major postoffices and delivery to most cities abroad takes about two days.

Useful phone numbers

(The Osaka area code is 06.)

● Airlines:

Air Canada, 277–1180.
Air France, 201–5161.
Air India, 264–1781.
Alitalia, 341–3591.
ANA, 374–5131.
British Airways, 345–2761.
Canadian Pacific, 346–5591.
Cathay Pacific, 245–6731.
Egyptair, 341–1575.
Japan Air Lines, 203–1212.
Japan Asia Airways, 231–0256.
KLM, 345–6691.
Korean Air Lines, 262–1110.
Lufthansa, 345–0231.
Northwest Orient, 228–0747.
Pakistan International, 341–3106.
Pan Am, 271–5951.
Philippine, 444–2541.

Qantas, 262–1341.
Sabena, 341–8081.
SAS, 202–5161.
Singapore, 364–0881.
Swissair, 227–0831.
TWA, 341–7131.
Varig, 341–3571.

● Consulates:

United Kingdom, 231–3355.
USA, 341–2754.

● Trade and travel sources:

JETRO (Japan External Trade Organization), 203–6301.
JTB (Japan Travel Bureau), 344–0022.
Osaka Chamber of Commerce and Industry, 944–6200.
Osaka City Tourist Information Office, 345–2189.
Osaka Federation of Tourists Associations, 945–0039.
Osaka Tourist Association, 261–3948.

Shopping

As with museums and sightseeing, shopping is probably better left to Tokyo, a shopper's paradise, or to Kyoto, where superb arts and crafts can be seen. If Osaka is your only stop, the best bet is the huge department stores, Osaka's are as circus-like as any in Japan; kimono floors, food floors, rooftop restaurants, art galleries.

Two of the biggest department stores are:

Hankyu, 8–7 Kakudacho, Kita-ku, tel. 361–1381. It has several floors stressing fashion, including the products of Issey Miyake, Mitsuhiro Matsuda and Rei Kawakubo.

Hanshin, 1–13–13, Umeda, Kita-ku, tel. 345–1201. Right at Umeda Station—clothing, toys, watches, computers, jewellery and kimonos.

A few specialty stores:

Mikimoto, Shin Hankyu Building, 1st Floor, 1–12–39, Umeda, Kita-ku, tel. 341–0247. Yes, those cultured pearls are here, and all sorts of other jewellery, in traditional and modern designs.

Kawahara Camera Co. Ltd., 2–2–30, Umeda, Kita-ku, tel. 345–0031. Established just after World War I, the store has a wide assortment of name-brand cameras and will happily ship overseas.

Asahiya Shoten Ltd., 2–12–6, Sonezaki, Kita-ku, tel. 313–1191. A huge selection of books, with a foreign-language section that has a wide selection of books in English on Japan.

Shikanko, 1–18 Shinsaibashisuji, Ninami-ku, tel. 251–9091 and Hankyu Sanbangai, tel. 311–6339. It has a broad choice of leather goods, including handbags and wallets. Tax-free facility and international mail department.

Note: One of Osaka's more unnerving experiences is a visit to the Umeda Chika (underground) Center, smack in the middle of things, that stretches for more than a mile and occupies 31,300 square meters. Getting lost in this labyrinth of shops and snack bars is inevitable—and also part of the entertainment.

▶ Hotels

Osaka is a business city and its hotels are appropriately businesslike; equipped with all the necessary facilities—telexes, typists, interpreters, international telephone service and (in most cases) facsimile transmitters. Rooms are clean, service is efficient, and the usual Japanese-style amenities (light cotton robe (*yukata*), slippers, toothbrushes and toothpaste and of course green tea) are all available. But these hotels don't rank with Asia's great luxury palaces.

A selection:

ANA Sheraton, 1–3–1 Dojimahama, Kita-ku, tel. 347–1112, telex 5236884. New and efficient, with a staff that speaks a startling amount of English, indoor pool, gym. (ANA stands for All Nippon Airways, a domestic airline.)

Miyake Osaka, 6–1–55 Uehomachi, tel. 773–1111. New, a member of the respected Miyake group.

Nikko Osaka, 7 Nishinocho, Daihojicho, Minami-ku, tel. 244–1111, telex 5227575. Excellent location for business travelers, run by Japan Air Lines.

New Otani, Shiromi 1–4 Shirami, Higashi-ku, tel. 06–361–7701, telex J5293330 OTNOSK. A cousin to the enormous caravanserai in Tokyo. VIP floor, super-modern business center. 20 restaurants.

Osaka Hilton, 3, Umeda 1-chome, Kita-ku, tel. 347–7111, telex 524–2201 HILOSA-J. Good location, sky lounge, pool, gym and tennis.

Osaka Terminal, 3–1–1 Umeda, Kita-ku, tel. 344–1235. A business favorite, it's atop the central station. Managed by Japan Travel Bureau.

Plaza, 2–2–49 Oyodo-Minami, Oyodo-ku, tel. 453–1111, telex 534555. Efficient, elegant, rooftop lounge atop tower, 24-hour room service, outdoor pool.

Royal, 3–608 Nakanoshima 5-chome, Kita-ku, tel. 448–1121, telex 63350. A comfortable business giant (1,459 rooms) that typifies Osaka right down to its curious waterfall, large shopping arcade, pool and health club, central location.

Toyo, Toyosaki 3–16–19 Oyodo-ku, tel. 372–8181, telex 5233886. Big and boxy, good English-speaking staff, upscale businessman's hotel.

▶ Restaurants

The city's better restaurants are geared to the expense-account trade: prices are high and quality is good. Osakans are vastly fond of *sushi*, perhaps more so than other Japanese, and gourmets say the area's edibles are more interesting and a bit less costly than in Tokyo. And Western food can be good here too. Japan's top school of French cuisine, L'Ecole Technique Hoteliere Tsuji of Shizuo Tsuji, is in Osaka. Not surprisingly, Tsuji's old grads head several good restaurants nearby.

Keep an eye open, and a palate ready, for Osaka's own style of *sushi*, which is called *oshi* (pressed) *sushi*. Unlike Tokyo's standard *sushi* (a piece of raw fish atop a riceball), *ozhizushi* is made by pressing rice and fish, eel and whatever else sounds good into a wooden mold. Once the ingredients are squeezed together, the resulting pellets are cut into square chunks and served.

● Japanese

Mimiu-Udonsuki, 3–20 Yokobori, Migashi-ku, near Yodobashi (but better phone for directions), tel. 231–5770. Old, traditional, small and unpretentious, with a garden and *tatami*-mat seating, best for small groups, all styles of noodles and vegetables, excellent cold *soba* in summertime. Moderate.

Wosa, Acty Building, 27th Floor, 3–11–1 Umeda, Kita-ku. tel. 344–4032. *Sushi*, with a loquacious and friendly chef behind the counter. Excellent rolled seaweed-cone *sushi*. A regular says 'it's very Osakan; bright, clean, pleasant and not much atmosphere'. Moderate.

Yamate ya Rinsa, Acty Building, 19th Floor, 3–11–1 Umeda, Kita-ku, tel. 345–3535. The works: *teriyaki*, *sushi*, *sukiyaki*, all sorts of Japanese specialties. A fine place to sample the basics, and to make your guests happy. Good location. Moderate to expensive.

● Western

Bistro Vingt-Cinq, 25 Daihojimachi, Nishinocho, near Nikko Hotel, tel. 245–6223. Formal French cuisine, surprisingly large portions, expensive.

Colosseo, 3–2–6 Minami Semba, Minami-ku, Shinsaibashi, near the Nikko, tel. 252–2024. Italian-owned, Italian chef, crisp service, wonderful bread and a stylish display of seasonal appetizers; excellent veal; serene, pleasant and not overly fancy, good for business dinners; moderate to expensive.

El Poncho, 20408 Shinsaibashi, near the Nikko, tel. 241–0588. Small, romantic and, believe it or not, Mexican. Noisy and busy, and there's a strolling guitarist. Food reasonable, drinks expensive.

● A bit further away

Perigord, at Shukagawa, 25 minutes from Osaka by express train, Meiji Seimi Building, B1, 8–3–7 Isigani-dori, Chuo-ku, tel. 078–251–4359. Good Indian food in a restaurant catering to Kobe's large and discriminating Indian colony, crowded, good service, recommended *tandjoori* dishes, elaborate decor, moderate.

Minsei, at Kobe, half an hour by express train, in Chinatown, tel. 070–331–5435, good food but no atmosphere, always crowded, closes at 21:00 like other spots in Kobe's Chinatown. Moderate.

► After hours

Beyond the hotel bars, which offer comfortable settings for conversation, Osaka's nightlife scene is wildly varied. There are big Western-style nightclubs, Japanese cultural shows, giant (and tiny) discos and plain old beer joints. There are hundreds of places to check out, but if one's Japanese is weak, one is best advised to make the rounds with a local friend. Be sure to find out what the drinks are costing: more than one visitor has been floored by a bill that closely resembles the US deficit.

● Worth a try

Misty, Marubiro near Umeda Station, tel. 345–5726. A hangout for professional jazz musicians and occasional celebrities too, Misty offers jazz of all vintages. The hostesses all sing jazz tunes; the boss likes Forties swing. Prices moderate.

Pig'n'Whistle, Izu Building, tel. 213–6911. Instant escape from Things Nipponese, if that's needed. Here's an English pub complete right down to dartboards, and a large proportion of speakers of the tongue of William Shakespeare and Spike Milligan.

Alcazar, 1–7–7, Sonezaki, Kita-ku, tel. 312–2020. Live Latin nightclub shows, Spanish and French food. Expensive.

St. Tropez, Nippo Dojima Center, 1–3–9 Dojima, Kita-ku, tel. 345–0131. A huge and popular disco, jazz pianist, buffet food. Expensive.

Royal Horse, 15–13, Toganocho, Kita-ku, tel. 312–8958. A jazz club and restaurant that features live music by local visiting musicians. Moderate.

● A bit further away

Casablanca Club, in Kobe, half an hour away by express train, tel. 078–241–0200. A big lively hangout, complete with live piano music (jazz and pop), singing waitresses, an Indian chef with variable talents and a lively mixture of foreigners and Japanese.

● A bit farther out

Tsutenkaku is one of Osaka's more lurid pleasure sections. It's near Dobutsuen-mae Station, south of Namba, and provides a bit of everything—with the accent on lowlife. This is the area where the notorious *'no pan kissas'*—coffee shops where the waitresses are conspicuously pantieless—originated. The center of action is Tsutenkaku Tower, and the amusements are varied, starting with pachniko parlors, *go* and *shoji* (Japanese chess) arcades, porn flicks and so on into the night. Unlike, say, New York's Times Square, this area isn't downright chancy, but it's not the best place to charm an important business contact.

► Sights and sounds

Though Osaka is distinctly not a cultural wasteland, as some of Tokyo's snobs maintain, tourist attractions are few and far between. When businessmen are in Osaka, they're talking business; when schedules slow down—Kyoto and Kobe aren't far away.

● Museums

Expo 1970 Memorial Park, 41–1 Yamada Ogawa, Suita-shi, accessible by cab or bus from Ibaraki-shi station. In the park there are three excellent museums devoted to, respectively, contemporary international art (tel. 876–2481), Japanese folk art (tel. 877–1971) and ethnology (tel. 876–2151). The ethnological collection offers dazzling artifacts from all over the world, from shrunken heads to gypsy caravans. All three museums are in modern buildings. Also on the grounds is a classic Japanese garden, spotlighting all the features that make them famous— rocks, water, trees, special shrubs and 'hills'. Don't be put off by the vast Coney Island amusement park near the museums; the funds this enterprise provides pay for the museums.

Osaka Castle, near the city center, 500 meters from the Ote-mae bus stop. Perhaps Osaka's most memorable sight, the castle was built in the 1500s, demolished by artillery fire in 1615 and finally rebuilt in ferroconcrete in 1931. From the top there's a fine panoramic view of the city. Lovely gardens.

● Japanese entertainments

Noh and *bunraku* drama thrives here, but be sure to check performance times before racing off to the theater. Useful for visitors is *Kansai Time Out*, published monthly, which lists cultural happenings in Osaka, Kyoto and Kobe.

Kokuritsu Bunraku Gekijo, 1–12 Nipponbashi, Minami-ku, tel. 212–1122, home of the world famous *bunraku* puppeteers.

Osaka Noh Gaku Kaikan, 2–3–17 Nakazaki-nishi, Kita-ku, tel. 373–1726. The city's center for *Noh* dramas.

Takarazuka Revue, 40 minutes away by train on the Hankyu line, tel. 0797–84–0321. An all-woman troupe sings and dances traditional Japanese set pieces and Broadway adaptations too. They're thoroughly drilled and put on an oddly appealing show, vastly appreciated by Japanese and a few Westerners as well.

▶ Weekends

Kyoto, Nara and Kobe are all close by, all superb in their own individual ways, and all very much worth a visit. Of the three, Kyoto is most strongly recommended.

Kyoto is 30 minutes away by express train and a powerful attraction for foreigners and Japanese alike. Its superb temples, shrines and castles are the Real Thing: for once touristic ballyhoo is on target, and only minor repairs have been needed over the centuries. (World War II passed it by.)

Japanese traditional culture is alive and thriving here. The place is home to dozens of *kimono* artists, potters, dollmakers, weavers, lacquer craftsmen and *kabuki* actors. There are probably more 'living national treasures' here than in any other Japanese city. But Kyoto is also a bit snobby, very confident and rather pleased with itself. True, it has a lot to offer, but it's stuck firmly in the past. Tokyo and, yes, Osaka, are much more aware of today's dizzy reality.

Kyoto is jammed with temples: more than 1500. One of the greatest is *Kiyomizu*, a dark wooden masterpiece more than 456 feet high and set in a lovely forest. It's a genuine don't-miss-it sight, one that manages to stir the spirit even though one usually cannot avoid seeing it without the company of a couple of hundred poorly disciplined schoolchildren. The street leading up to it is lined with curio shops, preceded by a clutch of pottery shops with some lovely wares.

Close to Kyoto station is *Sanjusangendo* Temple, also on the must list. Its chamber contains a thousand and one glittering images of *Kannon* (Kwan Yin), the goddess of mercy, all dating to the 13th Century.

A third splendid sight is *Nijo* Castle, home to the great *Shogun* Ieyasu during his Kyoto forays, which offers a fascinating look at how *shoguns* lived. The wooden floorboards emit high-pitched squawks as one walks through, explaining their nickname of 'nightingale boards'. Legend says they were designed to warn the *shogun* of unannounced and probably sword-swinging visitors.

There are two particularly pleasant Japanese inns (*ryokan*) if there's time to spend a night here. These are Chigiriyo Ryokan (tel. 075–211–1281) and Matsukichi Ryokan (tel. 075–221–7016) which has only 15 rooms. Both are expensive.

There's a good Western-style hotel as well: the Miyado (tel. 075--771–7111), which has some Japanese-style rooms too.

Nara, about an hour by train from Osaka, is smaller and less sniffy than Kyoto, and almost as beautiful. Most of the highpoints are in or near *Nara Koen*, a sprawling park within walking distance of the fine old Nara Hotel (tel. 0742–26–330). The biggest sight is the Great Buddha, built in 1709 and, unlike Kamakura's own statue of the Great One, is housed in an incense-scented temple of Todai-ji.

The park also includes the Nara Museum, which has a fine collection of Japanese art works. Each autumn, the museum exhibits the superb imperial Shosoin treasures—wonderful porcelains, carvings, textiles and musical instruments dating back to the Silk Road era of the 8th Century. The annual airing of the treasures attracts visitors from all over the nation and is very much a seasonal ritual. Equally famous are Nara's deer, a pack of Bambis who've probably posed for even more amateur photographs than Mt. Fuji.

Kobe, about 20 minutes by train from Osaka, is an easy day trip. An exceedingly pleasant, cosmopolitan town, Kobe has a long history of foreign residents: Americans, Koreans, Europeans, Chinese and Indians. There aren't many compelling tourist spots, but the shopping is pleasant and the restaurants good. This is a fine place, incidentally, to sample the world-famed Kobe beef, from the world's most pampered cattle. Not far away, in the surrounding hills, is Mt. Rokko, at 3,057 feet the area's loftiest. It can be reached by cable car or bus and offers a pleasant view of Osaka Bay.

Sports

During the baseball season (April through October), the Osaka area is a splendid place to see a game: three professional teams (the Hawks, Braves and Buffalos) make this region their home base. The Hawks, who play in the huge Osaka stadium, are the local favorite. Americans won't find their standard peanuts and popcorn...instead, it's dried fish chips and rice crackers.

In late March, the city also hosts one of the nation's half-dozen annual sumo tournaments. The site is the Osaka Prefectural Gymnasium, which holds up to 10,000 *sumo* worshippers.

> Note: A good book about Osaka is Junichiro Tanizaki's novel, *The Makioka Sisters*, which deals knowledgeably with the decline of a great Osaka merchant family and its Kansai mores.

Seoul

Whoever believes Korea is still the Land of the Morning Calm never spent much time in weekday Seoul. The ritual stampede to The Office brings private cars, taxis and buses out on the streets early on and successive waves of vehicles, borne on a pandemonium of horns, carry hundreds of thousands off to work.

But what happens when they arrive? First, a quiet cup of coffee, then a cigarette and some desultory chat about the children or sports or the coming weekend. Then, after a properly solemn interlude, comes the slow turning toward the pile of waiting paperwork.

The lesson: once a goal is set, Koreans will stop at nothing to achieve it. Then, once it's reached, a certain immobility sets in. Some foreigners say that Seoul businessmen are classic examples: anything goes to get a contract. Parties and feasts and *kisaeng* dancers by the score; lavish suites and country tours and expensive presents as well.

But once the contract is signed, watch out. Deadlines are missed as often as they're met; late deliveries are the rule and agreements are too often broken. Old Korean proverbs come into play to help avoid harsh yes-or-no answers. Some delays are purely bureaucratic, some are caused by inefficiency expectable in a still-developing country. But be cautious. Be patient. Koreans have a way of coming through when all seems desperate.

They've done just that for centuries. There is no tougher nation in Asia. Isolated as they are on a strategic peninsula halfway between Japan and China, Korea has suffered countless invasions and occupations in the past, to say nothing of the more recent vicious fratricidal war between North and South. Through it all, Koreans have preserved their language, customs and their very civilization.

Now, foreign observers theorize, they want recognition for that victory. The economic miracle of the three decades since the end of the Korean War restored national pride as well as the face of the country. Living standards are high by Asian standards and are climbing higher. And all this has been won by struggle.

Seoul, as the center of the Korean ego, is a city of struggle. On crowded streets, shoving and pushing is part of the game. Loud haggling in shops is common; so is shouting at friends and spouses in public. Foreigners may be appalled but Koreans won't be: they feel family-like in their homogeneity and

123

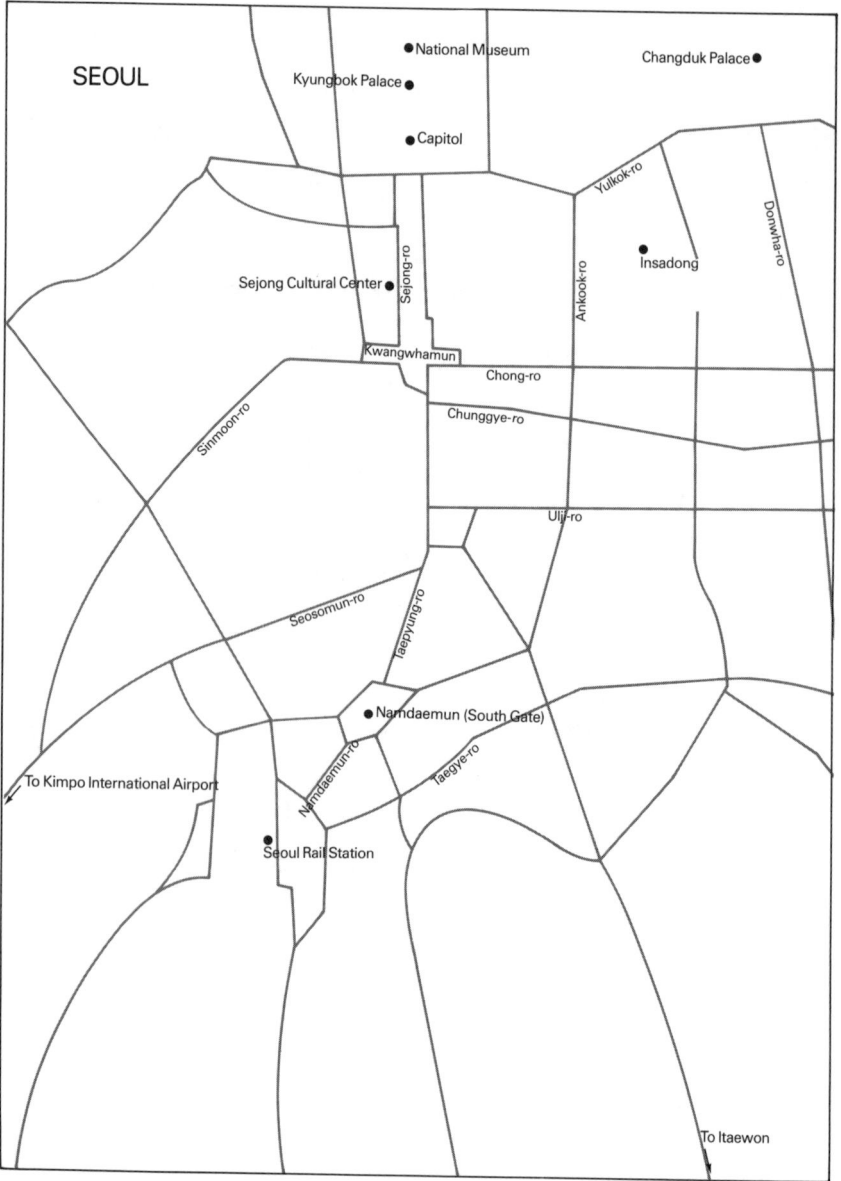

SEOUL

National Museum

Kyungbok Palace

Changduk Palace

Capitol

Yulkok-ro

Donwha-ro

Insadong

Ankook-ro

Sejong Cultural Center

Sejong-ro

Kwangwhamun

Chong-ro

Sinmoon-ro

Chunggye-ro

Ulji-ro

Seosomun-ro

Taepyung-ro

Namdaemun (South Gate)

To Kimpo International Airport

Namdaemun-ro

Taegye-ro

Seoul Rail Station

To Itaewon

treat one another like kin. No secrets, no beating about the bush.

But back home, personalities change radically. Korean Confucianism still defines the hierarchy. The elderly are granted the highest respect (Granny is even allowed to smoke), husbands rule the family and wives (who generally control the finances) smile quietly while they manipulate their men.

And foreigners, because they offer Koreans a chance to confirm their proud new self-image, are treated like VIPs. Not only businesspersons (men and women alike) who offer a chance of profit as well, but foreigners of every sort: students, teachers, journalists and tourists benefit from this status. To all concerned, Koreans broadcast their virtues and make no noise at all about their vices.

So here's something to keep in mind. Koreans are appallingly quick to anger—though they're almost as quick to calm down. Someone in fact once called them the Irish of Asia, and to be sure there's a wee bit of truth in the comparison. But never tell Koreans this. To them, the Irish are nothing but European Koreans, and damned lucky to merit the title.

▶ Spotlight

The campaign started almost as soon as Seoul was awarded the 1988 Olympics: 'For the Olympics: Don't spit on the streets'.

'For the Olympics: Don't litter'.

'For the Olympics: Obey traffic rules'

'For the Olympics: Be polite to others'.

The list could go on—and indeed, there's some gentle spoofing of the city's earnestness. But there's no doubting at all: if Seoul has its way, this is going to be the world's best organized and most profitable track meet ever. The city leaders are going all-out in preparations for the 25th Olympic Games—as they did for the huge dress rehearsal, the Asian games of 1986.

Thus far, at least US$128 million alone has been spent on the huge new Seoul Sports Complex. The Olympic stadium (capacity over 100,000 spectators) is the centerpiece of the complex, but the entire 54.5 hectares is crammed with other new sporting facilities.

Among these: A 20,000-spectator-capacity gymnasium, a 50,000-spectator baseball stadium that will be used for cultural shows and as a track-and-field exercise ground; a smaller gym and an indoor pool shaped to resemble the Gobukson, an ironclad 'turtle ship' with which Admiral Yi Sun-shin defeated the invading Japanese navy at the end of the 16th Century.

The sports complex and nearby athlete housing apartments are located 13 kilometers from central Seoul. A superhighway links it to the city, as do bus and subway routes.

New hotels are rising all over the capital, and local restaurants and nightspots are bracing for the arrival of the foreigners. Even Seoul's belles of the evening are being prepared: an all-out anti-VD campaign began in late 1985.

● Arriving

Formalities at Seoul's Kimpo International Airport are uncomplicated, though the line-waiting factor is as annoying as Hong-Kong's. Baggage inspection (on both arrival and departure) is thorough: a resident explains that this is because lots of deer antlers (a favorite cure for impotence) are smuggled into Korea. Once through immigration and customs, arriving passengers run a gauntlet of many greeters and a few would-be cabbies. Cab fares from the airport into central Seoul average about US$3. If you're arriving to sign a major deal, or have good friends in Seoul's Korean community, you may be met by business contacts at the airport and chauffered into town in style. (Warning: avoid the large brown cabs. These are known as 'call taxis' and tend to be twice as expensive as the smaller green, yellow or blue cabs.)

Fifteen-day visas can be obtained on arrival (save for Japanese and citizens of Communist nations) but extensions are very difficult to obtain. Tourist visas (30 to 60 days) can easily be obtained at all South Korean embassies, and business visas of varying duration are almost as easy to get.

> Note: There's a 5000-*won* airport tax to pay on leaving the country.

● Orientation

Seoul is the capital and most populous (10 million) city of the Republic of Korea, and is located just south of the central dividing line of the Korean peninsula. The government is a constitutional democracy with significant military influence. Major religions include Buddhism, Confucianism and Christianity. Most Koreans are of Mongol origin with traits quite unlike the Chinese or Japanese.

● Transportation

Public transportation is hectic but inexpensive, and rush hours are rushed indeed. There are plenty of taxis and the rates are low, but few drivers speak much English and foreigners are advised to have their destinations written out for them in advance. In central Seoul, there are taxi queue stations which instill some order into the usual scramble for cabs.

If appointments are scattered around the city, it's best to hire a chauffeured car (about US$70 a day), unless your local contacts offer you a car and driver. Don't drive yourself unless there's an emergency. Seoul's traffic is mad.

The bus and subway system is comprehensive and cheap, but getting around is tricky unless you speak and read Korean. At rush hours, all public transport is jammed.

● Money

The monetary unit is the *won*, and as of early 1987 it was trading at about 870 to the US dollar. Bills are in denominations of 1000, 5000 and 10,000; coins in 1, 5, 10, 50, 100 and 500. Unused *won* can be exchanged on departure, and exchange receipts are necessary if large amounts are involved.

● Tipping

Don't. Most restaurants add a 10% service charge. Otherwise, an offer of a tip may be regarded as offensive.

● Communications

International and domestic links are generally excellent. Most Seoul hotels offer direct-dialling facilities both internally and abroad, and telex and cable connections are first-rate. Postal services adequate.

● What to wear

Seoul, like Tokyo, is a four-season city. Winters can be bitterly cold and summers are sizzling. Humidity is high. Spring and autumn are superb—comparable to Paris or, say, Boston. Business suits are worn all through the year, and nylons are usual for working women. Evenings can be formal: dinner jackets and long dresses may be useful.

> Note: Professional tailoring is of fair quality. A three-piece suit will cost about US$250.

● Languages

Korean is a Ural-Altaic language that some say has more in common with Hungarian and Finnish than with Chinese or Japanese. In Seoul, however, the foreigner will discover (with some relief) that most hotel and office personnel speak at least some English. Japanese is also spoken in these areas—a consequence of the long Japanese occupation of the peninsula.

Written Korean has its own alphabet—*hangul*—which was invented by one of the nation's best-known rulers, King Sejong, in 1443. Hangul is supposed to be quite easy to learn and Koreans, perhaps as a result, have one of the world's highest literacy rates. Korea certainly is the only country in the world that celebrates a public holiday (Oct. 9) in honor of its alphabet.

Romanization of the language varies erratically. Seoul is always 'Seoul', but Pusan is sometimes 'Busan' and the name Lee is often written as Rhee. The government now has formally adopted the McCune-Reischauer Romanization system, but several letters are interchangeable: K for G, for instance, CH for J and B for P.

● Doing business

Koreans tend to be somewhat more open than Japanese or Chinese, but the usual Asian politenesses are still vital. When exchanging business cards, for instance, the traditional 'two-hands-in-Asia' rule still applies, but there's a slight variation: hand the card to your new acquaintance with the right hand, while your left hand touches the underside of your right wrist. And don't forget to nod slightly during the initial handshake.

Before a business meeting really gets under way, expect Koreans to spend some time drinking coffee, smoking a cigarette and making general conversation. Don't be startled by personal questions: you'll be asked about your wife and children, where precisely you live, your age and sometimes even your religion or salary. Women inevitably are asked whether they're married, and single women are always asked why they've chosen that status.

*Business cards in English are acceptable, but a Korean translation on the back can be useful.

> Note: Always speak English very slowly, and choose words and sentence structure with care. A Korean nod of 'understanding' doesn't always mean your thoughts have gotten across. And even a 'yes' or 'no' may not mean agreement, but rather that you've been understood—or just that it's time to be getting on to something else.

*Entertaining can be high-powered, and visiting males are expected to keep up with the hosts. (Korean males won't be distressed if a visiting businesswoman orders a Scotch or two during dinner, but Korean women are still forbidden these pleasures. Bear in mind that Korean men will never forget that the visiting female is indeed a woman.)

*Business hours are from 09:00 to 18:00, March through October, and from 09:00 to 17:00 the rest of the year. Some private businesses open a bit earlier and close a bit later, and match government and banking Saturday morning hours of 09:00 to 13:00 or even 13:30.

*All leading international-class hotels have efficient business centers.

*For domestic and international travel, there are agents in all top hotels. Korean express trains are comfortable and efficient. So is domestic air travel.

*Korean names provide a steady challenge to visitors. There are three major family names: Kim, Pak and Lee—and Romanization varies enormously. Pak is often written as Park, for instance, and Lee is also Li, Yi, Yee, Rii, Rhee, Ee and even I. (Another complication is that Korean women use their maiden names after marriage.) Thus trying to track down a Mr. Kim, or a Mr. Park, in a large office, is often frustrating. Try to pin down a new acquaintance's full name, and his exact business title as well.

Useful phone numbers

● Airlines:

China Air Lines, 281–523.
Cathay Pacific, 779–0321.
Japan Airlines, 776–9751.
Korean Airlines, 777–8221.
Malaysian Airlines, 777–7761.
Northwest Airlines, 753–6106.
Pan American, 777–2993.
Singapore Airlines, 281–226.
Thai International, 779–2621.

● Diplomatic Missions:

Argentina, 793–4062.
Australia, 70–6491.
Austria, 72–6649.
Belgium, 72–6822.
Brazil, 70–4769.
Canada, 776–4062.
Chile, 792–9519.
Colombia, 267–4761.
Costa Rica, 793–3721.
Denmark, 792–4187.
Finland, 23–2092.
France, 362–5547.
Gabon, 261–4634.

Germany (West), 22–40–37.
Guatemala, 793–3721.
India, 793–4142.
Indonesia, 782–5116.
Iran, 793–7751.
Italy, 74–7405.
Japan, 73–5626.
Malaysia, 794–7205.
Mexico, 793–0651.
Netherlands, 793–0651.
New Zealand, 70–4255.
Panama, 70–4164.
Peru, 792–2238.
Philippines, 58–9434.
Saudi Arabia, 75–9263.
Spain, 70–4564.
Sweden, 73–7876.
Switzerland, 70–4767.
Taiwan, 776–2721.
Thailand, 792–0197.
Turkey, 762–1571.
United Kingdom, 75–7341.
USA, 72–2601.
Uruguay, 33–4224.
Vatican, 72–5725.

● Government offices:

Construction Ministry, 593–2989.
Economic Planning Board, 732–5221.
Education Ministry, 730–3261.
Federation of Korean Industries, 783–0821.
Finance Ministry, 732–0011.
Immigration Office, 776–8858.
Korea Trade Promotion Corp., 753–4181.
Korean Traders Association, 28–8251.
Korea National Tourism Corp., 261–7001.
Patent Bureau, 633–9161.
Science and Technology Ministry, 753–0255.
Trade and Industry Ministry, 732–2671.

● Others:

American Chamber of Commerce, 23–6471.
Bank of Korea, 777–8611.

Japanese Chamber of Commerce, 28–6672.

Korean Chamber of Commerce and Industry, 757–0757.

● **Emergencies:**

National Medical Center, 265–9130.
Sacred Heart Hospital, 776–1002.
Severance Hospital, 322–0161.

Shopping

Shopping in Seoul has its own odd character. The favorite place for foreigners is the Itaewon area just outside the huge US Army base at Yongsan, not far from city center—and the area is fast becoming the preferred area for many Koreans as well. Why? Selection, quality and price. Inevitably, haggling is vital. So is careful inspection of the wares on offer. Be wary of name-brand items: they're often clever fakes.

Itaewon offers a broad selection of Korean curios—brassware, woodcarvings, gold and silver jewellery and the local topazes and amethysts. Leather goods—jackets, shoes, purses and briefcases—are plentiful and of fair quality, and the current best buy is eelskin, a soft and oddly slippery leather. Because Itaewon attracts many American service families, prices are often quoted in dollars, but Korean *won* are accepted without hesitation.

There's also a wide selection of tailors and dressmakers in the area, but prices and workmanship vary widely. First-timers are advised to seek a local friend's advice—or wait until they are safely back on Bond Street. Readymade clothing abounds, and some is of good quality. Much of the off-the-rack wares are bought by shopkeepers at the huge Namdaemun (South Gate Market), which opens up at 04:00. Clothes are thus cheaper here, but would-be hagglers must speak some Korean. There are good buys here, and at Tongdaemun (East Gate Market) as well.

Korean antiques are hard to find, but good-quality reproductions abound. Those ruggedly handsome Korean chests can still be found, but most of the best seem to have been shipped overseas years ago. Itaewon shops offer mostly reproductions, but some high-quality originals can sometimes be tracked down in Insadong, a center-city enclave where prices and quality are higher.

Avoid the major department stores, which are spectacularly well-stocked but which charge higher prices than the market areas. These stores have two advantages: they're much handier to the downtown hotels, and their labels (Lacoste, say, or Rayban) are trustworthy.

For some shoppers, Seoul's greatest single attraction is the Jindo fur salon. There's a retail outlet in Itaewon and a factory outlet in southern Seoul. Jindo buys its furs mostly in Scandinavia and brings them back to Seoul, where coats are stitched together by lowpaid young female workers. Jindo claims the savings in buying one of its coats can pay the cost of a trip to Korea. Well, maybe.

Hotels

Hilton, 395, 5-ka, Namdaemun-ro, Chung-ku, tel. 753–7788, telex K26695. A new top-ranking hotel with a fine French restaurant, pool; 10 minutes from city center by cab.

Hyatt Regency, 747–7 Hannam-dong, Yongsan-gu, tel. 798–0061, telex K24136. Hillside location with superb views, good restaurants, pool and gym; 15 minutes from city center by taxi.

Lotte, 1 Sokong-dong, Chung-gu, tel. 77110, telex K28313. Located smack in the center of downtown, huge lobby and many bars and restaurants, linked by underground passageway to Lotte Department Store, popular cocktail bar, pool.

President, 188–3, 1-ka, Ulchi-ro, Jung-gu, tel. 753–3131, telex K27521. Good location in city center, and less-expensive rooms. Caters to Japanese businessmen.

Seoul Plaza, 23, 2-ka, Taipyung-ro, Jung-gu, tel. 77122, telex K2615. Fine views, central location, busy bars and restaurants, excellent Japanese food.

Sheraton Walker Hill, San 21, Kwangjang-dong, Sungdong-ku, tel. 453–0121. Telex K22228. Resort hotel less than an hour from central district, offering a 24-hour gambling casino, dinner revues, outdoor pools and many sports facilities and villas for short or long-term rental.

Shilla, 202, 2-ka, Jangchung-dong, Jung-gu, tel. 233–3131, telex K24160. Beautifully located with fine views but sometimes short of taxis for the 10-minute ride to city center. Houses heads of state. Run by Tokyo's Okura Hotel group. Good Asian restaurants.

Westin Chosun, 87, Sogong-dong, Chung-ku, tel. 77105, telex K 28432. The oldest and smallest luxury hotel, with a good French restaurant and popular outdoor pool in the center of the city. Good shopping arcade.

Restaurants

Most Westerners discover an instant affection for Korean food, though *kimchi* (a peppery pickled cabbage) can be a deterrent. But Korea's best-known dish, *bulgogi*, is superb. It consists of strips of prime beef marinated in a mixture of soy sauce, garlic, sesame, green onions and grilled, usually by the diner himself, over a cooker embedded in the table. Surrounding the cooker is a variety of pickled vegetable dishes, sprouts, preserved fish and meat and of course rice. There are soups (hot and cold) as well, and everything is washed down by tea, beer or rice wine—and the Korean grape wine (Majuwang) is not bad. The whites are particularly recommended.

Another favorite Korean specialty is *kalbi*, grilled or steamed beef ribs. Hosts will also press *sinsollo* on their guests: an elaborate dish consisting of meat, eggs, fish and vegetables (and sometimes nuts), cooked in a special chafing dish. Many Koreans dote on a cold noodle dish called *naengmyon* which is something of an acquired taste.

If you're planning a business meal, be prepared to battle for the privilege of paying the check. Koreans love to entertain and seem to like paying even more. If you outwit them (by surreptitiously paying the bill on a visit to the lavatory, say) you'll gain points, but that trick only works once.

● Korean

Korea House, 80–2, 2-ga, Phildong, Jung-su, tel. 266–9101. Expensive, but it offers superb Korean food (at a buffet or in private rooms), and its post-dinner shows of traditional Korean singing and dancing are splendid. The gift shop stocks handsome artifacts. Not to be missed.

Monnijuh, Hannam-dong, Yongsan-gu, tel. 74017. Run by a retired actress and located in the nightclub area, Monnijuh's prices are moderate and its servings large. The *bulgogi* is delicious, though it's not on the menu. And the *dongdangju* (rice wine) is highly recommended.

Sanchon, 244–11 Huam-dong, Yongsan-gu, tel. 777–9696. An excellent vegetarian restaurant run by a former monk who knows his mountain herbs. Good selection of rice wines. Floor shows.

Warning: You'll sit crosslegged on the floor, *not* on chairs. A test for the less agile—and less fit.

● Other styles

La Cantina, 50, 1-ga, Ulchi-ro, Jung-gu, tel. 777–2579. The best Italian food available in Seoul and a favorite with many local businessmen.

The Moghul, 71–20 Chungdam-dong, Kangnam-gu, tel. 541–1257. Good spicy Pakistani food and an exotic treat for many Koreans. Prices on the high side.

Swiss Chalet, 104–4, Itaewon-dong, Yongsan-gu, tel. 792--1723. You've guessed it: Korean waitresses in dirndls, lots of beer, occasional yodelling and regular oom-pah music, and all the wienerschnitzel and sauerbraten you can hold. Moderate prices.

After hours

Seoul's nightlife is still many-splendored, though some veterans maintain the pace has slowed a bit. For the younger set, including US GIs, Itaewon is the place to go. Lots of cozy bars, fair jazz and attractive young ladies. Seoul is still going through the disco stage: the best is the Westin Chosun's Xanadu, closely followed by the Hilton's Rainforest. Avoid the others.

Kisaengs are the Korean version of Japanese *geishas*, though the comparison in Korean company is likely to cause a degree of ill-feeling. *Kisaengs* are trained to please male guests and do it superbly, though their after-hours company is nobody's business but their own. *Kisaeng* restaurants are hugely expensive and should not be visited without a Korean friend—who will offer all the necessary guidance.

Daewongak, 323-ho, Songbuk-dong, tel. 762–2818. This is perhaps the city's best *kisaeng* house: beautiful girls dressed in traditional costume, fine food and good drinks, and lots of very skilful entertainment. Very popular with very wealthy businessmen. Per-person charges start at about US$150 and rise with startling rapidity.

● Western style

All That Jazz, 168–17-ho, Itaewon-dong, Yongsan-gu, tel. 792–5701. Small, friendly, good sounds. The pizza's not bad.

Rumors, 34–145, Itaewon-dong, Yongsan-gu, tel. 793–1787. A trendy new disco, very small and very snooty. Seoul's gilded youth hang out here and dress to shock. Starts moving about midnight. Expensive.

The Warehouse, 52–4 ho, Seocho-dong, Kangnam-gu, tel. 568–8029. Good live jazz featuring the club's owner on sax. A favorite hangout for businessmen and government officials. Snacks available, but booze is the mainstay. Expensive.

Sights and sounds

Kyungbok Palace, Samchung-dong. Built by a Yi emperor in 1395, destroyed by fire 200 years later and rebuilt in the original style in 1867. Beautiful pavillions and residences, handsome park. Open 09:00 to 17:30. Houses the National Museum (below).

National Museum, Yungbok Palace, Samchung-dong, tel. 733--7274. A highly interesting collection of national treasures, including paintings, pottery, sculpture and metalwork dating back for centuries.

Changdok Palace. Built in 1405, restored in 1611. A feast of fine old Yi Dynasty buildings set in a lovely park. The main entrance gate itself is superb, and dates back to the 14th Century. It can be visited only in guided tours, conducted in English, Japanese and Korean. Ask your hotel to check for starting times.

Toksu Palace, Jung-dong, Jung-gu. A large statue of Buddha in a public park built on the site of a 1454 palace. Site of a Museum of Modern Art (tel. 752–7206), which offers monthly exhibitions of European and modern Korean art.

National Theater, San 14–67, Changchung-dong 2-ga, Jung-gu, tel. 274–1151. Large and small enclosures which present traditional Korean performances, large concerts and experimental student work.

Sejong Cultural Center, 81–3, Sejong-ro, Chung-gu, tel. 720–3671. Performances by visiting foreign artists and larger Korean groups such as the Seoul Philharmonic. Occasional film festivals.

Korean Folk Village, Suwon. An enormous and well-planned living museum of the past, with occasional dances and festivals tucked in among the old-style homes, farms and shops. Artisans produce items of iron, wood, cane, brass and even the splendid stovepipe hats made of horsehair. The houses and farms are samples of the country's widely varied regional architecture. An interesting country-style restaurant or two as well, where the beef is delicious and the rice wine flows freely. Less than an hour south of Seoul by car. Inexpensive. Spend the day.

Panmunjom. The truce talks village, symbol of Korea's continuing division, lies 35 miles north of Seoul. Part of the border area can be easily reached by private car, but the demilitarized zone itself, and the conference buildings, can be entered only with official permission. (Not all tourist agencies can obtain this permission: be sure your choice is the correct one.) Tours include the conference hall area, (site of several unpleasant incidents in past years), as well as the infiltration tunnels built by North Koreans. The trip offers important insights into the peninsula's continuing tensions.

◖▬▬▶ **Weekends**

Soraksan. This formidable cluster of spiky, steep mountains lies on the east coast just south of the demilitarized zone and is one of the country's favorite hiking and sightseeing areas. There are many well-marked paths, Buddhist temples and, in one spot, a cable car to haul the less-athletic aloft for a view. There are several acceptable hotels in the base area and a few mountain inns as well. Reachable by air in less than an hour from Seoul, or—preferably—by tourist bus in about five hours over a winding mountain highway that offers some spectacular views.

Kyongju. Site of the enormously productive Silla Dynasty from roughly 57 B.C. to A.D. 939, Kyongju is one of the world's most important ancient cities and as such is well worth a weekend—or a week. Its temples, tombs and fortresses have been lovingly restored, and there are several good hotels in the area. (Try the Chosun or the Tokyu, both on Pomun Lake). Recent tomb excavations have brought many interesting gold art objects to the surface, as well as a superbly preserved painting of a white horse that dates to the 5th Century. The Silla Dynasty coexisted with China's golden Tang Dynasty and the brilliant inspirations of those days are clearly manifest here. Pulguk-sa, one of Korea's largest and most important temples, is worth a careful visit.

And for a break from the temples and tombs, the area offers an 18-hole golf course, plenty of tennis and swimming, as well as water-skiing and boating in a swan boat oddly reminiscent of those on Boston Common.

Kyongju can be reached from Seoul by comfortable air-conditioned express train in less than five hours.

Cheju. Sixty miles south of the Korean peninsula and a 90-minute flight from Seoul, Cheju island is famous for its volcanos, its women and its superbly unspoiled scenery. The volcanos have been quiescent since A.D. 1007, the scenery is being changed a bit by resort development, but the women go on diving for shellfish in even the coldest winter weather while the men stay at home and tend the families. Cheju has been billed as 'Korea's Hawaii' by overenthusiastic flacks, but its mountains are lovely, its beaches largely unspoiled and its mystic artifacts fascinating. There are a few good hotels and the new Hyatt Cheju is a recommendable resort. (Readily booked via the Seoul Hyatt.)

Cheju can also be reached by air or ferry from Pusan.

Shanghai

New Life Among the Ruins

Carl Crow's many-splendored *Handbook for China*, in its 1933 edition, calls Shanghai 'the commercial metropolis of the China Coast and of Asia, and one of the most diverting and cosmopolitan cities of the world.'

Crow was an American advertising executive and writer who lived in Shanghai from 1911 to 1937, and his guidebook makes it clear that he was something of a booster for his city. But even allowing for Yankee exuberance, there is no denying the city's pre-war dominance. Shanghai combined the financial power of London and New York, the jazz and gangsterism of Chicago and even a bit of the elegance of Paris.

In those days, great ships regularly disgorged wealthy travelers onto the Bund, and the massive office buildings those travelers saw as they stepped ashore symbolized the city's solidity and power.

Hotels and restaurants were world-quality, merchants cunning and rich and department stores and shops full of the best from Europe, Asia and North America. Shanghai's inhabitants were wildly heterogeneous: Chinese and Japanese, Americans and Britons, Frenchmen and Russians and Germans thronged the streets of the foreign concessions.

Just below the city's glittering surface, however, was cruelty, corruption and abject poverty. Highly organized Chinese gangs ruled the ramshackle Chinese areas and ran the nightclubs and whorehouses of the foreign concessions as well. Thousands of overworked, underpaid coolies starved to death every year. That Shanghai died in 1949.

Today's huge (12 million) city on the Huangpu is in some ways a living museum of that rapacious colonial century. The big office buildings, now shabby, still stand along the Bund. Occasionally a gleaming white Scandinavian luxury liner unloads another band of nervous tourists. But the swanky hotels long ago lost their swagger, the elegant restaurants downgraded their menus and the huge old department stores now sell brummagem.

Shanghai these days is a hardworking daylight city, bursting with ambition to regain its old place as the nation's financial center, full of plans to catch up with other Chinese cities that so far have outpaced it in the race toward prosperity. In Beijing and Guangzhou, there's a certain condescension toward Shanghai, a feeling that the old leader will never make it back to pre-war heights.

SHANGHAI

Shanghai Gymnasium

Caoxi Lu

Hengshan Lu

To Hongqiao International Airport

Huaihai Zhonglu

Yan'an Zhonglu

Nanjing Xilu

Shanghai Exhibition Center

Jade Buddha Temple

Jiangning Lu

Wusong River (Suzhou Creek)

Nanjing Road

Tianmu Lu

Peoples Park

Yan'an Donglu

Shanghai Art and History Museum

Xizang Zhonglu

Zhejiang Zhonglu

shopping area

Nanjing Donglu

Xizang Beilu

Central Railway Station

Henan Nanlu

Yuyuan Garden

Henan Zhonglu

Henan Beilu

Sichuan Zhonglu

The Bund

Zhongshan Nanlu

Zhongshan Dong Y Lu

Huangpu River

135

But Shanghai's residents are as cocky as ever. They discount the heavy political damage they suffered during the Seventies, when Shanghai was smeared as the bastion of the now-discredited Gang of Four. They point instead to the fact that Shanghai now produces a ninth of China's total industrial output, a sixth of central budget revenues and much of, if not all of, the nation's better-quality consumer products. Shanghai claims to be China's cultural center as well, though artists in Beijing have their own ideas about that.

And central government leaders in Beijing, after ignoring Shanghai for many years, now seem prepared to forgive and forget. Renovation of the city's aging industrial plant began in 1983 under the impetus of a $1 billion grant from the capital. After Premier Zhao Ziyang's visit in late 1984, Shanghai won the autonomy it needed to expand in trade, finance, commerce and tourism. One specific area of improvement will be the city's shabby hotels, collectively the worst of any major Chinese city. At least 12 new hotels are scheduled to open by 1987.

Shanghai will never return to its status as, to requote Crow, 'one of the most diverting and cosmopolitan cities of the world'. But foreign businesspeople, attracted by the central government's growing largesse in the old city by the Huangpu, will find more pure entrepreneurial spirit here than in most other mainland cities.

➤ Spotlight

It is a testament to the glamor of old Shanghai that books about its reckless years still continue to flow off the presses of the world's publishers. A recent novel by a Hong Kong professor (*Shanghai*, by Christopher New, Futura, London, 1985) traces the city's history from the turn of the century to the Japanese occupation, through the life of an English businessman; another (*Empire of the Sun*, by J.G. Ballard, Gollancz, London, 1984) tells the story of a young English boy trapped in the city during the Japanese conquest. Both novels are accurate portrayals of the city, both are spellbinding, and Ballard won Britain's prestigious Booker Prize for *Empire*.

Yet the full story of old Shanghai probably never will be told, if only because the scope is so vast. For every story one hears of the old days, another will top it. Shanghai is a great deal larger than life. Today's city is a much better place in which to live, but is much less interesting.

Happily for the romantic, artifacts of the Old Shanghai still exist; some in the secondhand shops (try the Shaanxi Old Wares Store, at the corner of Shaanxi and Yenan West Roads) but more impressively in the old buildings along the Bund, Nanjing and Huaihai Roads, and elsewhere in the central city.

The old British Consulate on the Bund, for example, is now the Friendship Department Store. The snobbish old Shanghai Club (with its world-famed Long Bar) is now the Dongfeng Hotel—and the bar is still there. The huge headquarters building of the Hong Kong & Shanghai Bank, on the Bund, now houses the municipal government.

Out near the Zoo, at 2409 Hongqiao Road, is the elegant former home of multimillionaire Victor Sassoon, built in the 1930s and later occupied in turn by a gambling casino, Japanese naval headquarters, then by the now-disgraced Gang of Four. Present tenant? British Petroleum.

Sun Yat-sen, leader of the Chinese revolution, lived for several years at 7 Xiangshan Road, while his widow, Madame Soong Ching-Ling, sister of Mme. Chiang Kai-shek, spent much of her very active political life at 1843 Huaihai Road, and died there in 1981.

Perhaps the most ironic fate is that suffered by the former 'Great World', a gangster-run assortment of gambling, prostitution and cabarets. Today, it's the Shanghai Youth Palace—a center for chess matches, stamp exhibitions and painting and singing lessons.

● Arriving

Back in Shanghai's wilder days, most travelers arrived by passenger liner, up the Huangpu River from the Yangtze and the sea. Now, aircraft have replaced the liners. Hongqiao Airport, about 30 minutes by taxi west of the city center, is the terminal for both international and domestic flights and offers no more red tape than any other small town Asian airport.

Taxis wait just outside the airport exit, and drivers stalk passengers as they leave the money changer. Bargain a bit, if your Chinese is up to the task: the proper fare to central hotels is about 15 *yuan*. Bus service is undependable.

At Shanghai Central Railway Station, taxis queue outside the main exit—just follow the crowd.

● Orientation

Shanghai for the past century has been the industrial and financial capital of East China, though its predominance has eroded a bit in the last few decades. With a population of about 12 million, it ranks as one of the world's largest cities, and its sizzling summers and chilly winters don't seem to affect the verve of its inhabitants. A key domestic center of transportation (air, train, boat), it is also home base for much of China's high-technology industries.

● Transportation

For the business visitor, taxis or chauffered cars offer the most reliable ways of getting around. Public transport is usually jammed, and difficult for non-Chinese-speakers to fathom.

Cabbies are usually only too happy to drive one about for any number of hours, and rates are reasonable: start bargaining at about 70 *yuan* per hour. If your schedule of appointments keeps you in the vicinity of the major hotels, their reception desks can produce a taxi to the next destination. Unlike Canton, it's almost impossible to flag down taxis in the streets.

It's also worthwhile to try the Shanghai Friendship Taxi Service (tel. 584584 or 536363).

If you find yourself pursuing a contact in one of the city's suburbs, ask your driver to wait. Odds are against finding another cab out in the wilderness.

To hire a car, check first with the hotel desk, or with business contacts. If they cannot help, try the Car Rental Service at tel. 222999 or 224949.

● Money

Bear in mind that most credit cards are only sporadically accepted in China, outside the grand-luxe hotels of Canton and Beijing.

Thus most foreigners for the time being will find themselves using primarily the Foreign Exchange Certificates (FECs) issued by the Bank of China for travelers checks or foreign currency. These will be phased out soon, officials say. Bills should now be paid in FECs, which were issued in 1980 in an attempt to isolate the domestic economy from foreign exchange transactions. FECs are denominated in notes of 100, 50, 10, 5 and 1 *yuan*, and 5 and 1 *jiao*.

FECs are prized by local residents, who can use these notes to purchase goods at imported-goods Stores. This in part explains the presence of touts outside all major hotels, offering high premiums for FECs in exchange for national currency. Remember that such transactions are illegal, and that the local money (*renminbi*, or people's money) is not accepted from foreigners in payment for, say, hotel bills, air and rail tickets. Some major hotels simply double their rates for *renminbi* payments.

Renminbi can be used, however, for purchases by foreigners in some shops and restaurants. Its basic unit is the *yuan*, which breaks down into 10 *jiao* (also called *mao*). There are 10 *fen* to each *jiao* or *mao*. Bills: 10, 5, 2 and 1 *yuan*; coins, 5, 2 and 1 *fen*.

● Tipping

Tipping has been outlawed in China. Service charges are added to bills in the larger hotels. A few Shanghai cabbies and hotel workers now can bring themselves to accept small tips or gifts, but most still refuse.

● Communications

Telephoning is chancy, whether you're calling Nanking or New York. Hotel operators are helpful, but delays are common. If you're intent on making your own long-distance calls, dial 536266 for information on international calls and 116 for calls to other Chinese numbers.

Patience is a great virtue everywhere in Asia, but nowhere more useful than at the outgoing end of a Chinese phone line. And don't count on leaving messages for contacts who are out of their rooms or offices: somehow these rarely get passed on by hotel clerks.

Telex communications work reasonably well. The business center at the Jinjiang Hotel is small and generally ill-equipped by foreign standards, but the staff on occasion is helpful. The Jinjiang telex machines are do-it-yourself. Shanghai's main telex center is near the Peace Hotel, is open 24 hours a day and has a section for foreigners that also has self-service telex machines.

Postal services are slow but reasonably sure. Most hotels have small postal counters which enable visitors to evade long postoffice lines.

● What to wear

Spring and fall in Shanghai resemble those seasons in Paris or New York, but summers are steamy and winters are bonechilling. Central heating is rare, particularly in offices, so dress warmly. Ties and jackets are worn by businessmen from October to April or May, and safari suits are useful during the summer.

Foreign women will notice that their Shanghai counterparts have a higher sense of fashion than is found elsewhere in China. Beauty shops are found more frequently here as well, though customers have to endure a certain amount of staring. One salon, on Nanjing Road near the Park Hotel, attracts wondering crowds to its windows all day.

● Languages

Most business contacts will speak at least some English, but once talk gets technical be prepared to shift to interpreters. And be prepared as well for flaws in interpretation: some interpreters are much better than others.

Mandarin (*Putunghua*) is officially

spoken in Shanghai, just as it is elsewhere in China, but the guttural, sibilant Shanghai dialect is far more commonly used. Little English is spoken outside the larger hotels and shops, though in the city center, many shop signs are in English as well as Chinese.

English speakers and signs in English can be found at the airport and in the railway station, and many visitors strolling along the Bund will be accosted by students hoping to practice their English.

To avoid uncertainties, however, it's best to ask hotel staffers to write out destinations in Chinese.

● Doing business

*Shanghai's older hotels haven't yet geared themselves to aid business men and women, though the new hotels will include business centers equal to those in other Asian hotels. The Peace and Jinjiang hotels offer access to telex facilities, however, and a service center of sorts exists in the Jinjiang complex.

*Formed in 1983, the Service Center for Overseas Traders (SCOT) is semi-concealed in a building across the street from the hotel, 58 Mowming Road, tel. 370660, telex 33012 BTHJC CN. It offers a half-hearted commercial library, a few aged typewriters (Chinese as well as English), and a fairly helpful staff. SCOT will find translators on request.

*Another organization intended to help foreign businessmen is the Shanghai sub-council of the China Council for the Promotion of International Trade, 27 Zhongshan East Road, tel. 210–7221, telex 33280 SCPIT CN. It's the local version of a Chamber of Commerce.

*One of the few consulting agencies in the East China area is Shanghai Industrial Consultants, with two offices in the city: Room 109, 49 Sichuan Road, tel. 211818 and 231747, telex 33102 SICFU CN; and suite 101, Jingan Guest House, 370 Hua Shan Road, tel. 563050, ext. 101, telex 33148 SICIS CN. A non-governmental

operation, it offers trade consultation for both Chinese and foreign firms, has a mini-computer for data processing and other modern office machinery, slide projectors and video recorders. SIC can organize business conferences, including the furnishing of interpreters, meeting rooms, hotel and air reservations, and local transport.

*Business hours are from 08:00 to 12:00 and 14:00 to 18:00 Mondays through Saturdays.

*Temporary office space is almost impossible to find. Until the many promised new office buildings come on stream, hotel rooms will continue to double as offices.

*Always carry business cards with your name and firm in Chinese on the reverse. Use the so-called simplified characters in China, not the traditional characters still used in Taiwan.

Guanxi, or connections, are perhaps more important in Shanghai than other trade centers. Items unobtainable elsewhere, a bureaucratic favor, a key introduction: all can be arranged with the help of the right connection. Foreigners find themselves joining the *Guanxi* network almost on arrival—or sometimes before, when a request arrives for a couple of new pop tapes from Hong Kong or New York. In Shanghai, *quid pro quo* becomes high art. Bribery? Heaven forbid.

■ Useful phone numbers

● Diplomatic Missions:

Australia, 565050, ext. 301.
France, 377414.
Germany (West), 379951.
Japan, 372073.
Poland, 370952.
USA, 379880.

● **National import and export corporations:**

Animal Byproducts, 215630.
Arts and Crafts, 21200.
Foodstuffs, 216233.
Cereals and Oils, 219760.
Chemicals, 211540.
Foreign Transport, 213103.
Light Industry, 216858.
Machinery, 215066.
Metals and Minerals, 211220.
Silk, 215770.
Textiles, 218500.

● **Banks:**

Bank of China, 217466.
Bank of East Asia, 216863.
Banque Nationale de Paris, 582582, ext. 58142.
Bank of Overseas Chinese, 213176.
Bank of Tokyo, 582582, ext. 58135.
Chartered Bank, 218858.
Hongkong & Shanghai Bank, 218383.

Industrial Bank of Japan, 582582, ext. 58238.
People's Bank of China, 217466.
People's Insurance Co., 217466.

● **Travel:**

Cathay Pacific, 532582, ext. 123.
China International Travel Service, 217200.
Civil Aviation Administration of China (CAAC), domestic reservations, 535953; and International Reservations, 532255.
Hongqiao Airport Inquiries, 537664.
Japan Air Lines, 378467.
Pan Am, 563050.

● **Emergencies:**

Shanghai No.1 Hospital, 240100.

● **Taxis:**

Friendship Taxi, 536363. Municipal Taxi, 564444.

Shopping

Shoppers love Shanghai, and vice versa. The range of products is China's largest: clothing and shoes, radios and televisions, books and prints and bicycles and sewing machines. Many clerks in most shops speak at least a bit of English, and in the larger stores special sections are set aside for foreigners.

It's not true that all of Shanghai is one huge department store, but it seems that way at times. The dedicated shopper can start at the huge Friendship Store, at the north end of the Bund, then prowl Nanking Road along the five kilometers from the Bund to the Exhibition Center, and finally return to the Bund via Huaihai Road. Merely walking this stretch, however, will take up much of a day in itself. Along the way are the huge department stores taken from their capitalist owners after China's Communists won power in 1949, medium-sized specialty shops, and smaller stores as well.

Most visitors don't have the time for leisurely strolls—and fascinating though Nanjing Road may be, walking it during shopping hours is as scrimmagey as rush hour in a Manhattan or Paris subway. Instead, many visitors prefer the Friendship Store, which has a broad selection of handicrafts (including cashmere sweaters and scarves, silks and down-filled jackets) as well as rugs and wooden furniture and screens.

Other useful 'one-stop' stores such as the above are the Exhibition Hall on Yenan West Road, and the Chinese Arts and Crafts Store near the Park Hotel on Nanjing Road. All these shops will crate and ship purchases.

Shanghai's antique stores no longer hold the array of treasures of pre-war years, but are still worth a long visit. There's a large antique store attached to the Chinese Arts and Crafts Store on Nanjing Road, but a personal preference is the Antique and Curio Store at 218 Guangdong Road: good selection and pleasant staffers. Red or brown wax seals attest to the official authenticity of the wares.

Books and writing instruments are an old Shanghai specialty. Try the Foreign Languages Bookshop at 402 Fuzhou Road, or the Xinhua Bookstore on Nanjing Road. Fine stationery shops and seals can be found at Duoyunxuan, 422 Nanjing East Road (tel. 223410). Another lovely old shop is Lazhouhuchen, which specializes in writing brushes and inksticks, on Fuzhou Road.

Shanghai has two top department stores: No. 1, on Nanjing Road, with an enormous range of products, boasts that it serves 200,000 customers a day; Store No. 10, also on Nanjing Road, and formerly known as Wing On, is undergoing a complete renovation scheduled to end soon, at which time the store will be renamed Xinan.

For the curious, the Shanghai No. 1 Foodstore on Nanjing Road offers an intriguing variety of specialties including Sichuan white fungus, Henan dogmeat and Guangdong beetles.

◗ Hotels

Shanghai's hotels were once among Asia's best, but those luxurious days are long past. Until very recently, accommodations here lagged behind what's available in Guangzhou and Beijing. Now, Sheraton, Hilton, The Peninsula Group and Hyatt are moving in, but space in the mid-Eighties remains at a premium. Too many rooms are occupied by block-booked tourist groups: foreign business travelers were largely ignored unless they had the necessary local connection (*Guanxi*).

But relief is on the way. Sheraton opened the Hua Ting Hotel in 1986. The Jing An Hilton is scheduled to open in late 1987, and there will be a Hyatt in town by mid-1988. A Peninsula Group hotel is to open in 1989. There are reports that another 10 new hotels are scheduled.

Hua Ting Sheraton, 1200 Cao Xi Bei Lu, tel. 386000, telex 33589 SH HTH CN. New, with five restaurants and cafes including French, Chinese and English food, health club with tennis, bowling and a pool and full business center.

Shanghai Hilton, Hua Shan Road, opening soon, enquiries to sales office at Hong Kong Hilton, tel. 5–233111.

Executive floors, business center, central location, health club with squash, tennis and pool, roof restaurant, underground parking.

Hyatt Shanghai, opening mid-1988, enquiries to sales office at Hyatt Regency Hong Kong, tel. 3–662321. Five restaurants and bars, business center, health club with pool and sauna.

Here is some data on the older sisters of these bright new debutantes. Remember to triple-confirm reservations before arriving. Be warned that cables and telexes are regularly ignored at older Shanghai hotels.

Cypress Hotel (Longbai Fandian), 2419 Hongqiao Road, tel. 329388. Near the airport and 30 minutes from central Shanghai, this newish resort-style hotel has a handsome garden setting and Western and Chinese Restaurants.

International Hotel (Guiji Fandian), 170 Nanjing West Road, tel. 225225. A pre-war veteran, the International (once the Park) is nicely located in the city center but overflows with tour groups. Service and food very casual.

Jingan Guest House, 370 Huashan Road, tel. 563050. Another veteran of pre-war Shanghai, also located in the city's center, but far more comfortable than the International. Nicely appointed rooms with full air-conditioning, good restaurants and willing service.

Jinjiang Hotel, 58 Mowming South Road, tel. 534242. Preferred by most business travelers, the Jinjiang compound includes four buildings and two gardens and is located in what once was the French concession. Formerly an apartment complex, the buildings themselves are handsome and the rooms (720 of them) fairly comfortable. The 11th-floor restaurant offers good Sichuan food, and there are several shops in the compound. Business center across the street.

Peace Hotel (Heping Fandian), 20 Nanjing East Road, tel. 211244. In the Twenties and Thirties, the Cathay Hotel was Shanghai's fanciest, and traces of that vanished grandeur linger in the renamed place. But the staff's manners need mending, as does most of the furniture. Located on the Bund, the hotel's 8th-floor restaurant offers a wonderful view of the river. Legend says that Noel Coward wrote his play *Private Lives* in four days here. He wouldn't recognize the place today.

Shanghai Hotel (Shanghai Bingguan), 505 Wulumgi Road, tel. 312312, telex 33022 BTHSGA CN. The city's newest, geared to mass tourism, with 600 rooms in its 23-story tower. More than a dozen dining areas of varying quality, scanty shopping arcade, post office.

Xijao Guesthouse (Xijao Bingguan), 1921 Hongqiao Road, tel. 379643, telex 33004 BTHHQ CN. The compound includes several villas set in spacious gardens and is located near the airport, about half an hour from downtown Shanghai. Boating and fishing in its private pond, Chinese and Western food in its restaurant. Originally built for VIPs and very expensive.

Restaurants

Shanghai cuisine is a favorite all over China: its oily texture and slightly sweet taste makes it distinctive, though at least a few foreigners may find the sweetness disconcerting. Cooks here have an abundance of fresh vegetables and seafood to draw on, and a proper Shanghai restaurant will offer a menu leaning heavily on the latter.

A particularly favored delicacy is freshwater crab, in season from mid-October through early January. Another is eel, usually eaten in May and June. And the 'drunken chicken' soaked in wine before cooking, is worth a try.

In general, the major hotels have pretty fair restaurants, notably the Sichuan food at Jingan Guest House. Usually, hotels offer both Western and Chinese food. As is true elsewhere in China, dining hours are earlier than customary in the West. Lunch runs from 10:30 to 13:00 and supper from 16:30 to 19:30.

As well as eating at the large restaurants, find time to drop in at one of the many smaller food shops to try steamed dumplings (*jaudza*), for which Shanghai is famous. These come stuffed with pork, beef or seafood—rather like a fat ravioli—and are dangerously addictive.

And in the Yuyuan Bazaar (on Yuyuan Lu, just south of the central shopping area) many local specialties are available: dumplings (of course), spring rolls, sesame cakes, deep-fried dough sticks (*youtiao*), five-flavor beans (*wuxiangdou*), noodles, spiced beancurd and pear syrup candy (*ligaotang*). At night, there's a food bazaar at nearby Lishui Road.

A heritage of the century of foreign rule is the huge number of bakeries and cake shops selling very tasty lemon meringue pies and creamy cakes. Try the Deda Xicaishe (founded in 1897) at 359 Sichuan Road (near the Peace Hotel), or the Donghai Fandian (opened in the Thirties) at 143 Nanjing East Road.

● Chinese

Chengdu Restaurant, 795 Huaihai Road, tel. 376412. Good Sichuan food.

Huating Restaurant, 62 Songshan Road, just off Huaihai Road, tel. 263998. Good Western and Chinese food. Excellent service.

Luyangcun Restaurant, 763 Nanjing Road, tel. 537221. This old Shanghai favorite opened in 1931 and specializes in Sichuan and Jiangsu dishes. Good seafood too. Try the ham in honey sauce. Friendly service.

Meilongzhen Restaurant, 1081 Nanjing West Road, tel. 562718. A well-known Sichuan-style restaurant that boasts more than 200 specialties. Try the crispy chicken, Longyuan beancurd and smoked duck.

Old Town Restaurant (Lao Fandian), 242 Fuyou Road, tel. 289850. Located in the heart of the old Chinese city, Lao Fandian serves very good Shanghai dishes. Among its best: crisp roast duck, steamed carp and dumplings. Banquets can be arranged in the nearby Yu Garden.

Tianjin Guan, 1029 Huaihai Road, tel. 373992. Excellent Tianjin-style dumplings.

Xinya, 719 Nanjing East Road, tel. 224393. Another famed oldtimer, this one specializes in Cantonese food of high quality. Good service.

Yangzhou Restaurant, 308 Nanjing East Road, tel. 222779. Straightforward, high-quality Shanghai specialties.

● Western

Many hotel restaurants offer more-or-less accurate versions of Western food, and the inevitable fast-food palaces are coming to Shanghai. But there's a hardy survivor of the old days that's particularly worth a try.

The Red House, 37 Shaanxi South Road, tel. 565748. Located at the corner of what used to be Avenue Roi Albert and rue Bourgeat in the old French concession, the Red House opened its doors in 1935 as Chez Rovere, and became Chez Louis in 1945. After the communist government took power in 1949, it was renamed the Red House 'because of its exterior colour only', as its ads state. On the menu: clams in garlic sauce, beefsteak with mustard sauce, crêpes Suzette and souffle's Grand Marnier. Reservations advised.

▶ After hours

'Joy, gin and jazz,' says an old Shanghai guidebook: 'There's nothing puritanical about Shanghai.' But that was long ago: Shanghai nights now lean to tea and noodles. True, some travelers report plucking an occasional blossom of the night, but these tales usually involve overseas Chinese. Caucasians tend to spend their nights reviewing marketing strategies.

Exceptions? A few, in fact. The lobby coffee shop at the Peace Hotel turns into a jazz club from 20:30 to 23:00, and the music's not bad. The band consists of local musicians, some of whom claim to have played in nightclubs here after the war. Drinks are served and dancing occurs sporadically. Occasionally, there's jazz at the Jinjiang Hotel as well: ask the desk clerks. And the Jinjiang is scheduled to open a fancy US$500,000 disco soon. Its decor? 'Nouvelle Chinese', says its developer.

The disco fad moved into Shanghai about five years ago and local kids picked up on it quickly. Musicians are local but dancing styles are very Western indeed. There are discos of sorts at the International, Shanghai and Jingan—remember that everything closes down at 23:00.

There are bars and coffee shops along Nanjing Road as well as at the hotels, and these offer a good way to meet the younger Shanghainese. Foreigners are still very much objects of curiosity and you'll find yourself instantly popular. But don't mistake friendly conversation for a come-on.

Sights and sounds

The Bund. Much of Shanghai's history over the past century is summed up in this stirring riverside promenade, its legacy of colonial-style office buildings lined up facing the freighter-jammed river. In capitalist days, these huge buildings housed banks, trading firms and hotels; now, most have been transformed into government offices. At the northern end is the pleasant park famed for the sign that supposedly barred entrance to 'Dogs and Chinese', but which in fact never existed. (Despite this, the current sign, put up by the city government, perpetuates the legend.)

Jade Buddha Temple, 170 Anyuan Road. Famous for two jade statues brought from Burma before the turn of the century, the temple also displays several other jade images of the Buddha, as well as ancient statuary and scrolls. Daily Buddhist services, a good vegetarian restaurant and even an antique shop.

Longhua Pagoda and **Temple**, 2887 Longhua Road, southern suburbs. Built in 977, during the Song Dynasty, the seven-story octagonal pagoda is one of the nation's architectural treasures. The nearby temple consists of five ornate halls and drum and bell towers and dates back to the Ching Dynasty. Handsome gardens.

Lu Xun Museum, Hongkou Park. Dedicated to the memory of an early Twentieth Century writer and revolutionary, the display includes his residence, his tomb and a memorial hall.

Renmin (Peoples) Park, Nanjing Road. Once the old Shanghai race course, the flowery park is something of an oasis of calm for exhausted Nanjing Road shoppers, among others. The old grandstand and clubhouse now house the Municipal Library.

Shanghai Botanical Gardens, Longhua Lu. Built in 1954, the garden has a good general display and specializes in miniature trees—some of the latter being several hundred years old.

Shanghai Art and History Museum, 16 Henan Nan Lu, tel. 280160. A world-class collection of Chinese paintings, porcelain and pottery, and some superb bronzes as well. Well worth a careful inspection.

Port of Shanghai. A daily four-hour trip up the Huangpu River to its point of junction with the Yangtze aboard a pleasant-enough tour vessel, offering a great view of the city skyline, waterfront and dock area. Tickets on waterfront near Peace Hotel at Huangpu River Sightseeing, tel. 212098.

Xujiahui Cathedral, 158 Puxi Road, Xujiahuigu, tel. 371218. Closed during the Cultural Revolution but now offering regular services, it is Shanghai's largest Catholic Church and was built in 1906 as the Catholic Cathedral and Seminary of St. Ignatius.

Yuyuan Garden, Yuyuan Road. Shanghai's finest classical Chinese garden, of the Suchow school, built during the Ming Dynasty. Pavillions, bizarre rockeries, pool and artificial hills create a garden complex much loved by the Shanghainese. A small lake is spanned by a zigzag bridge leading from the park to a famed dumpling shop located in the wonderful market area just outside the gardens. The Yuyuan area is located in the Old Chinese City, itself an interesting area in which to wander.

Weekends

Songjiang, about 43 kilometers southwest of Shanghai. The Square Tower, a wooden building first errected in 949 during the Han Dynasty, was rebuilt a century later under the Northern Song Dynasty. Unusual for its square shape and height, it stands next to a glazed tile wall, built during the Ming Dynasty, that features a monster planning to eat the sun. Also worth seeing is the lovely Ching Dynasty garden of writer Gu Da-Shen, located just outside the west gate of Songjiang Town.

Jiading County, 25 kilometers northwest of Shanghai. In Jiading City are memorial tablets and steles of an ancient Song Dynasty Confucian temple. Near Huilong pond is the Garden of Autumn Clouds, once a scholar's haven.

Hangzhou. One of China's loveliest cities frames the beautiful West Lake, painted so often by artists down through the centuries. Hangzhou was the capital of the Southern Sung Dynasty in the 12th and 13th Centuries and much of its ancient character remains. The Hangzhou Hotel, now operated by the Shangri La hotel group, is recommended. (Huanghu North Road, tel. 22921.) Reachable by train from Shanghai in about three hours.

Suzhou. Settled first more than 3,000 years ago, Suzhou is on the Grand Canal and its network of smaller waterways has reminded visitors of Venice since the days of Marco Polo. Famed among Chinese for the beauty of its women, its superb gardens and flourishing silk industry, Suzhou is one of China's most beautiful cities.

Singapore

Synergistic Singapore

Singapore is in fact an Asian city, but not at first glance. Its shiny new skyscrapers, thousands of government-built apartments, clean streets and near-neurotic passion for organization all make it seem more of an Oriental Zurich than what it really is: one of the world's most complex and driven societies.

Just behind its 21st-Century façade is a synergistic mixture of races and religious lifestyles; 2.5 million Singaporeans (Chinese, Malay, Indians and Europeans) squeezed into an island republic of 618 square kilometers. Independent since 1965, when Prime Minister Lee Kuan Yew yanked his state out of Malaysia and made it a nation, Singapore then went through two decades of startling growth that came to an abrupt halt in 1985. No one doubts that Singapore will cope with the turn-around, and rather sooner than later.

During that stunning takeoff, per-capita income rose to US$6500 (second only to Japan in Asia). About 80% of its people live in comfortable, inexpensive government subsidized apartments (and those who don't mostly have costly private homes or condominiums). There is one telephone for every three people in the country, a television set for every five, a public bus for every 313 and a doctor for every 1060. Medical care, communications, transportation and port facilities are among the world's best—and 85% of the population is literate.

How did Lee and his Political Action Party (PAP) do it? Lee, a brilliant and disciplined Cambridge-educated lawyer, built on the British-conceived theory that Singapore should be the region's economic heart. Today it is the area's dynamo for communications, finance, commerce, travel and shipping. Starting in 1965, the economy grew at an annual average of 7% until 1985. Lee galvanized the republic with an almost Confucian, rigorously disciplined system of government. One example: Trucks must carry lights on their rooftops that blink as soon as the vehicles go over the speed limit, beckoning the hordes of Singapore police—who also hand out extraordinarily stiff fines for littering, jaywalking, gambling and spitting.

Regular big-brotherly newspaper and television campaigns preach productivity and courtesy and coax the Chinese majority to speak Mandarin Chinese instead of their regional dialects. Even Singapore's once-anarchy-loving cabbies now behave almost like little lambs (but how they grumble).

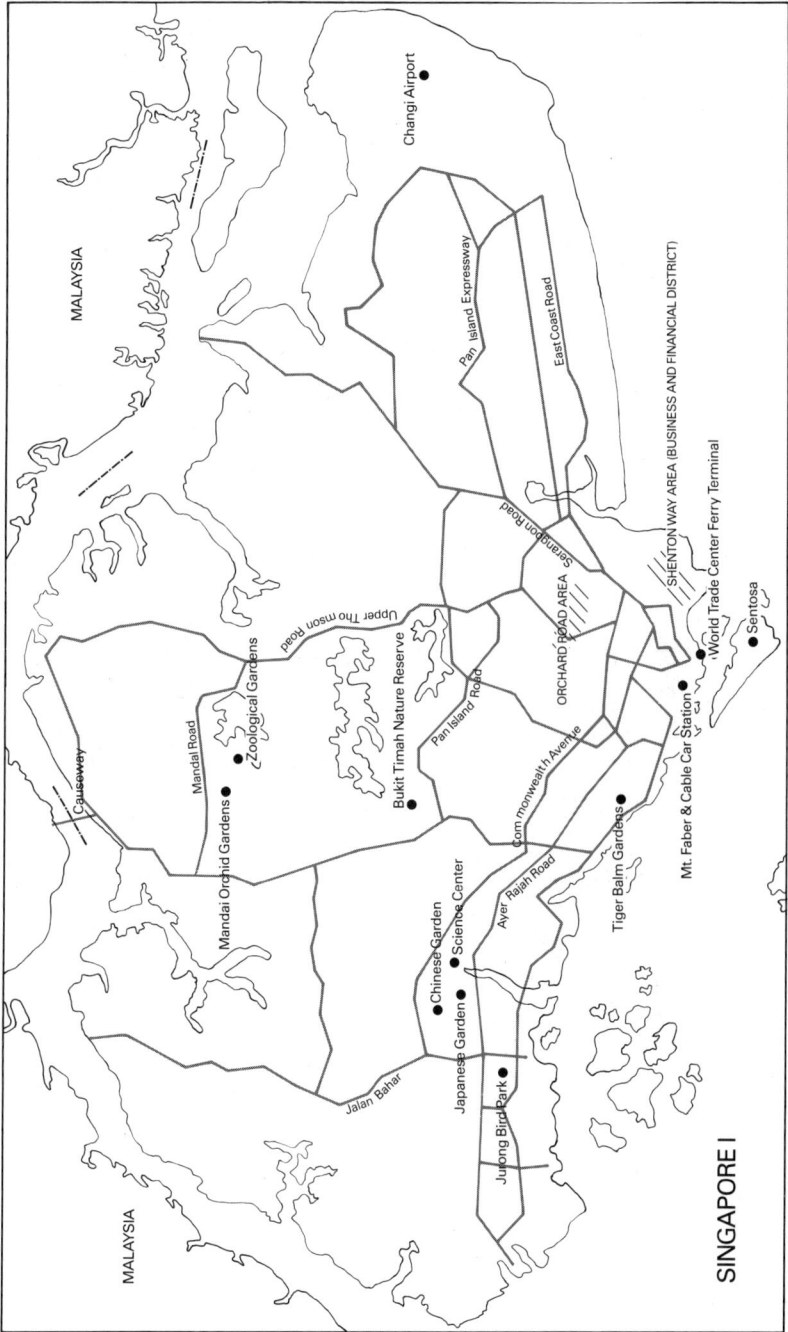

MALAYSIA

Changi Airport

Pan Island Expressway

East Coast Road

SHENTON WAY AREA (BUSINESS AND FINANCIAL DISTRICT)

Serangoon Road

World Trade Center Ferry Terminal

Sentosa

ORCHARD ROAD AREA

Upper Thomson Road

Bukit Timah Nature Reserve

Mt. Faber & Cable Car Station

Pan Island Road

Mandai Road

Zoological Gardens

Commonwealth Avenue

Mandai Orchid Gardens

Causeway

Tiger Balm Gardens

Ayer Rajah Road

Science Center

Chinese Garden

Japanese Garden

Jalan Bahar

Jurong Bird Park

MALAYSIA

SINGAPORE I

Not every Singaporean admires Lee and his policies, and there have been traces recently of at least the beginning of reasoned dissent to some of his more outrageous ideas. But the efficient, corruption-free bureaucracy that has emerged over the Lee years makes doing business here almost a pleasure, in contrast to the freewheeling ways of some neighbors. A bright new group of younger politicians has emerged, the austerity of the Seventies is yielding to a certain punk-mod influence, and at least a degree of criticism of the PAP pops up in the supervised local press. As Singapore works to cope with the sudden economic slowdown of the mid-Eighties, change seems very much on the horizon. But in which direction?

◖ Spotlight

Western businessmen feel more at home in Singapore than anywhere else in Asia, with the possible exception of Hong Kong. The formal stiffness of Tokyo, the Byzantine negotiations of nearby Jakarta or Kuala Lumpur, or the labyrinthine red tape of China, barely exist here. That Westernized first impression is a much truer reflection of actuality: the skyscrapers, modern offices and hotels, tidy streets and excellent communications are all evidence of the republic's go-ahead attitude.

For many European and American firms, Singapore's advantages are an old and respected story. The strategic location, political stability and well-known efficiency all combine to make Singapore a natural headquarters for many multinationals. Many senior government and business officials were educated and trained in Britain, Australia or the United States, and they have put that training into action. When, for example, it was decided to set up a gold and futures exchange, officials and traders were sent to the Chicago Mercantile Exchange for training. When SIMEX went into operation in 1984, Chicago experts were brought in to ensure a smooth startup.

A specifically American attitude many Singaporeans display is a distinct dislike for 'bullshit'. 'Talk straight with people here', advises one expatriate. 'Approach them with the assumption that they know as much as you do about the issue at hand. They probably do.' Nor is corruption much of a problem. Foreigners with shady propositions may in fact find themselves quickly escorted to the next flight out.

Don't talk business at social gatherings—of which there are apt to be plenty. Singaporeans enjoy their evenings out, but business deals are for office discussion. Nor is it wise to joke about local political or social foibles: Singaporeans may be sarcastic about their politicians, but they are proud of their republic and dislike outside criticism.

And Westernized though many businessmen may seem, the Chinese concept of 'face' remains very important. Never put a local aquaintance in a position where he might be publicly embarrassed. You'll lose your deal, you'll lose a friend, you'll do your own reputation no good at all.

● Arriving

Singapore's famous efficiency starts with arrival at its new, nicely engineered Changi International Airport. This is one of the very best airports in the world and boasts a wide range of facilities—including a supermarket if you've forgotten to bring home the bacon. Immigration and customs facilities are minimal and there are plenty of luggage carts available to scoop up your baggage—which arrives with the speed (almost) of light.

There's a useful duty-free shop for arriving passengers, just past immigration, which sells liquors and tobacco at half the downtown prices.

Changi has a plentiful supply of taxis, which will whisk arrivals to their hotels in about half an hour and charge between US$10.00 and US$14.00, depending on destination. And the strict taxi queues themselves are another example of Singapore's abhorrence of cheerful Asian anarchy: the republic is *organized*.

It's also tough. Like neighboring Malaysia, Singapore hangs drug traffickers.

● Orientation

Singapore is a republic, independent since 1965, located between the Malayan Peninsula and the Indonesian archipelago. Small (618 square kilometers) and situated just north of the Equator, its population of 2.5 million is about 78% Chinese, 15% Malay and 6% Indian.

● Transportation

There are plenty of taxis in Singapore, and fares are moderate, though there are occasional surcharges (night rates, baggage, airport extras) that may cause an occasional (but very mild surprise). Most drivers speak enough English to cope with your requests. In the government-demarcated Central Business District (CBD), there are scattered official queueing stations, but one can sometimes flag down a cab off-station.

Renting a car is simple enough, but avoid the airport firms: rates are lower in the city. Traffic is well-controlled. Ask the rental agent to explain the city's complicated car-park system. And remember that government, in order to minimize traffic in the CBD between 07:30 and 10:15, requires that autos carrying fewer than four riders purchase a S$5 daily permit to enter the zone (taxis pay S$2).

Oddly, in this otherwise very modern city, public transport is shaky. Buses are battered and slow.

● Money

Change only small amounts at the airport; save larger transactions for the downtown moneychangers who offer far better rates. The Singapore dollar (for the past decade it has hovered at 2.1 to 2.2 to the US dollar) comes in denominations of S$1, S$5, S$10, S$20, S$50, S$100, S$500, S$1000 and S$10,000. Coins: 50 cents, 20 cents, 10 cents, 5 cents and 1 cent.

Banks ask for a passport when changing money; moneychangers don't. Banking hours: 10:00–15:00 weekdays, 09:30–11:30 Saturdays.

● Tipping

A 10% service charge is usually included on bills; leave any small change as well. Same goes for taxis. A dollar or two handed round at hotels when checking in will bring a smile, but Singaporeans are not tip-hungry.

● Communications

The leading hotels have business centers with all the latest telex and telefax equipment, and international direct dialing is possible from almost all rooms. The Singapore Telecoms office in Killiney Road is open 24 hours a day for overseas calls and accepts phoned telexes and cables at tel. 7343344.

The postal service is reliable. Post office hours: 08:30 to 17:00 Monday–Friday, 08:30 to 13:00 Saturday—but offices at Killiney Road and Changi airport are open every day 08:00 to 21:00 (Sundays only, to 20:00).
Local phone calls are free.

● **What to wear**

Singapore is very tropical indeed. Temperatures year-round average around 30°C. During the day, humidity is about 85%. Wear light cottons and allow for regular changes. A short-sleeved shirt and tie is acceptable for office calls. Safari suits, perfectly okay in neighboring Indonesia and Malaysia, are not quite chic in snobby Singapore. Umbrellas are useful during the November–February monsoon rains.

● **Languages**

English, one of Singapore's three official languages, is widely if not beautifully spoken. The other official languages are Mandarin and Tamil, while Malay is the *national* language. Most Singaporeans speak at least two or three of the above, and also slip easily into one or more of the dozen dialects of Chinese and Indian languages to be heard here. Readers will find a good range of English titles in the MPH and Times bookshops.

● **Doing business**

*Business cards are useful. A Chinese translation on the back of your card is helpful.

*A useful address is the Economic Development Board, atop the World Trade Center (tel. 271–0844), which offers a broad range of advice to foreign businessmen.

*Many foreign embassies (notably Australia, France, West Germany, the United Kingdom and the United States) have well-stocked commercial libraries and competent trade advisers.

*There's plenty of new office space these days, even for short-term renters. World-Wide Business Centers (tel. 336–6577) has a daily/weekly/monthly rental service.

■ Useful phone numbers

● **Government agencies:**

Economic Development Board, 271–0844.
Institute of Standards and Industrial Research, 336–0933.
Monetary Authority, 222–5577.
Port of Singapore Authority, 271–2211.
Statistics Department, 533–6121.
Trade Development Board, 271–9388.
Tourist Promotion Board, 235–6611.

● **Trade and commerce organizations:**

British Council, 533–7644.
Chinese Chamber of Commerce and Industry, 337–8381.
Convention Bureau of Singapore, 235–6611.
Federation of Chambers of Commerce and Industry, 338–9761.
Indian Chamber of Commerce and Industry, 222–2855.
International Chamber of Commerce, 224–1255.
International Monetary Exchange, (SIMEX), 278–6363.
Japanese Chamber of Commerce and Industry, 221–0541.
Malay Chamber of Commerce and Industry, 221–1066.
Manufacturer's Association, 278–5211.
Pakistan Chamber of Commerce and Industry, 222–0723.
Stock Exchange, 220–9455.

● **Airlines:**

Aeroflot, 532–6711.
Air India, 220–5277.
Air Nauru, 222–6738.

Air New Zealand, 918–266.
Air Niugini, 250–4858.
ALIA, 292–1188. Alitalia, 737–6966.
Balkan, 264–2748.
Bangladesh Biman, 912–306.
British, 253–8444.
Cathay Pacific, 911–811.
China, 737–2144.
Czechoslovak, 737–9844.
Garuda, 250–5666.
Japan, 221–0522.
KLM, 737–7211.
Korean, 221–1333.
Lufthansa, 737–4444.
Malaysian, 336–6777.
Pakistan, 737–3233.
Pan American, 220–0488.
Philippine, 336–1611.
Qantas, 737–3744.
Royal Brunei, 235–4672.
Royal Nepal, 225–7575.
Sabena, 221–7010.
Saudi Arabian, 235–5660.
SAS, 225–1333.
Singapore, 223–8888.
Swissair, 737–7004.
Tarom, 338–1467.
Thai, 224–2024.
UTA, 737–7166.
Yugoslav (JAT), 235–3017.

● Embassies and Missions:

Argentina, 235–4231.
Australia, 737–9311.
Austria, 235–4088.
Bangladesh, 250–6323.
Belgium, 220–7677.
Brazil, 734–3435.
Brunei, 474–3393.
Bulgaria, 737–1111.
Burma, 235–8704.
Canada, 737–1322.
Chile, 223–8577.
Denmark, 250–3383.
Egypt, 737–1811.
Finland, 254–4042.
France, 466–4866.
Germany (West), 737–1355.
Greece, 220–8622.
Iceland, 777–7022.

India, 737–6809.
Indonesia, 737–7422.
Ireland, 916–377.
Israel, 235–0966.
Italy, 732–4822.
Japan, 235–8855.
Korea (North), 734–1737.
Korea (South), 256–1188.
Malaysia, 235–0111.
Netherlands, 737–1155.
New Zealand, 235–9966.
Norway, 220–7122.
Pakistan, 737–6988.
Panama, 221–8677.
Philippines, 737–3977.
Poland, 294–2513.
Romania, 468–3424.
Saudi Arabia, 734–5878.
Spain, 220–4222.
Sri Lanka, 254–4595.
Sweden, 734–2771.
Switzerland, 737–4666.
Thailand, 737–2644.
United Kingdom, 639–333.
USA, 339–0251.
USSR, 235–1834.

● Places of worship:

Anglican: St. Andrew's Cathedral, 337–6104.
Baptist: International Baptist Church, 466–4929.
Buddhist: Siong Lim Temple.
Catholic: Cathedral of the Good Shepherd, 337–2036.
Hindu: Chettiar Temple, 737–9393.
Interdenominational: Salvation Army, 737–9122.
Jewish: Synagogue, 336–0692.
Muslim: Fatimah Mosque.
Methodist: 336–1433.
Presbyterian: 337–6681.
Seventh Day Adventist: 256–4571.
Taoist: 222–2651.

● Miscellaneous numbers:

Police, 999.
Fire Brigade, 995.
Ambulance, 995.

Emergency, 995.
Airport Flight Information, 542–5680.
Taxis: 452–5555, 268–4233.

International Calls (Prefixes):
  To Malaysia, 109.
  To the rest of the world, 104.
  Time, 1711.

Shopping

There's bad news for those who thought they'd left shopping centers behind in Frankfurt or Manchester or Scarsdale. Singapore adopted the idea a decade ago, with what can only be called overkill. Some shoppers enjoy the chance to browse for hours—and miles—in air-conditioned comfort. But space in the plazas is expensive, and prices reflect it. Perhaps the first sign of Singapore's economic crunch of the mid-Eighties was the rising tide of bankruptcies of the small shopholders in the plazas.

That said, the range of goods is enormous. There's just about every name-brand item from Europe, Japan or the United States on Singapore's shelves, and a fine selection of regional handicraft goods as well. There's batik from Indonesia (preferred) and Malaysia, silks and saris from China and India, jade and ivory and ceramics, woodcarvings—and of course gold, which can be purchased in rings and chains and bracelets at prices just a fraction over the daily market price.

Two cautionary notes: if you're going on to Hong Kong, prices on some items may be a bit better there. And in any case, don't hesitate to bargain. This is indeed a duty-free port, but prices have a way of sliding up and down just the same.

Perhaps the most popular shopping cluster is in the Orchard Road area. Tang's Department Store, next to the Dynasty Hotel, is a favorite of the chic set. Other shopping plazas in the area include: Scott's, Lucky, the Promenade, the Adelphi, Far East Plaza and Lang Court. (The latter specializes in Japanese goods.)

For good selections of regional crafts, try Arab Street, in the older part of town, which hasn't yet been subsumed by shopping malls. The small shops here have an interesting selection of crafts, including basketwork, batik and silks. For handicrafts from China, Thailand and Burma, investigate the Tanglin Shopping Center—and don't pass up the basement and sub-basement.

The Singapore Handicraft Center is another spot to inspect regional goods, these from the Philippines, Indonesia, India and the Middle East. Locally made goods are on sale here during the night market (Pasar Malam).

Singaporeans browse for gold at People's Park, on North Bridge Road in Chinatown. The shops in this area sell simple gold jewellery at prices based on the daily gold market. For fancier gold gifts, try the shopping plazas.

Many countries of the world now ban imports of ivory, crocodile and lizard items. Before you buy that lovely crocodile bag or ivory elephant, be sure you can bring it back home legally.

Note: Salespeople here aren't as pushy as they used to be. Nonetheless, you may feel a bit too heavily pressured along the way. If so, *walk out*. Don't hang around and argue. File a complaint with the Tourist Promotion Board, tel. 235–6611.

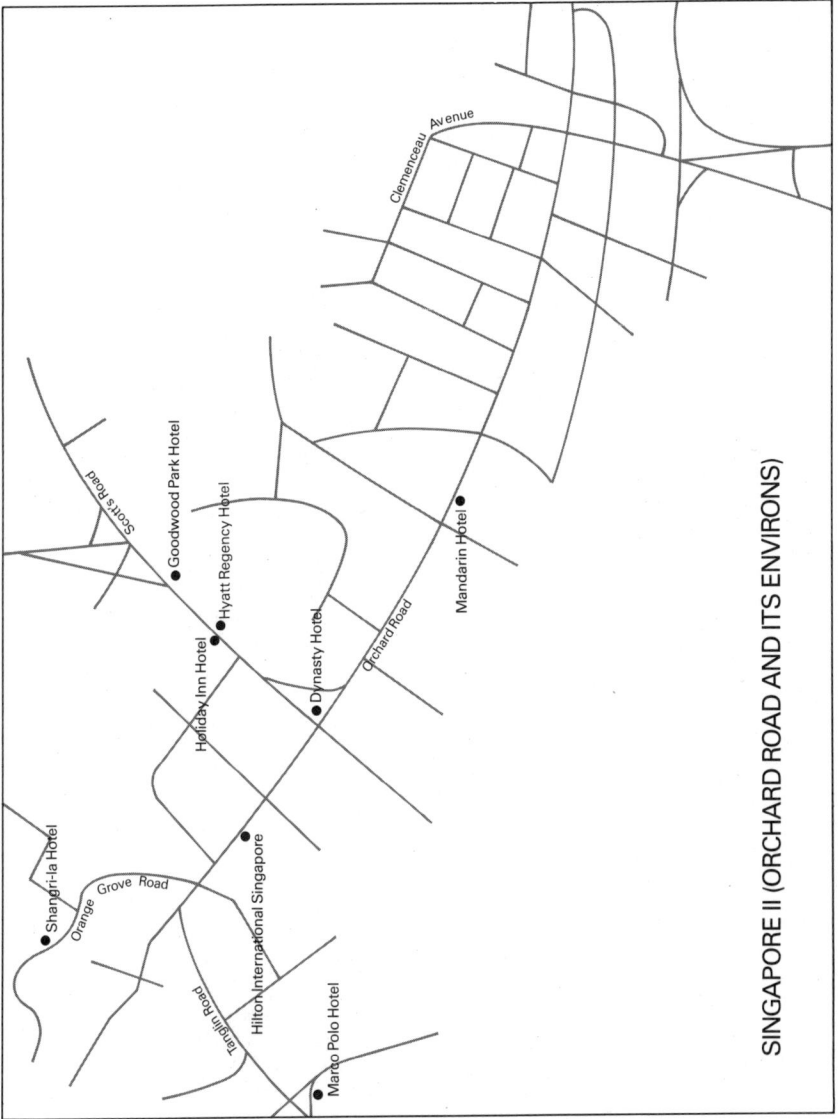

SINGAPORE II (ORCHARD ROAD AND ITS ENVIRONS)

Clemenceau Avenue

Scott's Road

Goodwood Park Hotel

Hyatt Regency Hotel

Holiday Inn Hotel

Dynasty Hotel

Orchard Road

Mandarin Hotel

Shangri-la Hotel

Orange Grove Road

Hilton International Singapore

Tanglin Road

Marco Polo Hotel

Hotels

Singapore, like Bangkok, has a definite oversupply of hotel rooms, and the situation will worsen in the later Eighties as still more new hotels come on stream. Thus, *bargain*. There are several varieties of packages and perks available and there is no reason not to take advantage of them.

The city offers an alternative to hotels, by the way. There are now plenty of service apartments available, which combine hotel services (phone answering, daily maid and laundry services, useful locations) with elements of private flats (video and sound systems, fully-equipped kitchens, dining rooms). For a longer-than-brief stay, costs may well be lower than a hotel. Among the better ones: **Ascott**, tel. 732–0033; **Plaza**, tel. 298–0011 and **Hotel New Otani**, 338–3333.

Note: Convention facilities are excellent in Singapore. Brand new complexes like Raffles City and Marina Square are of international class. Convention Bureau: tel. 235–6611.

Century Park Sheraton, Nassim Hill, tel. 737–9677. Quiet location, near Handicraft Center; disco, pool, Japanese tour groups.

Goodwood Park, 22 Scotts Road, tel. 737–7411. Built in 1899, turned into a hotel in 1929, just renovated (1984), elegant British-style rooms (half its 230-odd rooms are luxury suites), two pools and six restaurants. The superb Brunei suite is often occupied by the Sultan of Brunei...even though he controls the Royal Holiday Inn across the street. Old-style Asian elegance at its best.

Hilton, 581 Orchard Road, tel. 737–2233, telex 21491. Close to Orchard Road business and shopping area, renovated in early 1980s, rooftop pool, 12 executive suites by Parisian designer Hubert de Givenchy.

Hyatt Regency, 10/12 Scotts Road, tel. 733–1188, telex RS 24415. Another newly renovated hotel in the Orchard Road area. Good Italian food at Pete's Place, popular Chinoiserie disco, up-market shopping area nearby.

Marco Polo, 247 Tanglin Road, tel. 737–4411. A handsome member of Hong Kong's Peninsula group, regularly rated among the world's leading hotels, good restaurants and attentive service. Particularly attentive to businesswomen.

Meridien, 100 Orchard Road, tel. 733–8855. A new, very French hotel that offers excellent food, a pool with a restaurant alongside, and even the local branch of a well-known Paris department store.

New Otani, 177A River Road, tel. 338–3333, telex RS 20299 SINOTA. A recently opened affiliate of its well-known Tokyo namesake, it's located near the business district. Four restaurants, business center, pool and large shopping center.

Oriental, 6 Raffles Boulevard, Marina Square, tel. 338–0066, telex RS 29117, FAX 339–9537. Opened in early 1987. Member of Mandarin Oriental Hotel Group. Two restaurants and four bars, health club with pool and squash, business center, parking.

Park View Holiday Inn, Cuppage Road/Cavenagh Road, tel. 734–4448. Opened in 1985, the inn has a rooftop pool, three restaurants and coffee shop, as well as a shopping arcade.

Pavilion Intercontinental, 1 Cuscaden Road, tel. 733–8888, telex RS 37248. A pleasantly flowered atrium lobby, French and Cantonese restaurants, pool and health center.

Raffles, 13 Beach Road, tel. 337–8041. Singapore's best-known hotel, it overflows with atmosphere: Rudyard Kipling, Somerset Maugham and Joseph Conrad all stayed here during the palmy days. Try an original Singapore Sling, cast an eye at the Writer's Bar and the Elizabethan Grill, sip tea in the Palm Court and muse on the fleetness of time.

River View Hotel, Havelock Road, tel. 732-9922. A new hotel not far from the city's business center, there are three restaurants (Japanese, Chinese and Italian), a pool and disco.

Royal Holiday Inn, 25 Scotts Road, tel. 737-7966. An Austro-German emphasis with a 24-hour coffee house—and a Sichuan-style restaurant to spice the mixture. On the roof, a pool and minigolf.

Shangri-La, 22 Orange Grove Road, tel. 737-3644, telex SHANGLA RS 21505. A longtime favorite, now busy building new wings and perhaps losing a bit of its intimate atmosphere. Its

Japanese restaurant, Nadaman, remains the best in town.

Sheraton Towers, 39 Scotts Road, tel. 737-6888, telex RS 37750 SHNSIN. Six restaurants and bars, business center.

Westin Plaza, 2 Stamford Road, Raffles City, tel. 338-8585, telex RS 22206 RCHTLS, FAX 338-2862. Opened in 1986, it's part of what's already a regional landmark—the Raffles City Complex which includes many shops and restaurants, and huge conference facilities. The Westin Plaza itself offers eight restaurants and lounges, a health club with pools, tennis and squash courts, and a 24-hour business center.

Westin Stamford, Raffles City, tel. 338-8585, telex RS 22206 RCHTLS, FAX 338-2862. Opened in 1986. Fully equipped executive center, squash and tennis courts. Its 1,253 rooms help make this one of the tallest hotels in the world.

Restaurants

Singapore cuisine is enormously varied and enormously tasty. There are few greater pleasures here (or anywhere) than gathering friends around one of the tables in the city's famed hawker centers, heaping plates and eating to the bursting point. There's nothing fancy about the hawker centers save the food: all sorts of Indian, Malay and of course Chinese dishes, all made before your eyes and served hot and fresh, accompanied by superb fruit, heaps of rice and wonderful fruit or cane juice, or good cold local beer, to wash it all down. The government makes sure that high standards of hygiene are maintained. One favorite is at Newton Circus, not far from the Scotts Road Hotel area. Some prefer Rasa Singapura, behind the Handicrafts Center. Also very much worth a try is the so-called 'Satay Club' on the Esplanade.

● Dishes to try:

Satay: meat, chicken or seafood grilled on wooden skewers over charcoal and dipped into spicy peanut sauce.

Hainan chicken rice: steam-boiled white meat served with chilis, soy sauce and soup.

Kway Teow: thick Chinese noodles stir-fried with meat, bean sprouts and other ingredients.

Murtabak: an Indian omelette containing onion, chicken and lamb, fried, then dipped into a spicy cream sauce.

Laksa: noodles, rice cakes, prawns or oysters with a thick hot gravy.

*Fish-head curry: for reasons that escape a few Westerners, this is one of the city's great favorites, and it is exactly

what the name implies; a fish head, staring eyes, gills and all, cooked in a blend of spicy sauces. Connoisseurs claim the muscle around the eyeball is extremely tasty.

*Durian: this fruit, about the size of a green rugby ball and covered with nasty spikes, has such a revolting smell that hotels ban it from their rooms and aircraft won't let it be brought aboard. Its enthusiasts—and there are many—swear that its taste is superb and beyond words. Try it. (Warning: it's ill-making with liquor.)

The hawker centers are perfectly acceptable places to entertain clients—but for the less adventurous, here's a list of the more usual sort of restaurants:

Banana Leaf Apolo (sic): 56 Race Course Road, tel. 293–8682. and Muthu's Curry Restaurant, 76 Race Course Road (just down the road), tel. 293–2389. Tasty, spicy South Indian food, served on banana leaves and eaten with the hands (for purists), but dining tackle is available. Buffet style, Muslim approved, inexpensive.

Chico 'n' Charlie's, 5th floor. Liat Towers, tel. 734–1753. Popular with resident foreigners, serves steaks, chicken and Tex-Mex specials (enchiladas, tostadas, burritos). Excellent Margaritas. Reserve on weekends.

Happy Valley Seafood and Sharksfin Restaurant, Singapore Shopping Center, 190 Clemenceau Avenue, tel. 338–7286. One way to one-up Chinese contacts is to tell them you've a reservation at this superb but painfully expensive restaurant. Fine sharksfin soup, bear paws and drunken prawns, and a good wine list.

Luna Coffee House, Apollo Hotel, 405 Havelock Road, tel. 733–2081. One of Singapore's most unusual cuisines—and of the world's rarest—is the so-called 'nonya' food, a combination of South Chinese edibles and Malay spices. Pungent, delicious, with a distinctive, faintly sour echo, it's served here in daily luncheon buffets. Take a Singaporean friend to help explain the dishes, or else ask the friendly staff. Don't miss it.

Maharani, Far East Plaza, Scotts Road (next to Hyatt Regency), tel. 235–8840. Excellent North Indian food, though service is slow; small and usually crowded. Prices in high-moderate range.

Pete's Place, Hyatt Regency, 10–12 Scotts Road, tel. 733–1188. Good Italian food (pasta, pizza, veal, chicken) and a popular salad bar. Rich desserts at the dessert bar at Nutmeg's, upstairs. Reservations a must; moderate. Nutmeg's itself has a fine reputation for American-style cooking.

Pine Court, 35th floor of the Mandarin Hotel, 333 Orchard Road, tel. 737–4411. Beijing cuisine in elegant surroundings; noted for Beijing duck and baked tench (a fish), the perfect place to take a Chinese contact. Expensive.

Red House, 512 Upper East Coast Road, tel. 442–3112. Once on the sea, this old home has been landlocked by the reclamation program that has added 2,000 hectares to the republic since 1966. But the meaty chili crab is still superb (don't wear a white shirt!) and so is the *sotong* (fried baby squid). Beer available. Parking free but difficult. Inexpensive.

Le Restaurant de France, Hotel Meridien, 100 Orchard Road, tel. 733–8855. Perhaps Singapore's best Western restaurant; recommended by resident Frenchmen, plush Louis XV decor, fine wines, attentive service. Reservations recommended. Expensive.

Swatow Teochew Restaurant, Centrepoint Shopping Plaza (fifth floor), 176 Orchard Road, tel. 235–4717. The Teochew are one of the city's major Chinese ethnic groups and their special cuisine is served here in rich style. House favorites: pomegranate chicken, goose meat, stuffed crab claw, roast suckling pig. Lavish decor, Expensive.

After hours

The word on Singapore is that the night life is deathly: the word is wrong. Check the phone book: six solid pages of escort ads, ten of massage parlors. There are even two escort services that specialize in male escorts and guides for the ladies (High Society and Fair Lady). Big Chinese nightclubs abound. So do tiny hostess bars, where charges run about US$12 an hour for drinks and a dance.

Avoid the Desker Road redlight district, avoid Bugis Street (the rowdy transvestites of yesteryear have flounced away) and avoid cabbies touting thrills. And be wary at the Rasa Sayang bar in the Tropicana nightclub, on Scotts Road. Lighten up at the Jockey Pub in Shaw Tower, across the street. Better still, check the classier scenes, where Singapore residents turn up regularly.

> Note: A 10% service charge is routinely added to most bills. No more tipping is necessary.

Grand Palace Deluxe Nite (sic) Club: 1 Grange Road, Orchard Building, tel. 737–8922. Taiwanese, Singaporean and Malaysian singers backed by Filipino bands, lots of good-looking hostesses. Noisy and fun.

Hollywood East, Furama Hotel, 10 Eu Tong Sen Street, tel. 534–1181. A branch of the popular Hong Kong disco, young, loud and amusing. Opens at 20:00, moderate.

Matthew's, Orchard Tower, 400 Orchard Road, tel. 732–6000. Of all things, Country & Western music, from Singapore's own singing cowboy, Matthew Tan—who (with his band) has starred at Grand Ole Opry in Nashville, Tennessee. Guest musicians. Tex-Mex food. Moderate.

The Neptune, Overseas Union House, Collyer Quay, tel. 224–3922. Lavish Chinese nightclub revues, seats 1,200; expensive.

Peppermint Park, 4th floor, Parkway Parade Shopping Complex, 80 Marine Parade Road, tel. 344–5888. Three pop bands (usually Filipino). Disneyworldy decor including artificial rainstorms with taped thunder and crickets, icy air-conditioning. Recommendable as a hassle-free evening for women travelers. Moderate.

Rainbow, Ming Arcade, Cuscaden Road, tel. 733–3779. High-tech rock (three bands each evening), disco, dancing, a great place to meet people but it's difficult to hear them. Moderate.

Top Ten, Orchard Tower, 400 Orchard Road, tel. 732–3077. One of the newest spots, features big-name talent. Very popular. Expensive.

Sights and sounds

Chinatown: A colorful morning (and evening) market at Trengganu, Smith and Banda Streets, is worth an hour or two. Interesting shops on Temple and Sago streets, a large department store at the People's Park Complex. Fortune-tellers, herbal medicine vendors, pots and pans and sauces and oils, and the expectable assortment of curios.

Little India: Its center is Serangoon Road, where shops offer saris and silks, incense and jasmine and bangles and—just the thing for Aunt Em—a nose stud.

Arab Street: Batik, precious and semi-precious stones (be wary), cane and straw products, velvet Malay *songkoks* (caps), wood and brass work.

The Padang: Singapore's colonial core, a group of splendidly stodgy buildings left over from the days of 'Empah': the Cricket Club, Supreme Court, City Hall, Victoria Hall and St. Andrew's Cathedral. Nearby is the new, 8-meter-high fountain statue of the Merlion, a creature half-lion, half-fish, symbolizing Singapore's dual heritage. (Singa Pura means Lion City; Temasek (Sea Town) was the island's earliest recorded name).

Chinese and Japanese Gardens, Yuan Ching Road, Jurong. The Chinese Garden is spectacular, with a seven-story pagoda, pools full of fat lordly carp, bamboo groves and a pine forest. The Japanese Garden is subtler, meticulously arranged to create a feeling of peace.

Sentosa Island: Just south of Singapore Island, it can be reached by ferry or, more spectacularly, by cable car from Mt. Faber. Developed as a resort by the government, it has a golf course, small hotel, and a beach, all linked up by a 6-km monorail which circles the island. An old fortress, Ft. Siloso, can be visited, and there is a wax museum depicting scenes from Singapore's history as well as the two wartime surrenders.

Armenian Church: The oldest in town, it dates back to 1835, just 16 years after Sir Stamford Raffles got things moving in Singapore. A national monument, it is no longer used for services.

Haw Par Villa (Tiger Balm Gardens), Pasir Panjang Road. Grotesque statues from Chinese mythology. Not for the squeamish, or the tasteful.

Jurong Bird Park, Jalan Ahmad Ibrahim, tel. 265–0022. A lovely park with spectacular walk-in aviary that holds many free-flying rarities and a noisy manmade waterfall. Outside the aviary, talkative mynahs and parrots, vultures, flamingos, eagles and owls and lots, lots more. Wonderful.

MacCritchie Reservoir: enter from Lornie Road. The closest thing to a natural attraction on the island—tropical vegetation, wild monkeys, good jogging trails, hiking.

National Museum and Art Gallery, Stamford Road, tel. 337--6077. Houses the famed Haw Par jade collection, as well as prehistoric artifacts from Southeast and East Asia, fine ceramics, bronzes and articles of local historical interest.

Temple of 1000 Lights (Quian Fo Si), Race Course Road. A 15-meter-high statue of Buddha and a mother-of-pearl replica of Buddha's footprint.

Thian Hock Keng Temple (Tian Fu Gong), 158 Telok Ayer Street, tel. 222–2651. The city's oldest Chinese house of worship, built in 1840 to honor Ma Chu Poh, queen of heaven. The smoke of thousands of joss sticks, burned by grateful immigrants thanking her for safe passage, has thoroughly blackened the temple ceiling.

Zoological Gardens, Mandai Lake Road, tel. 269–3411. One of Southeast Asia's best, set in a pleasantly hilly landscape. Most animals are displayed cageless, including orangutans and gibbons and lions and hippos—and the otters will win your heart. Keep your eye open for Mousedeer.

▶ Weekends

Getting out of Singapore for a weekend means going to Malaysia or (less likely) Indonesia, but there are a lot of Singaporeans who have the same idea. Make your plans—and reservations—early. And be aware that the Johore causeway, which links Singapore and Malaysia, can be a most-annoying bottleneck as weekends begin and end.

For most getawayers, the destination is the beautiful east coast of peninsular Malaysia. And to avoid the causeway nuisance, it's possible to fly by Singapore Airlines subsidiary Trade Winds (tel. 222–4611) in 50 minutes, from Seletar Air Base in Singapore to Pulau Tioman, an island that offers fine beaches, fishing and water skiing. (The flight saves a four-hour drive plus three-hour boat trip.) Another popular island, Pulau Rawa, is a bit more rustic and does not have an airstrip. Thus, it takes seven hours to get there.

Slightly closer and a bit busier is Desaru beach resort, about two and a half hours by car or bus from Singapore. There's also a ferry, from Changi Point, that links with a Desaru bus which is faster and pleasanter. Two hotels, the Desaru View (Singapore tel. 737–5570). Beach chalets (about US$100 daily for four) can be rented by phoning Kota Tinggi, Malaysia (07/838–240): these have kitchenettes.

Desaru has a beach that's 16 kilometers long, an outstanding 18-hole golf course designed by Robert Trent Jones (wild monkeys love golf balls: be alert), good windsurfing and sailboarding.

Further north, there's a Club Méditerranée branch at Cherating, Asia's first.

Note: Cars rented in Singapore are not allowed to enter Malaysia. For the trip, take a bus or cab or train across the causeway, then rent a car in Johore Bahru on the Malaysian side.

If Indonesia attracts you, the flight to Medan, in northern Sumatra, takes about an hour from Changi by Garuda or SIA. But Medan itself is of no great interest, and the area's great attraction, Lake Toba and its resorts, is just over three hours farther by road. Berastagi, which features a volcano, hot springs and a few resort hotels, is slightly closer.

Taipei

Another World

Taipei residents and foreign visitors find a lot to like about this maddening city—and a lot to dislike too. Its seemingly permanent shroud of cloud, for instance, or its death-defying cabbies and the general traffic confusion, or the steady nattering of government officials about the evils of communism Chinese-style. Taipei still suffers from its old identity problem: Is it the capital of all China, or of just a cadet branch, or simply of an island province?

But set aside boring weather, and boring politics, and take another look at the new Taipei. Over the past two decades, no city in Asia has shot up so rapidly. A backwater village in the Fifties, then fuelled mostly by anti-Communist fanaticism, Taipei blossomed in the Sixties and is still growing fast today. Not only physically but psychologically too: Taiwan surged out of the Third World long ago and these days is one of Asia's latest success stories.

Taipei's skyline illuminates it. There are high buildings now where only rice paddies existed 20 years ago. A new elevated expressway speeds traffic over still-crammed streets. There is a host of splendid new hotels, not concentrated in the city's heart along Chung Shan North Road but scattered elsewhere too—sign of continuing expansion. Perhaps the single most stunning monument is the enormous—and beautiful—mausoleum built to honor the late Chiang Kai-shek in center city. A huge new international airport, also honoring the Generalissimo, opened in 1979 and is one of Asia's best—though customs and immigration controls are among Asia's most annoying.

Figures document the success. Taiwan's per capita GNP, about US$45 in 1949, when the Nationalist government fled the mainland, rose to about US$300 in the early Sixties. Now the GNP has hit US$3000 (more than ten times the mainland's figure) and it is rising at about 8.5% a year. Taiwan is now the fifth-ranking US trading partner: the US imported US$16.4 billion worth of goods from Taiwan in 1983—and is running a US$10 billion deficit.

There's still poverty, though the gap between rich and poor has been narrowed dramatically by, of all things, government planning. In 1953, for example, the income of the wealthiest 20% of the population was 20 times that of the poorest 20%. By 1980, that gap had been narrowed to 4.2%. Unemployment is under 2%. So is inflation. This adds up to a steady rise in consumer spending. Accordingly, shops are full. Department stores, proliferating at a positively alarming rate, offer

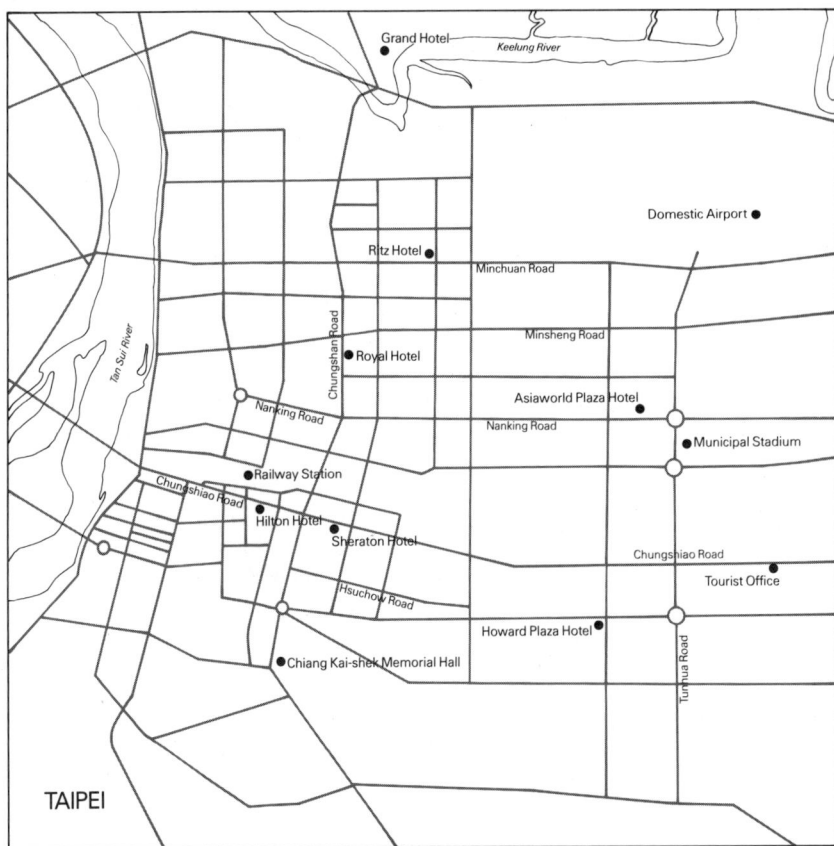

a wide selection of foreign (Japanese and French) styles; food is inexpensive and superb, and there are new Taiwan-built cars everywhere.

The contrast to the other China—just across the Taiwan Straits—is stark. There are those who argue that Taipei's economic revolution can be the pattern for a similar transformation over there. The continuing economic tinkering in Beijing makes that an increasingly interesting hypothesis.

▶ Spotlight

Cantonese, one hears, will eat anything on four legs except a table, and anything that flies except an airplane. Chinese from other regions are not far behind: meats like cat, dog and bear are not impossible to find. Neither is duck blood, or fried snake, or even snake wine. Bees? Grasshoppers? Beetles? Enough said: it's best not to ask too many questions when a savory dish is steaming before your hungry eyes.

Remember this: if it's edible, you can probably find it in Taipei. Every school of Chinese cooking is represented here, and at its epicurian best. The range of food in Taipei makes it the undisputed capital of Chinese gastronomy. That's not far from saying that Taipei is the world capital of eating.

Perhaps the single most resplendent cuisine on offer here is that of Szechuan, that agriculturally rich province of Southwest China which sheltered (1938–45) the Nationalist government during the war against the Japanese. Many officials and generals recruited their cooks in Chungking, the wartime capital, and brought them along when they fled to Taiwan in 1949. Today, these cooks (and their apprentices) set the pace for the more than 200 Szechuanese restaurants in Taipei alone. Heavily spiced and peppered, Szechuan food is dangerously addictive.

But so is Cantonese cuisine, which has been highly esteemed throughout China for centuries. In Imperial times, Cantonese cooks were prized in the emperor's kitchens in Beijing. Delicate and multiflavored, lightly cooked and carefully balanced, Cantonese food properly served has little to do with the tepid slop that passes for much of Chinese cuisine in the West. A *dimsum* lunch—a delicious marathon of endlessly varied snacks and tea—has been known to halt even the most frenzied business talk for at least half a day.

Less varied, less spicy and much heartier is Beijing food, including wheat noodles, much barbecued meat and above all that gift of the gods, Beijing Duck. Thin, crusty slices of roast duck skin, wrapped with scallions in a thin pancake and dipped in plum sauce...there's nothing tastier in this city. Taiwanese cuisine, closely allied to Fukien and Chiu-chow food, stresses fresh seafood, richly accompanied by a sea of sauces.

There are hundreds of good restaurants in Taipei, and many of them make a special effort (and charge accordingly) to please foreigners. Old hands know it's by far the best to go exploring with a Chinese friend or colleague. Tell him you've heard about the pavillion restaurants perched on the hills across from the National Palace Museum, and the chicken-in-wine delights beside the Grass Mountain hot springs, or the fresh seafood restaurants of Minsheng East Road. That will show you've already learned a thing or two about Taipei's favorite diversion and he—being Chinese—will be happy to tell you about a few others as well.

● Arriving

Most visitors will ride their hotel's bus into town (US$5) or arrange for a hotel limousine (US$30). An airport bus leaves for the Taipei railway station or the domestic airport every 15 minutes from the right-hand exit of the international arrival terminal. Cost: US$1.80. Taxis charge about US$20; driving style is terrifying.

All visitors need visas. These can be obtained at Taiwan's diplomatic or representational offices in most capitals: some of these offices provide a letter which is exchanged for a visa on arrival at the airport. Persons who have visited mainland China are no longer automatically barred from Taiwan.

● Transportation

Take taxis: the *kamikaze* style will remind newcomers of Tokyo—or Rome—but there are startingly few accidents, and fares are inexpensive. Have instructions in Chinese ready: ask the hotel or business contacts to write out addresses. Don't rent a self-drive car until you've had a chance to study the chaos that passes for rules-of-the-road here. For destinations further away: domestic air service is cheap and quick; trains passable. Book via the hotel.

● Money

The New Taiwan (NT) dollar is worth about 2.5 US cents. You'll see few coins smaller than the dollar. There are NT$1, NT$5 and NT$10 coins; NT$10, NT$50, NT$100, NT$500 and NT$1,000 bills.

● Tipping

In hotels and restaurants, a 10% service charge is built-in, but the staff almost never sees any of that. Instead, leave another 5%, say, with the waitress, or put it in the tip box near the cash register—if you've been pleased by the service. Taxi drivers will be happy if you leave them the odd bit of change. Bribes for good tables aren't usually necessary in Taipei.

● Communications

International direct dialling hasn't yet spread to all exchanges but is on its way, and dial-up communications (computer to computer) are now available to domestic points and internationally through packet-switching. Telex and cable links work well. Postal service is reliable and there's a cheap 'speedpost' service to major world destinations that's almost as fast as couriers. For example: next-morning delivery in Hong Kong; three days to New York.

● What to wear

Taipei's climate is subtropical. Summers (May–October) are hot and muggy; cool winters (January–February) require medium-weight clothes and a sweater now and then. Spring and fall are temperately pleasant. Casual clothing is very much the rule here: safari suits are normal summer business wear. The

Filipino *barong tagalog* passes for formal wear in Taipei. Carry an umbrella—it will be useful about 365 days a year.

● Languages

Mandarin Chinese is the basic language. Taiwanese—the local Chinese dialect—is usually understood. Good English is spoken by businesspeople and ranking government officials, but man-in-the-street standards are shaky. Older Taiwanese often speak Japanese.

● Doing business

*Offices are generally open between 08:00 and 18:00, with a lunch break for an hour or so at noon. Small shops open earlier and close later.

*The Taipei American Chamber of Commerce is at room N12, Chia Hsin Building Annex, 96 Chung Shan North Road, Section 2. Phones: (02) 551–2515, 581–7089, 551–5211 extensions 441 and 475. Telex 27841 AMCHAM Taipei; cables AMCHAM Taipei.

*Temporary office facilities: Most major hotels, including the Royal, the Ritz, the Grand, the Hilton and the Lai Lai Sheraton, offer well-equipped working rooms for businesspeople and will guide you to secretarial and translation services.

*Business cards: It's useful to have your cards printed in Chinese as well as English. Your hotel, or a business contact, can arrange this quickly.

■■▶ Useful phone numbers

● Airlines (international):

Cathay Pacific, 712–8228.
China Airlines, 715–1212.
Continental, 715–2766.
Korean, 521–4242.
Malaysian, 561–1174.
Northwest Orient, 596–5951.

Pan American, 767–3161.
Philippine, 581–4111.
Singapore, 511–5291.
Thai, 715–4622.

● **Airlines (domestic):**

China Airlines, 715–1122.
Far Eastern, 361–5431.
Formosa Airlines, 501–7766.
Taiwan Airlines, 537–3660.

● **Banks:**

American Express, 715–1581.
Bank of America, 715–4162.
Bangkok Bank, 571–3215.
Bank of Taiwan, 371–9111.
Central Bank of China, 393–6161.
Chase Manhattan, 521–3262.
Citibank, 715–5931.
Irving Trust, 311–4682.
Lloyds Bank, 521–8521.
Royal Bank of Canada, 713–0911.

● **Embassies/Foreign Trade Organizations:**

Since the 1970s, when Taiwan left the United Nations, many countries have closed their embassies in Taipei and instead set up trade offices. In most cases,

these offices maintain consular services.
Embassy of Bolivia, 836–9800.
Embassy of Korea, 761–9360/65.
Embassy of Panama, 596–8563.
Embassy of Saudi Arabia, 703–5855.
Embassy of South Africa, 715–3250.
American Institute, 709–2000.
Anglo-Taiwan Trade Committee, 521–4116.
Australian Commerce and Industry Office, 542–7950.
Austrian Trade Delegation, 715–5221.
Belgian Trade Association, 715–1215.
Danish Trade Organization, 721–3386.
France-Asia Trade Promotion Association, 561–0109.
German Trade Office, 596–5565.
Indonesia Chamber of Commerce, 571–9131.
Sino-Japanese Interchange Association, 351–7250/4.
Netherlands Council for Trade Promotion, 713–6560.
Singapore Trade Representative, 772–1940.
Spanish Chamber of Commerce, 721–9730.
Swedish Industries Representative Office, 562–7601/3.
Swiss Industries Trade Office, 551–8276.

Shopping

Taiwan's great bargains these days are, embarrassingly, its counterfeits. For years, manufacturers here have merrily defied international sanctions against fakery. Now there are grave official warnings against the practice, but it continues, a bit more discreetly. Standbys are books and tapes. Try Cave's Bookshop on Chungshan North Road for a wide selection. (Warning: quality replicas these aren't.) Fake watches, in just about every brand known to mankind, are harder to find now: these generally have inexpensive Japanese innards, glitzy fake Swiss cases. Copies of chic brand-name bags and suitcases abound: the best are made in Taiwan but there are also versions from South Korea, Hong Kong and Japan.

Taipei's shops and department stores stock a good selection of consumer goods, such as clothing and electronic apparatus, but no great bargains are to be had. Chinese antiques and curios are worth a look. A sampling of markets:

Cloisonné Alley, running between Chungshan North Road, Section 3, and Shuangcheng Street, from Minchu East Road to Nungan Street. Here you'll find original cloisonné products and inexpensive copies as well. Bargain!

Haggler's Alley (Chunghwa Road): Just about everything imaginable, from records to paintings to electronic parts. And antiques and semi-antiques and quite new antiques. *Caveat emptor.* Haggle!

China Handicraft Center, 1 Hsuchow Road. Good, inexpensive examples of Chinese handicrafts.

China Pottery Company, Peitou. Reproductions of celebrated ceramics—and you can watch the pieces being made. The company can ship the larger purchases.

National Palace Museum, Waishuanghsi, Shihlin, 881–2021. Reproductions of famous Chinese paintings and calligraphy.

Far Eastern Department Store, Hsimenting branch. A special section sells paintings, Taiwan jade, bamboo products, coral and fans.

◢◣◤ Hotels

Many new hotels have sprung up in Taipei over the past decade, and there are occasional gluts. It's always worth asking for a 'special rate'—the usual euphemism for a cheaper room price. Both business travel and tourism have slumped recently. On the other hand, there are occasional crunches—particularly in spring and fall. For top hotels, reservations are almost always necessary.

Note: Now and then, surprised visitors will receive phone calls at their hotels from friendly sounding chaps who seem to know them well—right down to the birthdate. These callers will try to entice travelers to come along to special 'factory outlets' for jade, coral and other treasures. Their information is accurate—it's taken from the passport data turned over to the police by every hotel. Some less-than-scrupulous hotel clerks, or even policemen, sell this data to touts.

To avoid this nuisance, simply give your hotel switchboard a list of potential callers and ask that only these be connected to your room.

Hilton, 38 Chunghsiao West Road, 311–5151, telex 22513. Five restaurants, disco, central location, health club with sauna.

Lai Lai Sheraton, 12 Chunghsiao East Road, Section 1, 321–5511, telex 23939. Four Chinese restaurants, two Japanese, one French (excellent) and one Italian. Four bars. Business center. A welcome new feature: the 'ladies only' section, with 24-hour security, an array of small gifts and special features.

Asiaworld Plaza, 100 Tunhwa North Road, 715–0077, telex 26299 ASIAWRD. Expansive is the word for this huge

complex. There are 1,057 rooms and suites, including two presidential suites with private gardens, 57 food and drink outlets.

Fortuna, 122 Chung Shan North Road, Section 2, 563–111. telex 21578 FORTREL. The high point is the revolving restaurant, the only one in Taipei, in this recently remodelled and renamed hotel; the Cantonese restaurant offers feasters gold cutlery. Health center.

Grand Hotel, 1 Chungshan North Road, Section 4, 596–5565, telex 11646. Perched high above the city and built to resemble an imperial palace, the Grand's scale and sweep are stunning—despite a certain old-fashioned air to its restaurants and bar and its distance from midtown. Great noodle shop. Health club, pool and tennis.

Howard Plaza, 160 Jen Ai Road, Section 3, 700–2323, telex 10702. A four-story waterfall in the skylit atrium lobby sets off this formal new hotel. Health club and pool.

Ritz, 155 Minchuan East Road, 597–1234, telex 27345 The Ritz. Small (210 rooms), select (no tour groups) and, with the Royal, Taipei's most elegant. Fine Chinese and Western food. Special rooms for women traveling alone, complimentary health center, business cards and personalized stationary.

Royal, 37–1 Chungshan North Road, Section 2, 542–3266, telex 23915. A cheerful European oasis (French designers, Italian marble, Austrian chandeliers) that stresses individual attention. Great rooftop pool, gym and sauna, personalized stationery, secretarial service around the clock.

Restaurants

● Western

Chalet Suisse, 47 Nanking East Road, Section 4, 715–2051, all major credit

cards. Alpine decor, fondue, veal, (try the roast lamb Provençale).

Les Celebrités, Royal Hotel, 37–1 Chungshan North Road, Section 2, 542–3266. Imaginative French cuisine, fine desserts, fair wines.

● Szechuan

Rong Hsing, 45 Chilin Road, 521–5431. Perhaps the best known of all Taipei's more than 200 Szechuan-style restaurants. For non-Chinese speakers, there's a menu with colored photos of specialties. Just shut your eyes and point—or ask for that dish your neighbors are enjoying.

● Beijing

Celestial, 12 Nanking West Road, 4th Floor, 563–2380. This reasonably priced spot offers good Peking duck, and freshwater eel with rice noodles.

Tao Jan Ting, 16 Alley 4, Chunghsiao Road, Section 4, 711–4015. Perhaps the best Beijing duck in Taipei, and a good selection of other northern specialties. Try their onion-oil cake.

After hours

Taipei nightlife is lively, and the city fathers are fairly relaxed about fun-seekers. There's almost always action in the clubs off Chungshan North Road, near the old US military compound, and some don't even charge minimums for drinks and companionship. To ransom one of the ladies, you'll pay the club about US$35, then negotiate. A conservative total: US$125. And it could go *much, much* higher.

It is also worth noting that after midnight, some nightlife areas can get ugly. Foreign visitors are advised to keep a low profile.

Most top hotels offer pleasant drinking areas open until late. Listed below are some of the good spots.

The Horseshoe, 2 Lane 28, Shuang Cheng Street, 591–6856. Live jazz and rock 'n' roll nightly. One of the few non-piano-bar spots that offer good music. No cover charge, average prices.

Ploughman's Inn (formerly Pepe el Mongol), 8, Lane 460, Tun Hwa South Road, 773–3286. Rock combo Friday and Saturday evenings, which draws crowds. Good mix of local residents and expatriates. Prices moderate. Western food upstairs, Mongolian fare (in yurts, yet) downstairs, at US$7 per person.

Sam's Place, 2–2 Shuang Cheng Street, Lane 32, 594–2402. A hole-in-the-wall bar next to the Aloha Club that's favored by many expatriate businessmen and some colorful locals. Prices moderate, fair pizza, darts. No credit cards.

A word to the wise: male strollers will notice, in certain areas off Chungshan North Road, a plethora of luxurious barbershops, some small and discreet, some enormous, all staffed by scads of agreeable young women. At least a few Westerners have been forced to visit two or three before finally managing to talk someone into actually performing a haircut.

Sights and sounds

The National Palace Museum, Waishuanghsi, Shihlin, 881–2021. Open daily, 09:00–17:00. The cream of China's imperial collections of painting, sculpture and pottery, brought here from the mainland with the retreating Nationalists in 1949. This is one of the world's greatest collections, sadly not well displayed. Explanatory films (often in English), guided tours in six languages. Best on weekdays when crowds are scantier.

Taipei Fine Arts Museum, 181 Chungshan North Road, Section 3, 595–7656. Paintings by Chinese artists since 1911, the year of the overthrow of the last dynasty. Also sculpture, calligraphy, printing, carving, ceramics and textiles.

Sun Yat-sen Memorial Hall, 505 Jen Ai Road, Section 4, 702–2411. Concerts, opera, ballet and modern dance (Chinese and Western). Schedules and ticket information from your hotel.

Night Market: Wanhwa and Shihlin are the best known. Crowds of strollers, hundreds of sidewalk vendors of goods and food. A good way to get the feel of Taipei—and to pick up a trinket or two.

Street Theater: Taiwanese opera, traditional tales acted or sung by wandering players on temporary stages. They're usually hired as part of a family event: birth, marriage or death. The whole neighborhood attends. Deafening but fun.

Weekends

Taiwan's compactness makes for easy touring. There are regular down-island flights to points like Kaohsiung and Hualien as well as the Pescadore islands. Fares are inexpensive, hops are short. And Taiwan has some of Asia's loveliest scenery.

Hualien and the Taroko Gorge: Fly to Hualien (40 minutes), hire a taxi (US$30) to drive you up to Tienhsiang. Spectacular mountain gorge, pavillions nestled in the cliffs, impressive highway engineering and a pleasant pagoda and restaurant at Tienhsiang. A one-day trip from Taipei, if you're rushed...a must see.

Cross-Island Highway: Chopped through the mountains thirty years ago, at a cost of hundreds of lives. If you've more than a day, continue on from Taroko Gorge along this highway across to the island's west side, then return to Taipei via Taichung. More superb scenery.

Kenting-Oluanpi: Near Taiwan's southern tip, Kenting has a lovely beach and a nearby national forest which began existence underwater until volcanic activity brought it above sea-level. Inexpensive accommodation in a recently built guest house in traditional Taiwan-Fukien style.

Alishan: a four-hour trip by narrow-gauge railway from Chiayi in the island's south brings travelers to the highest railway station in the Far East (2274 meters or 7459 feet). Superb view over the 'Sea of Clouds' at Yushan (Jade Mountain). Quiet mountain village.

Yangmingshan: About half an hour by taxi from Taipei is the Hotel China Yangmingshan, on Kochi Road (tel. 861–6661). For a short break from Taipei bustle, try the natural hot-spring baths here, a traditional therapy for just about any aches and pains. The hotel has fine scenery in a quiet setting, offers 50 twin rooms at US$28, a dining room and coffee shop and an outdoor pool.

Tokyo

Tokyo makes a terrible first impression—all that smog, traffic and ersatz-modern buildings. The city sprawls: it has no shape, no articulation, no notable river or peak or boulevard to attract the eye and quicken the pulse. Enthusiasts insist that on a clear day you can see Mount Fuji, but clear days are rare. They point to the Imperial Palace, with its gardens, trees and moat—but which is almost completely hidden from view. Versailles it's not. Tourists have been known to arrive, glance quickly about, shudder and hop the next train to Kyoto.

They're wrong.

Tokyo is a city of subtle qualities, of hazy delights that come into focus only gradually. It's a cerebral experience. And those who stay awhile inevitably reach the same conclusion: this is the city with *everything*.

Perhaps most important, it is thoroughly Japanese. Visitors who grouse that the place seems too Western have missed the point; the word they're fumbling for is *modern*. What makes Tokyo so fascinating is the fact that while it's totally of its time—and, some might say, ahead of its time—this is no Asian Los Angeles. Tokyo is contemporary Japan at its best and its worst, mindful of its traditions but aimed squarely at what is to come. Kyoto, with its shrines and temples, is lovely, a living museum. But Tokyo is the place to see how and why Japan is a formidable international economic and cultural force today.

The city's form is a prime example of its 'Japaneseness'. What at first seems to be undefined urban sprawl is in fact a cluster of little villages straight out of the Japan of the past. Each village has its distinct character—this in an enormous city that is more than 800 square miles large, more than 12 million people strong. The villages also make the place navigable; they give residents and visitor alike a means of understanding and enjoying it.

There are, for example, the business districts, with tall buildings, wide streets and anonymous storefronts: Ginza, Nihonbashi, West Shinjuku. There are the old districts dotted with low wooden structures, craftsmen's shops, small factories: Asakusa, Ueno, Nippori. Trendy Tokyo resides in the west, in the fashion jungles of Harajuku, Roppongi and Aoyama. To pass from one village to another is to enter a different world. One reason Tokyo can be so exhausting is that it offers the full gamut of human experiences, all linked by a whippet-quick subway system and a tangle of roads that can produce some of Asia's most monumental traffic jams.

What can business travelers expect from Tokyo? First, everything works: phones, telexes, taxis, interpreters—name it and you've got it. Hotels here cosset

TOKYO

businessmen and leave tourists to their own bewildered devices. It's nice to know that creature comforts will be pleasant—because business negotiations themselves may be less so. In many instances, the Japanese still view foreigners with wariness and suspicion: They're much more at ease dealing with other Japanese. Foreign women are at a special disadvantage, particularly when it comes to the great Japanese ritual of the business dinner with all the drinks and trimmings. But things are changing, however gradually. Foreign women on business here no longer are regarded as exotic. And ultimately it's the business that matters, not who's negotiating the deal.

A quick note on Tokyo's clichés: they're mostly true. The place really is clean, efficient and in many ways polite. One can walk the streets late at night and, though a groggy businessman or two may pop up, money and life won't be endangered. Perhaps the biggest myth is that all Japanese speak English. Wrong. They speak Japanese. Indeed, don't be surprised when the women in the party are greeted with an enthusiastic and quite well meant 'Good afternoon, Sir.'

National holidays: Business grinds to a halt on national holidays; banks and post offices close. In addition, there are two periods during which businessmen should avoid Japan: Golden Week (April 29–May 6) and Shogatsu (December 28– January 4), which are the year's most popular vacation times. (Christmas, however, is a working day). In mid-August, many businesses slow down for the O-Bon holidays, reserved for visiting the graves of loved ones.

Here are the national holidays so dreaded by visiting business travelers: January 1 (New Year's Day) (*Ganjitsu*). January 15 Coming-of-Age Day (*Seijin no hi*). February 11 National Foundation Day (*Kenkoku Kinen no hi*). March 21 Vernal Equinox Day (*Shunbun no hi*). April 29 Emperor's birthday (*Tenno Tanjo bi*). May 3 Constitution Day (*Kenpo Kinen bi*). May 5 Children's Day (*Komodo no hi*). September 15 Respect-for-the-Aged Day (*Neiro no hi*). September 23 Autumnal Equinox Day (*Shubun no hi*). October 10 Health Sports Day (*Taiiku no hi*). November 3 Culture Day (*Bunka no hi*). November 23 Labor Thanksgiving Day (*Kinro kansha no hi*).

Spotlight

So here you are, standing beside the *gelato* stand in the thick of Tokyo's modish Harajuku district, certain that the Japanese are the most adventurous dressers in the world. Passers-by look like runway models, all decked out in bright colors, baggy post-mod suits and dresses, sculpted hair and dark glasses. It's all a casual salute to the whimsical ways of local talents like Kensho Abe, Rei Kawakubo, Yohji Yamamoto and Mitsuhiro Matsuda.

But wait a minute. Over in Otemachi, a quick cab ride away, everything's different. It's the business district, and here the men are wearing plain white shirts, downright timid neckties and shiny blue suits...jokingly referred to as the *dobunizumo iro* or 'sewer-rat look'. The women turn out in prim company uniforms or sober dresses, in designs that make the Queen Mother's wardrobe look madcap.

So which is the 'Real Japan'? Both, really. Everything depends on one's occupation—or still more important, age. Indeed, age is the key to determining on which side of the great stylistic divide an individual stands. Those on the youthful side (between 18 and 25, say) include some of the world's most dynamic and devoted clothes buffs, happy to invest huge amounts of time, money and energy into eye-boggling arrays of sartorial delights. As a Matsuda staffer points out, 'People outside Japan usually don't realize that the biggest influence on fashion here comes from the 20-year olds.'

They're known informally, in fact, as the *dokushinki zoku* or unmarried aristocrats. During the halcyon days between school and marriage, most live rent-free with their parents and spend all their pocket money on clothes, travel and fancy food. Japanese youngsters know that this is their designated playtime, and they play hard. They vacation in Hawaii, New Zealand and Guam. They frequent scores of trendy Tokyo cafe bars, where $2 coffee and $4 beers lubricate conversation and flirtation. And they dance their shoes off in Yoyogi Park every Sunday afternoon, dressed to slay in tight trousers, leather jackets, drop-dead skirts and huge bangly earrings, heads artistically honed or tinted as the mood strikes.

Far from incurring parental wrath as did Haight-Ashbury hippies in San Francisco 20 years ago, the fashion kids are considered amusing—and even cute. And most in fact play by the unwritten rules: at 25, they slip into the proper mold, oats flamboyantly sown, with marriage and a company job. Even the wildest Yamamoto freak pulls on a sober business suit and joins Japan Inc. The women, in turn, trade in their short skirts and shoulder pads for silk dresses and Vuitton handbags—and maternity tops.

But this is becoming a madly mobile society in many ways, and some unsettling cracks are beginning to appear in the Japan Inc. mold. Not everyone these days seems ready to pack it in at 25. Younger Japanese are more deeply involved with leisure than their sweat-soaked elders and are increasingly reluctant to hang up their hang gliders with the official arrival of Adult Responsibility Day.

In fact top designers like Matsuda and Yoshie Inaba are now making styling lines for the slightly older customer—those who've (gasp) turned 30. The Japanese *are* getting more stylish. And if the current crop of *dokushinki zoku* has its way, the party may never end.

● Arriving

Narita International Airport ranks right up there with Chicago's O'Hare or Beirut International on the miss-at-any-cost list. Not quite as people-crammed as O'Hare, or as nervous as Beirut, Narita outranks both in sheer inconvenience. And in its sadder moments (particularly in the transit lounges), it can be confusing, poorly organized and smelly: its restrooms are unpleasant and often untouched by human hand.

Most startling is the fact that although Narita is well into its first decade, its managers still haven't figured out how to get passengers into town quickly, conveniently and cheaply. If one is not being met by a chauffeured host, it'll cost around US$100 for a taxi to cover the 60 kilometers into downtown Tokyo. And in the best of conditions, the ride takes well over an hour; at any time near rush hour, count on two hours and don't be shocked at three. The traffic is abominable.

To save money, take the airport limousines, which wait outside the exit. Ask for help in sorting out which line to wait in—the signs are not at all clear. These air-conditioned buses will drop you at, or close to, most major hotels, (and the downtown air terminal) for about US$15. But traffic slows them down just as it does taxis.

Faster and cheaper still is the Keisei Railway's train into East Tokyo's Ueno Station. It costs about US$9, but it's not practical for travelers with lots of baggage: Keisei terminals have an abundance of stairs and a paucity of porters.

There's talk of a helicopter service into the city, but it has not yet materialized. There's also talk of a 'bullet train' (*shinkansen*) but that's not yet on track either.

Much more convenient is Tokyo's old international airport, Haneda, only 20 minutes from downtown. But it serves only domestic flights, with one very stark exception. Taiwan's China Airlines still flies to Haneda, though all other international carriers were chivvied out to Narita. How did CAL manage to avoid the pressure? Because the Republic of China is no longer recognized diplomatically by Japan. Unsurprisingly, CAL Tokyo flights are usually fully booked.

From central Tokyo, taxi fare to Haneda runs between US$25 to US$35. There's a cheaper monorail from Hamamatsucho subway station which costs a bit more than US$1, gets to Haneda in 17 minutes, and offers a fine view of Tokyo Bay. But it's recommended only for passengers traveling light.

● Orientation

Tokyo, the capital of Japan, is a sprawling city of more than 800 square miles and 12 million residents. It lies on Tokyo Bay, on the island of Honshu, which is one of the country's four main islands. (The others are Hokkaido, Shikoku and Kyushu.) Formerly known as Edo, it was the seat of the Tokugawa Shogunate from 1603 to 1867. When Japan returned to the imperial system in 1868, Edo was renamed Tokyo and became the national capital.

● Transportation

There are plenty of taxis—more than 45,000—and they're in good shape, with doors that pop open automatically and cabbies in clean white cotton gloves. Many taxis are equipped with pay-TV: just drop a 100-*yen* coin into the slot. There are days, however, that you may be able to watch complete episodes of Dallas (pronounced Darris, of course)—the traffic can be miserable, particularly during peak morning and evening hours.

Another complication is the maze-like quality of most Tokyo neighborhoods. Streets are often unnamed, and the numbering system for blocks or buildings is very puzzling indeed. Always ask your hotel clerks to write out your destination in Japanese; even then, tracking down some addresses will be time-consuming. And always carry a hotel matchbook or card to help cabbies get you back safely. (Even if you pronounce Hilton Hotel as Hurton Hoteru, you may wind up in Asakusa just the same.)

Tokyo's subway system is one of the world's best. It's color coded; signboarded in Roman letters and reasonably easy to decode with the aid of a good map. Best of all, it's fast and clean, though jammed at rush hour—when those fabled pushers are cramming riders into cars. Trains are frequent: they start at 05:00 and stop at midnight. Security is good. For claustrophobes, a green elevated train called the Yamanote line circles the city regularly.

There are plenty of buses too, but they're best avoided if you do not speak Japanese. The same goes for rental cars: road signs are mostly in Japanese, parking is impossible and penalties for accidents astronomical. A particularly Japanese twist is that the transgressor is expected to bring gifts and apologies with him on the obligatory and regular visits to his victim in the hospital.

> Note: Getting around Japan is a breeze. Trains and planes to all points are frequent and fast. Try the bullet trains, to Osaka, Kyoto and Nagoya. They're fast and interesting, right down to the box-lunch salesmen who even offer *misuware* (whisky and water), the milk of Japanese businessmen.

● Money

Japanese money is handsome. Bills are sized and color-coded in denominations of Y10,000, Y5000, Y1000 and Y500. Coins: 500, 100, 50, 10, 5 and 1. In late 1984, new notes were issued; those outsized Y10,000 and Y5000 notes you get on occasion are merely old, not fake. The new Y10,000 bill has a round blank space in the center that is watermarked with the stern face of a progressive Meiji-era leader, Yukichi Kukuzawa. It's also marked in Braille. The *yen* is one of the world's major currencies and is easily obtained and exchanged abroad. At Narita, there's a 24-hour exchange service.

● Tipping

Do not tip. Most folks routinely hand tips back. Exception: tip cabbies about 20% of the fare *after midnight only*. Leading restaurants and hotels usually add a 10% service charge. And there's a 1% luxury tax for meals that cost more than Y2000.

● Communications

Phones and telexes and all other modern communications impedimenta can be found everywhere in Tokyo, and they're as dependable as any in North American or Western Europe. Top hotels routinely offer well-equipped business centers; translators, secretaries and conference rooms are easily arranged.

Public phones are color-coded: red, pink or blue for local calls, yellow for local and long-distance, and apple-green for everywhere, including points overseas. Local calls cost Y10 for three minutes, but it's wise to feed in a few extra coins at the outset, to avoid being cut off in mid-phrase (spare change is refunded). (Yellow and large red phones swallow Y100 coins but *don't* spit up change.) Remember that telephone books are scarce, but that English-language phone books (astonishingly complete) can often be purchased from your hotel.

> Note: More and more hotels are installing direct-dial facilities, but there are still a few laggards. Ask before you check in. Long-distance and overseas rates tend to be very expensive.

Postal service is uniformly excellent.

● What to wear

Japan has four distinct seasons: three good ones and one horror. The latter is summer, which starts with a one-month (June–July) rainy season, then becomes hot and sultry. Autumn and Spring are lovely though punctuated by occasional spells of chills and fever. Winter is usually mild—rather like San Francisco. Tokyo gets one big snow a year, which inevitably first surprises, then paralyzes and finally delights Tokyoites.

Thus wardrobes won't differ much from clothing in Western Europe or most of the United States as the seasons roll past. Remember that the Tokyo business climate is fairly formal: suit and tie are required for men. For women, suits and silk dresses, *never* slacks. After-hours wear is on the formal side as well, unless one is visiting some under-25s, when almost anything goes. Most Japanese, over or under 25, are horrified by anything scruffy. Even in the heat of August, for instance, most Japanese women wear nylons and most men wear ties.

● Languages

It's a one-language nation. All that fractured English, French and even German you see on t-shirts and signs and ads doesn't mean a thing. It's there merely for decoration, providing what the Japanese consider to be a 'modern look'. Chances are slim that many Japanese will understand spoken English, or anything else, but most younger Japanese have studied *written* English for at least six years and some are actually obsessed with it. So: carry a notebook. If verbal communication fails, write out the question in large, simplified letters. Sometimes this works.

Remember also that spoken Japanese is based on a collection of phonetic signs that differ startlingly in most cases from those used in English. Thus, coffee mysteriously becomes '*kohi*', beer is '*biru*' and steak is '*suteki*'.

● Doing business

*Business hours: Usually, 09:00 to 17:00, or 10:00 to 18:00, though individuals may work much longer hours. A half-day on Saturdays is not unusual.

*Banking hours: Weekdays from 09:00 to 15:00, and 09:00 to noon of the first, third and fifth Saturdays. Changing money tends to be laborious, though most cashiers speak some English.

*When introduced to a business contact, at least try to sketch a bow (hands at sides, back and neck straight, bend at waist), *then* shake hands. Please *don't* hiss.

*You can phone a friend on the *shinkansen* (bullet train) by dialling the operator at (03) 248–9311 and telling her the contact's name and train. Ships in port and near the coast can also be reached by phone; ask the operator.

*Don't wear shoes inside traditional Japanese homes. Remove them at the door; slippers are provided.

*Most public toilets do not provide paper. Carry some.

*Private cars can be hired via hotel business centers at about US$120 a day including chauffeur.

*Business cards (*meishi*) are extremely important and must be printed in English on one side, Japanese on the other. Business centers at hotels can handle this in 24 hours. Here's how to receive a card: hold it by the corners. Look at it with great interest. Leave it on the table or desk in front of you during the interview. Then, and only then, put it away, carefully.

*Business reading: *From Bonsai to Levis*, by George Fields, an amusing marketing guide; *Shadows of the Rising Sun*, by Jared Taylor, a critical and insightful guide to Japan, its business and culture; *Miti and the Japanese Miracle*, by Chalmers Johnson, which is not exactly

light reading but offers thorough background information. These and many others are available in the well-stocked bookshops of most hotels.

*Courier services: DHL and others are readily available here. Also keep in mind the postoffice's International Business Mail service. A packet dropped off at either the Central Post Office or the International Post Office (both near Tokyo Central Rail Station) can be delivered in most major cities abroad within 48 hours.

*Electricity is 100 volts AC: eastern Japan (including Tokyo) is on 50 cycles; western Japan (Osaka) on 60. Most hotels have adaptors.

*One can drink the water, but the taste isn't great. If the swimming-pool flavor isn't a thrill, try Fuji, a good local bottled water.

*Japan is on the metric system as far as weights, temperatures and most measurements are concerned. But rooms are still measured by the number of straw *tatami* mats that will cover its floors, and a 1.8 liter *sake* bottle translates as 1 *sho*.

*Credit cards are at last becoming commonly accepted, though most Japanese still carry huge wads of cash around.

◼▶ Useful phone numbers

● Chambers of commerce:

Australia, 245–0385.
Belgium, 285–1655.
France, 587–0061.
Germany (West), 581–9881.
Hong Kong Trade Development Council, 502–3251.
Italy, 580–2350.
India, (06) 261–1741.
Japan Chamber of Commerce, 283–7823.
JETRO (Japan Economic Trade Relations Organization), 582–5511.

Tokyo Chamber of Commerce, 283–7500.
United Kingdom, 265–5511.
United States of America, 433–5381.
Japan Travel Bureau, 276–7771.
Tokyo Information Center, 502–1461.

● Airlines:

Aeroflot, 272–5311.
Aerolineas Argentinas, 433–1195.
Air Canada, 586–3891.
Air France, 475–2211.
Air India, 214–7631.
Air Nauru, 581–9271.
Air New Zealand, 213–0968.
Alaska Airlines, 407–8386.
Alitalia, 580–2181.
All Nippon Airways, 580–4711.
Aloha Airlines, 216–5877.
American Airlines, 212–0861.
Ansett, 214–6876.
Austrian, 213–1751.
Bangladesh Biman, 593–1252.
British Airways, 214–4161.
Canadian Pacific, 504–1531.
China Air Lines, 436–1661.
Continental Air Micronesia, 592–1731.
Delta Air Lines, 213–8781.
Egypt Air, 211–4524.
Ethiopian Air Lines, 501–0782.
Finnair, 580–9231.
Garuda, 593–1181.
Iberia, 213–4306.
Iran Air, 586–2101.
Japan Air Lines, 747–1111
(international), 456–2111 (domestic).
Japan Asia Airways, 747–4911.
JAT (Yugoslav), 434–3842.
Kenya Airways, 214–4595.
KLM, 216–0771.
Korean Air Lines, 211–3311.
LOT (Polish), 437–5741.
Lufthansa, 580–2111.
Malaysian (MAS), 432–8501.
Mexicana, 593–2573.
Northwest Orient, 433–8151.
Olympic, 501–5651.
Pakistan International, 216–4641.
Pan Am, 240–8888.
Philippine Airlines, 593–2421.

Qantas, 211–4481.
Sabena, 585–6551. SAS, 503–8101.
Singapore Airlines, 213–3431.
South African Airways, 470–1901.
Swissair, 212–1016.
Thai International, 503–8101.
Trans Australia, 216–5828.
TWA, 212–1477.
United Airlines, 213–4511.
UTA French Airlines, 593–0773.
Varig, 211–7651.
Western, 213–2777.

● Embassies:

Afghanistan, 407–7900.
Algeria, 499–2661.
Argentina, 592–0321.
Australia, 453–0251.
Austria, 451–8281.
Bangladesh, 442–1501.
Belgium, 262–0191.
Bolivia, 499–5441.
Brazil, 404–5211.
Bulgaria, 465–1021.
Burma, 441–9291.
Canada, 408–2101.
Central African Republic, 499–5162.
Chile, 400–4522.
China, 403–3380.
Colombia, 409–0424.
Costa Rica, 486–1812.
Cuba, 449–7511.
Cyprus, 543–6555.
Czechoslovakia, 400–8122.
Denmark, 496–3001.
Dominican Republic, 499–6020.
Ecuador, 499–2800.
Egypt, 463–4564.
El Salvador, 499–4461.
Ethiopia, 585–3151.
European Economic Community, 239–0441.
Fiji, 587–2038.
Finland, 442–2231.
France, 473–0171.
Gabon, 409–5119.
Germany (East), 585–5404.
Germany (West), 473–0151.
Ghana, 409–3861.
Greece, 403–0871.

Guatemala, 400–1830.
Guinea, 499–3281.
Haiti, 486–7070.
Honduras, 409–1150.
Hungary, 476–6061.
Iceland, 531–8776.
India, 262–2391.
Indonesia, 441–4201.
Iran, 446–8011.
Iraq, 423–1727.
Ireland, 263–0695.
Israel, 264–0911.
Italy, 453–5291.
Ivory Coast, 499–7021.
Jordan, 580–5856.
Kenya, 479–4006.
Korea (South), 452–7611.
Kuwait, 455–0361.
Laos, 408–1166.
Lebanon, 580–1227.
Liberia, 499–2451.
Libya, 586–1886.
Madagascar, 446–7252.
Malaysia, 463–0241.
Mexico, 581–1131.
Mongolia, 469–2088.
Morocco, 478–3271.
Nauru, 581–9277.
Nepal, 444–7303.
Netherlands, 431–5126.
New Zealand, 460–8711.
Nicaragua, 499–0400.
Nigeria, 468–5531.
Norway, 440–2611.
Oman, 402–0877.
Pakistan, 454–4861.
Panama, 499–3741.
Papua New Guinea, 454–7801.
Paraguay, 447–7496.
Peru, 406–4241.
Philippines, 496–2731.
Poland, 711–5224.
Portugal, 400–7007.
Qatar, 446–7561.
Romania, 479–0311.
Rwanda, 486–7800.
Saudi Arabia, 409–8291.
Senegal, 464–8451.
Singapore, 586–9111.
South Africa, 265–3366.

Spain, 583–8531.
Sri Lanka, 585–7431.
Sudan, 406–0811.
Sweden, 582–6981.
Switzerland, 473–0121.
Syria, 586–8977.
Taiwan Visitors Association, 501–3591.
Tanzania, 425–4531.
Thailand, 441–1386.
Tunisia, 262–7724.
Turkey, 470–5131.
Uganda, 469–3641.
United Arab Emirates, 478–0659.
United Kingdom, 265–5511.
Uruguay, 486–1888.
USA, 583–7141.
USSR, 583–4224.
Vatican, 263–6851.
Venezuela, 409–1501.
Vietnam, 466–3311.
Yemen (Yemen Arab Republic), 499–7151.
Yugoslavia, 447–3571.
Zaire, 406–4981.
Zambia, 445–1041.

● **Emergencies:**

Dialling 110 (police) or 119 (fire, ambulance) will put you in touch immediately with the authorities. But there's a catch. One must give the alarm in Japanese. See the first page of the English-language telephone directories for details. Or ask a local friend to help.

Hotel desks can put one in contact with English-speaking doctors and hospitals.

St. Luke's International Hospital, 541–5151.

Tokyo Seventh Day Adventist Hospital, 392–6151.

International Catholic Hospital, 951–1111.

Confidential counselling by telephone is available through the Tokyo English lifeline, 264–4347.

● **Religious services:**

Christian:
Christian Science, 499–3951.

Church of Christ, 303–3336.
Church of the Latter Day Saints, 482–2985.
Holy Trinity Episcopal, 421–3646.
Presbyterian, 312–3071.
Quaker, 451–7002.
Russian Orthodox, 341–1171.
Seventh Day Adventist, 401–1171.
St. Alban's Episcopal, 431–8534.
St. Andrew's Episcopal, 431–2822.
St. Ignatius Catholic, 263–4584.

St. Mary's Catholic, 941–3029.
St. Paul's International Lutheran, 261–3740.
Tokyo Baptist, 461–8425.
Tokyo Union, 400–0047.
Islam: Tokyo Islamic Masjid, 469–9284.
Bahai: Bahai Center, 209–7521.
Jewish: Jewish Community of Japan, 400–2559.

Shopping

The Japanese department stores are a rousing part of Tokyo's cultural scene, designed to entertain as well as sell. Big and flashy, they have a dazzling display of goods, pretty young ladies posted at escalators to bow to patrons, whole floors dedicated to flossy designers or *kimonos* or palate-teasing displays of food.

The big *depaatos*, as they're called in Japlish, are mostly open from 10:00 to 18:00, and almost always on Saturdays and Sundays. Each major *depaato* observes a different weekday closing day: call your favorite one to find out which. Some stay open later: a good rule of thumb is that trendiness equals lateness, which means a 19:00 or 20:00 closing time.

One of the best of the old-style department stores is **Matsuya**, at 6–1 Ginza, 3-chome, Chuo-ku, tel. 567–1211. It has a *kimono* floor, a vast selection of Japanese tableware and several floors dedicated to designer fashions. Nearby **Mitsukoshi** is out of the same mold, as is the dignified and slightly starchy **Takashimaya**, 2–4–1 Nihombashi, Chuo-ku, tel. 211–4111.

For Japanese Yuppies, **Ginza Seibu**, a few blocks south of Takashimaya, is crammed with clothes by Ralph Lauren, Issey Miyake and Yohji Yamamoto. And 177 video screens beam rock music and videoclips at buyers—even in the elevators. Those looking for fashionable gear should check the designer floors at **Matsuya, Seibu** and the old branch of **Hankyu**, across the street from Seibu. (The new **Hankyu**, next door to Seibu, is a bit more traditional.)

> Note: Upper-floor restaurants in the *depaatos* usually offer quick and inexpensive rations for hungry, hurried shoppers. Gourmet foods are in the basement.

One-stop designer shopping? Try the **Parco Stores** in Shibuya: Parts I and II for fashion, Part III for sports and home decor. Parts I and II are huge: they all but overflow with designer boutiques such as Matsuda, Comme des Garcons, Pink House, Bigi, Yamasoto and so on.

To see what the young trendies are wearing, stroll along Omote-Sando Dori, near Harajuku Station. This street, built wide so the Emperor could move to the Meiji Shrine in style, is lined with dozens of stylish boutiques, from **Hanae Mori** to the **Vivre 21** building (a miniature Parco). Sundays are especially lively.

Tokyo has hundreds of shops offering trendy electronic goods, but the prices are unkind: it's often better to buy this sort of product in Hong Kong or New York, or even at the neighborhood shops back home. **Akibahara**, Tokyo's vast electronic bazaar, is a good place to find out what's new and available. Several shops in this area, such as **Laox** and **Yamagiwa**, cater to foreign customers and foreign electricity, but prices are sometimes a bit high. To get a good cheap camera, try **Shinjuku's** shops, including **Yodabashi Camera, Camera Sakuraya** and **Miyami Shokai**. All are easily spotted by their garish signs and blaring loudspeakers.

The best gifts for the folks at home, however, are Japanese craft items. Visit the *kimono* floor of any department store and stock up on the lovely *yukatas*, the lightweight blue-and-white *kimonos* many Japanese wear around the house. In the same areas are *furoshiki*, the decorative squares of cloth (usually cotton or silk) which the Japanese use for wrapping and toting packets. Lacquer, which is light, elegant and stylish, comes in a dizzying variety of styles (bowls, trays and bracelets for example) and prices, which range from modest to expensive.

A popular novelty item is plastic food: unsettlingly lifelike renderings of spaghetti, *sushi* and salad greens that fill restaurant display cases all over Japan. They're sold in **Kappabashi**, near Tawaramachi Station on the Ginza subway line, five minutes on foot from the famous Asakusa Kannon Temple.

Also near the temple are scores of small shops selling traditional Japanalia: kites, combs, fabrics, paper lanterns and *geta* (sandals). And **Hyakusuke**, 2–2–14 Asakusa, Taito-ku, tel. 841–7058, sells the traditional makeup used by *kabuki* actors and *geisha*, right down to a traditional facial mask made from nightingale droppings.

◆ Hotels

Tokyo's hotels are among Asia's best: comfortable rooms, good service, fine though pricey bars and restaurants. Good hotels exist in almost all of Tokyo's widely scattered 'centers': if most of your appointments are in a specific area, pick a hotel nearby to avoid being regularly stuck in traffic jams—a Tokyo specialty.

A selection:

Akasaka Prince, 1–2 Koi-cho, Chiyoda-ku, tel. 234–1111, telex 2324028. A big white-on-white building designed by Kenzo Tange and nicknamed 'The Hospital'. Forty stories high with a crowning cocktail lounge and restaurant serving one of the city's few buffet breakfasts. Excellent executive services center.

Capital Tokyo (formerly the Tokyo Hilton), 10–3 Nagata-cho, 2-chome, Chiyoda-ku, tel. 581–4511. Cheerfully gaudy East-West decor, *shoji* screens in all rooms, wonderful Japanese garden. Expensive coffee shop, good Keiyaki Grill. Executive service center, outdoor pool.

Century Hyatt, 2–7–2 Nishi-Shinjuku, Shinjuku-ku, tel. 349–0111, telex J29411 CENHYATT. French, Japanese and Western restaurants, penthouse swimming pool, Regency Club.

Hilton, 6–2 Nishi-Shinjuku 6-chome, Shinjuku, tel. 344–5111, telex 232–4515. New and beautifully designed, wonderful views and good restaurants. Three 'executive floors' offer private check-in service, express elevators, and complimentary breakfasts. Gym and indoor pool, business center, tennis, shopping arcade.

Note: The **Tokyo Bay Hilton** is scheduled to open in July 1988, in Tokyo's Disneyland. Several restaurants and bars are planned, as well as a gym, tennis and squash courts, and indoor and outdoor pool.

Imperial, 1–1 Uchisaiwaicho, 1-chome, Chiyoda-ku, tel. 504–1111, telex 222–2346. Tokyo's oldest Western-style hotel, with two new towers built in 1970 and 1983. Tasteful surroundings, well-trained staff and unbeatable Ginza-area location. Many restaurants, plenty of shops featuring all the fancy labels (Meissen, Chanel, Gucci), business center, sauna and indoor pool overlooking Tokyo Bay.

Keio Plaza Intercontinental, 2–2–1 Nishi-Shinjuku, 2-chome, Shinjuku-ku, tel. 344–0111, telex J26874. Tokyo's tallest hotel at 45 stories. Good business center, pool. A 'golden oldie'.

Miyako, 1–1–50 Shirogandei, Minato-ku, tel. 447–3111, telex 242–3222. The hotel overlooks a lush 5.5-acre Japanese garden, has good amenities, huge indoor pool, is located slightly out of the way but is good for those doing business in the Gotanda-Shinagawa districts of southern Tokyo.

New Otani, 4–1 Koi-cho, Chiyoda-ku, tel. 265–0111, telex J24719. Perhaps the largest hotel in Asia: certainly one of the splashiest. It's a popular site for celebrity weddings—pop singers, *sumo* wrestlers, ballet stars and their like. A splendid 400-year-old garden, many restaurants, including the Tokyo branch of La Tour d'Argent, tennis courts, pool and a good business center.

Okura, 10–4 Toranomon, 2-chome, Minato-ku, tel. 582–0111, telex J22790. Probably the city's most elegant; quiet and understated with superb service, East-West decor. Pleasant rooms, health club, Japanese-style suites if desired. Business center offers computers.

Palace, 1–1 Marunouchi, 1-chome, Chiyoda-ku, tel. 211–5211, telex 0222–2580. Spacious rooms, good service, superb view of the Imperial Palace and moat from the 10th floor cocktail lounge. Topnotch location in the center of the Marunouchi business district.

▶ Restaurants

At last count, Tokyo had more than 45,000 restaurants in a dizzying variety of styles. Almost every street is sprinkled with eating places, from mom-and-pop noodle shops to the would-be-bohemian *kissatens* (coffee shops) where one can rent a table with a Y400 cup of coffee and find what passes for privacy in this crowded city.

There are plenty of topnotch restaurants as well, from Chinese to French, Italian, American, German and, of course, Japanese. Of the latter, there are restaurants specializing in *sushi*, or *tempura* or *yakitori*, or the exquisitely refined *kaiseki ryori* at the Takamura (see below). Some eating places devote themselves exclusively to eel, or *tofu* or even blowfish, the notorious fish that can kill a banqueter if he gets the wrong piece (don't worry, this won't happen to you).

Most leading hotels have very good restaurants. The **Okura's Toh-Ka-Lin** is one of the best Chinese restaurants in town. And the **New Otani's** garden restaurant is excellent.

If one is out in Shinjuku, remember that most of those shiny new skyscrapers have restaurant arcades at the very top. Some are quite good, others are only moderately appealing. Try the **NS Building**, which has a flashy outdoor elevator and a wide selection of restaurants topside. Probably the best-quality food is at the top of the 50-story **Nomura Building**, where there's a branch of **Toh-Ka-Lin**.

● Japanese

Goemon, 1–1–26 Komagome, Bunkyo-ku, tel. 811–2015. Everything's made from *tofu* (high-protein soybean curd) and it's delicious, garnished as it is with all sorts of vegetables, chicken, fish and so on. The setting is wonderful—next to a classic garden complete with waterfall. Located a bit off the beaten path and worth the detour. Moderate.

Kuremutsu, 2–2–13 Asakusa, Taito-ku, tel. 842–0906. A handsome old Japanese farmhouse, transplanted to Asakusa. Comfortable and cozy, just right for a light meal and some *sake*. Moderate to expensive.

Takamura, 3–4–27 Roppongi, Minato-ku, tel. 585–6600. An exquisite restaurant with the look and feel of a mountain teahouse, featuring *kaiseki ryori* or tea ceremony cooking, which is a highly refined and expensive style of preparing food in which appearance counts as much as taste. Its courses change with the seasons. Best enjoyed if someone in your group speaks Japanese. Reservations a must. Expensive.

Tenichi, 6–6–5 Ginza, Chuo-ku, tel. 571–1949. A popular and high-quality tempura restaurant with nearly a dozen branches around town and a 50-year legacy of good eating. *Tatami* or table seating, so specify which is wanted when making reservations. Not exactly unknown, but a sound choice for business dinners. Moderate to expensive.

Tochigiya, 1–3–15 Nishi Shinjuku, tel. 342–5871. Game is the specialty here; bear, deer or wild boar *sukiyaki*. Being able to speak Japanese is useful. Moderate to expensive.

● Western

Aux Six Arbres, 7–13–10 Roppongi, Minato-ku, tel. 479–2888. Many consider this the best French restaurant in town. Tiny, chic and charming; small portions and large prices. Reservations a must.

La Columba, 2–1–33 Kudan Minami, Chiyoda-ku, tel. 230–1933. Northern Italian cuisine in a delightful white-walled room. Excellent veal. Avoid the thicker sauces. Sinful desserts, wonderful atmosphere. Expensive.

Prunier, atop the Kasumigaseki Building, Chiyoda-ku, tel. 581–9161. French, with the emphasis on seafood. Excellent location, superb view.

> Note: Business breakfasts are popular in Tokyo. Most business visitors simply take cornflakes at their hotel (the coffee shops at the Okura and the Imperial are very good). But you might consider trying a traditional Japanese breakfast: broiled fish, hot soybean soup, vegetables, an egg dish, fruit and steamed rice. Though high in sodium, it's low in cholesterol.

◣ After hours

Tokyo nightlife is wearing, and many visiting business men and women find that a certain amount of revelry is expected of them by their free-spending

Japanese hosts. Wiser heads will slow down their drinking pace as much as possible, spill one out of three highballs and vanish early. More convivial types may well surface in a Japanese steam bath three days later, wondering what hit them.

Revellers also have been known to awake in something that feels remarkably like a coffin. Not to worry. It's just one of these capsule hotels, which were in fact built primarily to house drunks who miss the last train home. (These hotels are men-only affairs: women have more sense.)

There are clipjoints: stories about walking out of a Ginza bar Y30,000 poorer after one beer are too-often true. Always check prices first.

Closing hours vary widely. Many bars close around midnight, but others, notably in Roppongi and Shinjuku, roll on much later.

The variety is enormous. There are nightclubs with the traditional floor shows (and where prices are terrifying), jazz bars, discos, folk-song bars, English-style pubs and raucous (and cheap) beer halls.

Some of the pleasantest bars in town are in the newer hotels. The cocktail lounge atop the Palace Hotel is one of the town's joys—it has a splendid view. The Old Imperial Bar at the Imperial Hotel is a delight; its chairs designed by Frank Lloyd Wright (the architect for the original Imperial in the Twenties), its walls adorned with bricks from the old hotel. (Women, incidentally, should expect no problems with would-be suitors in the better bars.)

At the other end of the scale are some very sleazy areas. The best-known is Shinjuku's Kabukicho district, a maze of porn shops, massage parlors, *no pan kissas* (coffee shops where waitresses work sans underwear) and other *pinku* entertainments, as these indulgences are called. Kabukicho isn't as nasty as Manhattan's Times Square, but it can get rough very quickly.

Other areas around Shinjuku's station are much pleasanter. There are lots of jazz bars and discos, straight and gay, and a wealth of color. With Roppongi and Asakusa, Shinjuku is one of the city's livelier nightlife areas. The Ginza, once the heart of the circuit, is beginning to price itself out of competition.

A popular local institution is the 'love hotel', where couples can go for a few hours of privacy. These are usually windowless buildings with a sort of Disneyland theme: castles, for instance, or boats.

A peculiarly Japanese fad is the *karaoke* bar, and one of your business contacts is almost sure to take you to one. The drill is to call for one of your favorite tunes, then step to the microphone and sing along at top volume. It's something of an endurance test, and an extra drink or two is often needed to stiffen one's nerves. Though most tunes are Japanese, a few *karaoke* bars will provide Western classics: *Home on the Range*, for example, or *The Yellow Rose of Texas*.

As in other cities, bars rise and fall rapidly in popularity. Listed here are a few that may be good for the long run.

Charleston, 3–8–11 Roppongi, Minatu-ku, tel. 402–0372. Funky, popular with foreigners and the fashion-model crowd, it can get wild as the hours roll on.

Ink Stick, Casa Grande Miwa Building, B1, 7–5–11 Roppongi, Minato-ku, tel. 401–0429. Great for listening to contemporary Japanese rock, slick high-tech interior, popular big-name visiting stars who occasionally get on stage themselves to perform. Restaurant attached. Chic.

Kotsu Kaikan Lounge, Yuracho 2-chome near the JNR station, revolving bar with a great view.

Lexington Queen, Daisan Goto Building, B1, 3–13–14 Roppongi, Minato-

ku, tel. 401–1661. Though it opened way back in 1980, it's still a popular disco for models, visiting celebrities and star-watchers.

Misty, 4–5–2 Roppongi, Minato-ku, tel. 403–403–7707. A small downstairs club, with good but garden-variety jazz.

◖ Sights and sounds

Check on current attractions in the local English-language press: the Saturday edition of the *Japan Times* prints reasonably complete listings. *Tokyo Journal*, a monthly English magazine, serves as a guide (with maps) to films, theater, dance, museums and art shows and costs Y1500.

Good local guidebooks include *Tokyo Access* (Access Press, Y1500) and *Tokyo City Guide* (Ryuko Tsushin Co., Y2200). Far more wide-ranging is Paul Waley's *Tokyo Now and Then: An Explorer's Guide* (Weatherhill. US$35).

● Museums

Tokyo has plenty, but many of the best collections are housed in aged, poorly lit buildings. Some first-rate exhibitions show up on the ground floor of an insurance company's building, simply because the works can be better seen. And because museum space is tight, some curators choose to keep their permanent collections locked away while displaying borrowed works. This is a fine way to increase attendance, but disappointing to visitors who hope to see a specific work.

Department stores such as Takashimaya, Seibu and Ginza Printemps often stage excellent worthwhile art shows. Details can be found in the daily press.

Bridgestone Museum of Art, 10–1 Kyobashi, 1-chome, Chuo-ku, tel. 563–0241. Probably the nation's finest collection of Western art, offering among other things a fascinating insight into Japanese taste.

Metropolitan Teien Museum of Art, 5–21–9 Shiroganedai, Minato-ku, tel. 443–0201. A classic Art Deco house once owned by a Japanese prince, now a showcase for loan shows, usually of Western art. The expansive garden is fine for a stroll. Don't miss the upstairs bathroom: wall-to-wall green marble.

National Museum, 13–9 Ueno-Koen, Taito-ku (Ueno Park), tel. 822–1111. The country's largest museum, with a first-class collection of Japanese art and

archaeology and fine special exhibitions as well, all unfortunately displayed in a dreary hall.

Nihon Mingeikan, 4–3–33 Komaba, Meguro-ku, tel. 467–4527. A fine folk art museum with an interesting collection of the crafts, textiles and pottery used by everyday Japanese up to the start of World War II, set in a cheerful Japanese-style house.

Yamatane Museum of Art, 7–12 Nihonbashi, Kabuto-cho, Chuo-ku, tel. 669–4056. One of Japan's most appealing museum interiors (beamed ceilings, *shoji*, even a rock garden), all nicely showcasing a superb collection of *nihonga*—contemporary paintings by artists using traditional materials and techniques.

● Theaters and concert halls

Rather sooner than later, Tokyo gets just about every world-class symphony orchestra, pop singer, rock group, dance company or Broadway musical. Check press listings.

Nihon Budokan, 2–3 Kitanomaru-Koen, Chiyoda-ku, tel. 216–0781.

NHK Hall, 2–2–1 Jinnan, Shibuya-ku, tel. 465–1111.

Tokyo Bunka Kaikan, 5–45 Ueno-Koan, Taito-ku, tel. 828–2111.

Tokyo Koseinenkin Kaikan, 5–3–1 Shinjuku, Shinjuku-ku, tel. 356–1111.

Among the more accessible Tokyo theater offerings are *bunraku* puppetry, *noh* plays and, especially, *kabuki*. Do not miss *kabuki* actors like Kanzaburo Nakamura (a living National Treasure), Ennosuke Ichikawa and Tamasaburo Bando, a willowy actor who plays female roles.

The country's leading ballet company is the Matsuyama, graced by world-famous ballerina Yoko Morishita. Local symphonies of note include the NHK Orchestra, the Tokyo Metropolitan Philharmonic and the Japan Philharmonic. End-of-the-year visitors to Tokyo shouldn't miss the latter's performance of Beethoven's Ninth Symphony, which is to Japan what Handel's Messiah is to Europe and North America.

● Sports and games

Sumo, some smitten Westerners argue, is one of the best things about Japan. The spectacle of these G-stringed monsters bashing into one another, sweating and straining to hoist an opponent off his feet and out of the ring, is memorable, and a great argument for the Hollywood Diet.

Tokyo is host to three 15-day tournaments, in January, May and September, at its shiny new stadium, Ryogoku Kokugikan, 2–1–9 Kuramae, Taito-ku, tel. 866–8700. For 36,000 *yen*, you'll get a *tatami*-matted box for four people, complete with seat cushions, a huge supply of tea and snacks and a complimentary *sumo* teacup (which usually features the blubbery, scowling visage of one of the wrestlers). The grunting and groaning starts at about 15:30.

If a *basho*, as the tournaments are called, is not in progress, phone one of the stables where the wrestlers live and train, and ask to watch morning practice (which usually begins at 08:00). Try Takasago-beya, 1–22–5 Yanagibashi, Taito-ku, tel. 861–4600, or Kokonoe-beya, 1–16–1 Kamezawa, Sumida-ku, tel. 621–1800.

Baseball, the all-American game, has long been welcomed here and, with some local twists, is a wildly popular sport. Tokyo's home team, the Yomiuri Giants, play at Korakuen Stadium, 1–3 Koraku, Bunkyo-ku, tel. 811–2111. If a stadium trip cannot be arranged, don't despair: local television covers games right down to the final out.

Golf is enormously popular in Japan, but public courses are few and private club fees astronomical. Business acquaintances can usually be counted on to arrange a game. If not, at least there are golf driving ranges seemingly everywhere in Tokyo.

Running and/or jogging is extremely popular in Japan, as indeed it is in many other parts of Asia. In Tokyo, the most popular path is the trail around the Imperial Palace, about 5 kilometers long with a gentle slope or two and a variety of sights. Ask the hotel desk clerks to guide you to other jogging areas.

Weekends

There are plenty of weekendable destinations in the Tokyo area and one of the very best is **Nikko**, just under two hours north by train. What's there? A lovely national park, temples and shrines and pleasant, modern hotels.

To reach its lake, waterfall and most of the other attractions, take a cab from the station to the top of a mountain, an unforgettable ride that includes 45 hairpin turns. Once up top, there's a good selection of Japanese and Western-style lodgings. One of the better ones is the Nikko Prince Hotel (tel. 0288–55–0661): its larger rooms are built to overlook both the mountains and the lake.

Nikko's best-known shrine is **Toshugu**, which with its elaborate carvings and liberal use of red and gold ornamentation looks almost Chinese and is a world away from the ascetic elegance of Kyoto's religious landmarks. It was in fact built as a baroque mausoleum for the mighty Tokugawa *shogun* Ieyasu, who died in 1616.

There are several impressive shrines nearby, including the exquisite **Chuzenji Temple**, which has an 8th Century rendering of the goddess Kannon (Kuan Yin) as its centerpiece.

Hakone, about two hours by train southwest of the capital, is as verdant as Nikko, and it has an added bonus: it's near Mount Fuji, the national symbol. Hakone itself lies in the crater of an extinct volcano. In its immediate area are more than a dozen hot springs resorts, three of which—**Gora**, **Kowakidani** and **Miyanoshita**—are particularly popular with foreign visitors.

The latter, well above sea level, is surrounded by good hiking trails and postcard-pretty forests. It's also the location of the legendary **Fujiya Hotel** (tel. 0460–22211, telex 3892718), one of the first Western-style hotels built in Japan and one of today's less-conventional lodging establishments. To get there, take the so-called Romance Train—ask for the 'lomansu'—and book seats in the front row of the first car. You'll thus get a superb panoramic view—almost like a rollercoaster at times.

Other easy trips include the run to **Kamakura**, the nation's 12th Century capital and site of the statue of the **Great Buddha**. The effigy, which is indeed huge, has survived typhoons, earthquakes, fires and tourists. And the town itself is charming, crammed with endless shrines and temples. There's a beach nearby, but it should be avoided at all costs during the summer: a problem of people.

Yokohama, a half-hour away by train, was for years a home to many foreigners, who were herded here by the emperor's minions in the 19th Century. Yokohoma is low-key and relaxed compared to Tokyo. Among its attractions is the country's biggest Chinatown, a delightful array of old buildings, the former foreigners quarter and the **New Grand Hotel**, a funky old building rebuilt after the 1923 earthquake and briefly headquarters for Gen. Douglas MacArthur during the early days of the American Occupation. **Yamashita Park**, just across the street, offers a good view of the harbor. And one can spend a pleasant afternoon at Yokohama Stadium, watching the baseballers of the local Taiho Whales sink another foe.

Finally, if the family has come along, there's **Tokyo Disneyland**, 45 minutes from Tokyo by train and packed with all the Disney amusements that have drawn millions to California and Florida. Appropriately enough, Mickey Mouse speaks Japanese and Donald Duck bows with grave Japanese courtesy—but the best sights in the park are the old *obasan* (grandmothers), kitted out in fine old *kimonos* and big black mouse ears.

LANGUAGE AND TRAVEL BOOKS
FROM PASSPORT BOOKS

Dictionaries and References
Vox Spanish and English Dictionaries
Harrap's Concise Spanish and English
  Dictionary
Harrap's French and English Dictionaries
Klett German and English Dictionary
Harrap's Concise German and English
  Dictionary
Everyday American English Dictionary
Beginner's Dictionary of American
  English Usage
Diccionario Inglés
El Diccionario del Español Chicano
Diccionario Básico Norteamericano
British/American Language Dictionary
The French Businessmate
The German Businessmate
The Spanish Businessmate
Harrap's Slang Dictionary (French and English)
English Picture Dictionary
French Picture Dictionary
Spanish Picture Dictionary
German Picture Dictionary
Guide to Spanish Idioms
Guide to German Idioms
Guide to French Idioms
Guide to Correspondence in Spanish
Guide to Correspondence in French
Español para los Hispanos
Business Russian
Yes! You Can Learn a Foreign Language
Everyday Japanese
Japanese in Plain English
Korean in Plain English
Robin Hyman's Dictionary of Quotations
NTC's American Idioms Dictionary
Passport's Japan Almanac
Japanese Etiquette and Ethics in
  Business
How To Do Business With The Japanese
Korean Etiquette And Ethics In Business

Verb References
Complete Handbook of Spanish Verbs
Spanish Verb Drills
French Verb Drills
German Verb Drills

Grammar References
Spanish Verbs and Essentials of Grammar
Nice 'n Easy Spanish Grammar
French Verbs and Essentials of Grammar
Nice 'n Easy French Grammar
German Verbs and Essentials of Grammar
Nice 'n Easy German Grammar
Italian Verbs and Essentials of Grammar
Essentials of Russian Grammar

Welcome Books
Welcome to Spain
Welcome to France
Welcome to Ancient Greece
Welcome to Ancient Rome

Language Programs
Just Listen 'n Learn: Spanish, French, Italian,
  German and Greek
Just Listen 'n Learn Plus: Spanish, French,
  and German
Japanese For Children
Basic French Conversation
Basic Spanish Conversation

Phrase Books
Just Enough Dutch
Just Enough French
Just Enough German
Just Enough Greek
Just Enough Italian
Just Enough Japanese
Just Enough Portuguese
Just Enough Scandinavian
Just Enough Serbo-Croat
Just Enough Spanish
Multilingual Phrase Book
International Traveler's Phrasebook

Language Game Books
Easy French Crossword Puzzles
Easy French Word Games and Puzzles
Easy Spanish Crossword Puzzles
Easy Spanish Word Games and Puzzles
Let's Learn About Series: Italy, France,
  Germany, Spain, America
Let's Learn Coloring Books In Spanish,
  French, German, Italian, And English

Humor in Five Languages
The Insult Dictionary: How to Give 'Em
  Hell in 5 Nasty Languages
The Lover's Dictionary: How to Be
  Amorous in 5 Delectable Languages

Technical Dictionaries
Complete Multilingual Dictionary of
  Computer Terminology
Complete Multilingual Dictionary of
  Aviation and Aeronautical Terminology
Complete Multilingual Dictionary of
  Advertising, Marketing and Communications
Harrap's French and English
  Business Dictionary
Harrap's French and English
  Science Dictionary

Travel
Nagel's Encyclopedia Guides
World at Its Best Travel Series
Runaway Travel Guides
Mystery Reader's Walking Guide: London
Japan Today
Japan at Night
Discovering Cultural Japan
Bon Voyage!
Business Capitals of the World
Hiking and Walking Guide to Europe
Frequent Flyer's Award Book
Ethnic London
European Atlas
Health Guide for International Travelers
Passport's Travel Paks: Britain, Italy,
  France, Germany, Spain
Passport's China Guides
On Your Own Series: Brazil, Israel
Spain Under the Sun Series: Barcelona, Toledo
  Seville and Marbella

Getting Started Books
Introductory language books for Spanish,
  French, German and Italian.

For Beginners Series
Introductory language books for children
  in Spanish, French, German and Italian.

PASSPORT BOOKS

Trade Imprint of National Textbook Company
4255 West Touhy Avenue
Lincolnwood, Illinois 60646-1975 U.S.A.